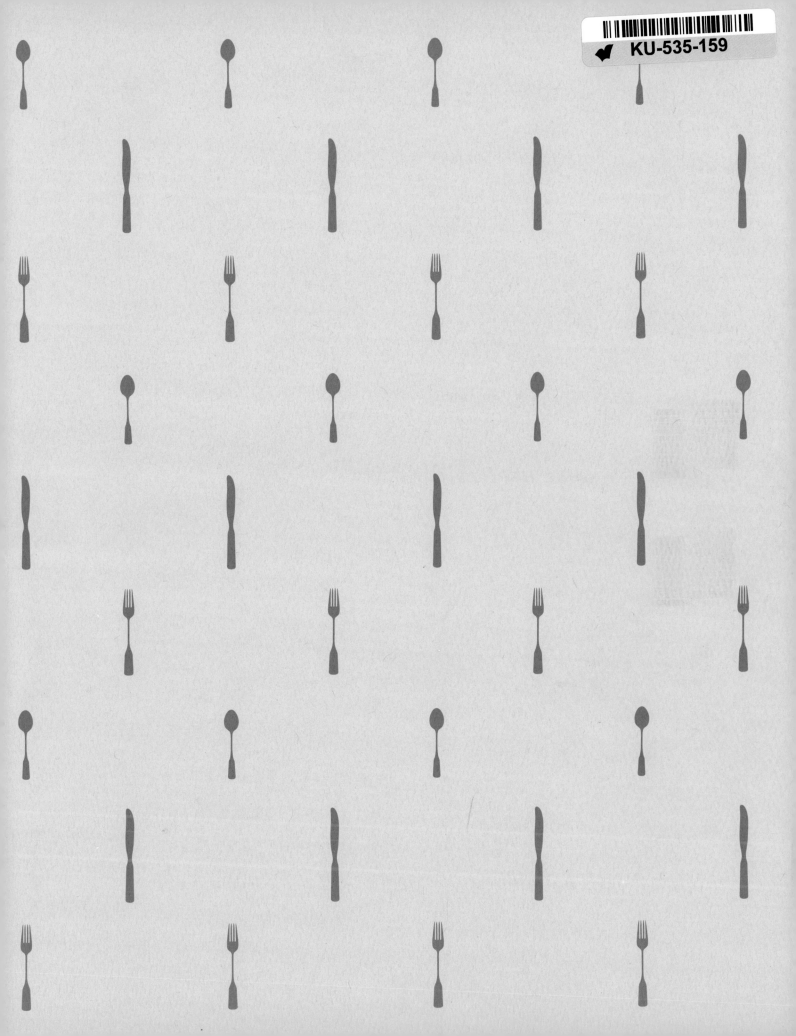

Fresh Ways with
Poultry

TIME LIFE BOOKS

COVER
Glowing with saffron, an aromatic stew of chicken, herbs and fresh vegetables stands ready for serving (recipe, page 34). The chicken pieces were skinned beforehand to reduce the amount of fat and then gently simmered with the vegetables. French bread, crisply toasted, is an ideal accompaniment.

TIME-LIFE BOOKS

EDITOR-IN-CHIEF (Europe): Sue Joiner
European Executive Editor: Gillian Moore
Design Director: Ed Skyner
Assistant Design Director: Mary Staples
Chief of Research: Vanessa Kramer
Chief Sub-Editor: Ilse Gray

Correspondents: Elisabeth Kraemer-Singh (Bonn); Dorothy Bacon (London); Maria Vincenza Aloisi, Josephine du Brusle (Paris); Ann Natanson (Rome).

A CHILD'S FIRST LIBRARY OF LEARNING
VOYAGE THROUGH THE UNIVERSE
MYSTERIES OF THE UNKNOWN
TIME-LIFE HISTORY OF THE WORLD
FITNESS, HEALTH & NUTRITION
HEALTHY HOME COOKING
UNDERSTANDING COMPUTERS
THE ENCHANTED WORLD
LIBRARY OF NATIONS
HOME REPAIR AND IMPROVEMENT
CLASSICS OF EXPLORATION
PLANET EARTH
PEOPLES OF THE WILD
THE EPIC OF FLIGHT
THE SEAFARERS
WORLD WAR II
THE GOOD COOK
THE TIME-LIFE ENCYCLOPAEDIA
OF GARDENING
THE GREAT CITIES
THE OLD WEST
THE WORLD'S WILD PLACES
LIFE LIBRARY OF PHOTOGRAPHY
TIME-LIFE LIBRARY OF ART
GREAT AGES OF MAN
LIFE SCIENCE LIBRARY
LIFE NATURE LIBRARY

HEALTHY HOME COOKING

SERIES DIRECTOR: Dale M. Brown
Deputy Editor: Barbara Fleming
Series Administrator: Elise Ritter Gibson
Designer: Herbert H. Quarmby
Picture Editor: Sally Collins
Photographer: Renée Comet
Text Editor: Allan Fallow
Editorial Assistant: Rebecca C. Christoffersen

Editorial Staff for *Fresh Ways with Poultry:*
Book Managers: Jean Getlein, Barbara Sause
Assistant Picture Editor: Scarlet Cheng
Researcher/Writers: Susan Benesch, Andrea E. Reynolds, Susan Stuck.
Copy Co-ordinators: Marfé Ferguson, Elizabeth Graham
Picture Co-ordinator: Linda Yates

Special Contributors: Carol Gvozdich (nutrition analysis), Nancy Lendved (props)

European Edition:
Sub-Editor: Wendy Gibbons
Production Co-ordinator: Nikki Allen
Production Assistant: Maureen Kelly

THE COOKS

ADAM DE VITO began his cooking apprenticeship when he was only 14. He has worked at Le Pavillon restaurant in Washington, D.C., taught with cookery author Madeleine Kamman, and conducted classes at L'Académie de Cuisine in Maryland. He developed most of the recipes in this volume.

HENRY GROSSI was awarded a Grand Diplôme at the École de Cuisine La Varenne in Paris. He then served as the school's assistant director and its North American business and publications co-ordinator.

JOHN T. SHAFFER is a graduate of The Culinary Institute of America at Hyde Park, New York. He has had broad experience as a chef, including five years at The Four Seasons Hotel in Washington, D.C.

CONSULTANTS

CAROL CUTLER is the author of many cookery books. During the 12 years she lived in France, she studied at the Cordon Bleu and the École des Trois Gourmandes, as well as with private chefs. She is a member of the Cercle des Gourmettes and a charter member and past president of Les Dames d'Escoffier.

NORMA MACMILLAN has written several cookery books and edited many others. She has worked on various cookery publications, including *Grand Diplôme* and *Supercook*. She lives and works in London.

NUTRITION CONSULTANTS

JANET TENNEY has been involved in nutrition and consumer affairs since she received her master's degree in human nutrition from Columbia University. She is the manager for developing and implementing nutritional programmes for a major chain of supermarkets in the Washington, D.C., area.

PATRICIA JUDD trained as a dietician and worked in hospital practice before returning to university to obtain her MSc and PhD degrees. For the last 10 years she has lectured in Nutrition and Dietetics at London University.

Nutritional analyses for *Fresh Ways with Poultry* were derived from Practicare's Nutriplanner System and other current data.

This volume is one of a series of illustrated cookery books that emphasizes the preparation of healthy dishes for today's weight-conscious, nutrition-minded eaters.

Fresh Ways with Poultry

BY

THE EDITORS OF TIME-LIFE BOOKS

TIME-LIFE BOOKS/AMSTERDAM

Contents

*Poultry's Boundless
Possibilities* 6

A Basic Chicken Stock 9

1 Chicken: Today's Perfect Meat 11

Stir-Fried Chopped Chicken
on Lettuce Leaves 12
Sautéed Chicken Breasts
with Livers and Grapes 13
Chicken Cutlets with Summer
Herbs and Tomato Sauce 14
Chicken Breasts Sautéed
with Coriander 15
Sautéed Chicken Breasts
with Raspberry Sauce 15
Chicken with Peanuts
and Ginger Sauce 16
Sautéed Chicken with Mustard,
Caraway Seeds and Chervil 17
Chicken Breasts Stuffed
with Garlic and Carrots 18
Chicken Riesling 18
Chicken, Aubergine and
Tomato Sauté 20
Chicken Paprika with Yogurt 21
Chicken Breasts with Tarragon
and Tomato 22

Chicken Legs with Dark Rum,
Papaya, Mango and Banana 43
Chicken Drumsticks Cacciatore 44
Chicken Breasts with Courgettes
in Red Wine Sauce 44
Chicken Legs Stewed with Prunes 46
Lemon-Mustard Chicken
with Root Vegetables 47
Braised Chicken, Almonds
and Chick-Peas 48
Chicken Casserole with Dried
Fruits and Caramelized Onions 48
Chicken Fricassee
with Watercress 50
Braised Chicken with Potatoes,
Leeks and Kale 51

Chicken with Peanuts and Ginger Sauce

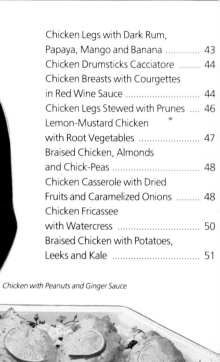

Poached Chicken with Fennel 26
Poached Chicken Strips
in Gingered Orange Sauce 27
Red Pepper and Chicken Spirals 28
Poached Chicken with
Black Bean Onion Sauce 28
Cranberried Chicken 29

Spicy Yogurt-Baked Chicken Thighs

Stir-Fried Chicken with Broccoli, Red Onions and Cashew Nuts

Stir-Fried Chicken with Broccoli,
Red Onions and Cashew Nuts 23
Sautéed Chicken Breasts with
Apricots, Bourbon and Pecans 24
Stir-Fried Chicken with Red
Cabbage and Chilies 25

Chicken Poached in Milk
and Curry 30
Chicken Fan with Basil-
Tomato Sauce 31
Braised Chicken Legs with Celery,
Shallots and Red Onion 32

Spanish-Style Chicken
and Saffron Rice 33
Orange-Glazed Chicken 34
Saffron Chicken Stew 34
Braised Chicken with Plums
and Lemons 36
Chicken with Orange and Onion 37
Braised Chicken with
Red and Green Apples 38
Chicken Braised with Haricot
Beans and Tomatoes 39
Jellied Chicken with Lemon
and Dill 40
Chicken Mole 41
Curried Chicken with Chutney
and Raisins 42

Chicken Rolled in Vine Leaves 52
Plum-Coated Chicken
with Chinese Cabbage 53
Honey-Basil Chicken 54
Baked Chicken Breasts
Stuffed with Tahini 55
Baked Chicken Legs
Stuffed with Millet 56
Chicken Pillows 57
Spicy Yogurt-Baked
Chicken Thighs 58
Spinach-Stuffed Chicken Breasts 59
Cajun Chicken Wings 60
Chicken Wrapped in Crisp Phyllo 61
Chicken-and-Cheese-Filled
Calzones 62

Yogurt-Baked Chicken
with Pimientos and Chives 64
Crêpes Filled with Chicken
and Sweetcorn 65
Peach-Glazed Poussins
with Ginger 66
Oven-Fried Cinnamon Chicken 67
Chicken on a Bed of
Savoy Cabbage 68
Lime and Mint Chicken 69
Saffron Chicken with Yogurt 70
Grilled Chicken with Malt Vinegar
and Basil 71
Chicken Breasts with Radishes 72
Chicken Thighs Grilled with
Sherry and Honey 73
Dry Martini Poussins 74
Poussins with Pineapple
and Mint 75
Roast Capon with
Sage Cornbread Stuffing 76
Roast Chicken with Apples,
Turnips and Garlic 77
Thyme-Roasted Chicken 78
Emerald Chicken Roll 79
Cold Chicken and Asparagus with
Lemon-Tarragon Vinaigrette 80
Spatchcocked Chicken with Basil-
Yogurt Sauce 81
Chilled Chicken Couscous
with Lime 82
Sage-Flavoured Chicken Pie
with Phyllo Crust 82

Roast Gingered Turkey Breast

2 Turkey Transformed 85

Turkey Patties with Beetroot Sauce ... 86
Turkey Crust Pizza 87
Turkey Rolled with Ham
and Mozzarella 88
Turkey Legs Baked with Yams
and Apples 89
Turkey and Green Chili
Enchiladas 90
Turkey Curry with Puréed Yams 91
Turkey Escalopes with Citrus 92
Chopped Turkey with Lime
and Coriander 93

Chilled Turkey with
Creamy Tuna Sauce 94
Turkey Escalopes with Pine-Nuts
and Currants 95
Turkey-Stuffed Pittas 97
Turkey Escalopes with Red
and Green Peppers 97
Stir-Fried Turkey with
Mixed Vegetables 98
Turkey Satays with Peanut Sauce 99
Turkey Rolls with Parsley Sauce 100
Rolled Turkey Escalopes
Stuffed with Buckwheat 100
Turkey Salad with Feta Cheese 102
Turkey Salad with Yogurt
and Buttermilk Dressing 102
Turkey and Black Bean Salad 103
Roast Breast of Turkey
with Fruit Stuffing 104
Roast Gingered Turkey Breast .. 105
Honey-Glazed Roast Turkey .. 106
Buckwheat Stuffing 108
Spinach, Beet Green
and Pine-Nut Stuffing 108
Red Pepper, Sweetcorn and
Aubergine Stuffing 109
Turkey Galantine 110

3 Updating Some Old Favourites 113

Duck Breasts with Red Wine
and Juniper Berries 114
Duck Breasts with Sour Apple 115
Duck with Mushrooms
and Mange-Tout 116
Roast Duck Stuffed with Pears
and Garlic 117
Roast Duck
with Cranberry Compote 118
Goose Breasts
with Blackberry Sauce 119
Braised Goose Legs
with Shiitake Mushrooms 120
Goose with Apple and
Red Cabbage Stuffing 121
Twice-Cooked Quail 122
Quail Stuffed with Wild Mushrooms
and Rice 122
Squab Breasts
with Shallot-Cream Sauce 124

Pheasant Breasts
in Parchment 124

Braised Goose Legs with Shiitake Mushrooms

4 Poultry in the Microwave Oven 127

Chicken Stew with
Soufflé Topping 127
Teriyaki Chicken 128
Chicken in a Tortilla Pie 128
Chicken Parmesan 130
Barbecued Chicken 131
Turkey Ring 132
Poussins with
Barley Stuffing 133
Roast Turkey
with Tarragon-Cream Sauce 134

Techniques 136

Cutting a Chicken
into Serving Pieces 136
Boning a Breast 138
Boning a Thigh 138
Trussing a Bird 138
Slicing Escalopes from
a Turkey Breast 139

Glossary 140
Index 141
*Picture Credits and
Acknowledgements* 144

Turkey Escalopes with Citrus

Poultry's Boundless Possibilities

Surely one of nature's greatest gifts to cooks the world over is poultry. No food can be treated more variously in the kitchen and brought to the table in more delicious guises; nor is there meat with more innate goodness than that of the two most popular birds — chicken and turkey. When skinned, both are wonderfully low in fat and therefore in calories, yet they are high in protein. Even duck and goose, long considered so rich as to be indulged in only at holidays or other festive occasions, can be eaten year round when measures are taken to relieve them of much of their fat.

This book celebrates the limitless possibilities of poultry. It presents 119 recipes — for sautéing, braising, grilling, baking, roasting and poaching birds. All were evolved in Time-Life Books' test kitchens by experienced cooks and nutritionists seeking ways to prepare poultry so that it has maximum flavour but still meets today's preference for light, healthy food.

In these recipes, the dual goal of nutritional soundness and eating pleasure is achieved in a number of ways. For example, since most of the fat in chicken and turkey is contained in and under the skin, the recipes frequently call for the skin to be removed and steps to be taken to keep the exposed flesh from drying out. Coatings or liquids provide protection in certain cases. In most sauté recipes, salt is sprinkled on the meat during cooking rather than at the outset, when it would draw out juices. In several dishes, vegetables are partially precooked and then added to the meat so that the cooking time can be shortened, further ensuring the meat's tenderness and moistness. Where the skin is essential to the success of a dish, as in a roast, the exuded fat is skimmed from the juices before the preparation of a sauce.

Few ingredients offer more rewards in the cooking of poultry than stock made at home from vegetables, herbs, and poultry trimmings and bones that might otherwise be discarded (trimmings can be frozen and saved until enough have accumulated). Stock serves variously as a moistener, as a cooking medium in braising or poaching poultry, and as a base for sauces. To add extra flavour, even the skin may be incorporated into the stockpot, providing the fat is removed later *(recipe, page 9)*. When the strained liquid is allowed

to cool, most of the fat will rise to the surface and congeal. It can then be lifted off easily and thrown away — or, in waste-not families, placed outdoors in winter as a cold-weather treat for wild birds.

Homemade stock may be stored safely in the refrigerator for three or four days, or it can be frozen: pouring it into small plastic containers in pre-measured amounts, freezing it, and then drawing upon it as it is needed without having to melt the whole batch can be a boon to the busy cook. Stock may be stored frozen in tightly covered containers for up to six months. Stock cubes or granules may be substituted in recipes where stock is used as a moistener; but because they are often excessively salty, a low-sodium product should be used, or any salt that is called for in the recipe should be eliminated or reduced.

In stock's role as a flavour-rich base for sauces, a little cream or butter may be added for enrichment or as a thickening agent — but always judiciously. In sauces where tartness is welcome, yogurt or buttermilk can be included (mixing a little cornflour with the yogurt will keep it from separating).

How to use this volume

The book is organized simply. The first and by far the largest section is devoted to chicken in all its delicious variety including its smaller version, the poussin. Chicken is followed by turkey, another bird that lends itself to many diverse and delicious preparations. For the cook's convenience, these two sections are broken down by cooking method; thus all the sautés appear together, as do the braises, the poaches, and so on. A third section of the book offers recipes for duck, goose, pheasant, quail and pigeon squab; it is organized by type of bird. In a final recipe section, several pages deal with the cooking of poultry in the microwave oven.

For every recipe in the book, there is a photograph of the actual dish. Metric and imperial weights for each ingredient are given in separate columns and, although close equivalents, the two systems should not be mixed for the same recipe.

The volume also includes instructions for generalized techniques common to a number of the recipes, such as jointing a chicken or boning a breast. These are demonstrated in a series of how-to photographs. Finally, there is a glossary that describes many of the foods and terms in the book.

The recipes treat poultry as a delicate meat that can all too easily spoil and that can all too easily be overcooked. Ideally, poultry should be bought fresh — and the fresher the better. Some cooks have taken to seeking out fresh-killed, free-range chickens, reared as of old on farms where the birds can strut around the farmyard and peck at seeds and other titbits to their hearts' content. These free-range chickens have an excellent flavour, and are again becoming more widely available.

Poultry tips

Poultry can be bought fresh, chilled or frozen. A bird should have a clean skin without blemishes, bruises or pinfeathers. A pliable breastbone and soft, thin skin indicate a bird's youthfulness (skin colour, which may range from white to yellow, is of little significance). Packaged chickens generally have a "sell by" or "use by" date on the label. Sometimes even the freshest of packaged chickens can emit a chickeny odour when unwrapped, but the smell will quickly dissipate; the odour of a spoiled chicken, however, will not go away, and the bird should be returned.

Fresh poultry should be treated carefully to curtail bacterial growth. It should be refrigerated as soon after purchase as possible. If the package contains a large amount of pinkish juices, discard them, rinse the bird under cold running water, and pat it dry. The drying is important, because bacteria thrive in a moist environment. The bird should then be wrapped tightly and stored in the coldest part of the refrigerator at 5°C (40°F) or below, but for no longer than two days. (Although refrigeration retards the growth of bacteria, food-spoiling bacteria grow even in the cold.) Cooked poultry can be kept as long as four days, but when covered with a sauce or liquid, it should be kept only one or two days. Poultry should never be cooked partially and then refrigerated: bacteria will continue to multiply in the raw portions.

Just before poultry is to be used, it should be rinsed and dried. The cavity of a bird intended for stuffing should be washed to flush out any bacteria and remaining bits of organs. The stuffing itself should be inserted cool but not chilled — do not pack it tightly since it will expand — and the bird should be placed in a preheated oven immediately. Cooks should wash their hands in warm, soapy water before and after handling poultry, as well as any knives, cutting boards or worktops used during its preparation to avoid the transference of bacteria to other foods.

Fresh poultry pieces that will be stored longer than a couple of days should be frozen immediately: to avoid freezer burn, remove the pieces from the shop wrapper and rewrap them tightly in a moistureproof, vapourproof material such as freezer paper or heavy aluminium foil. When a fresh whole bird is to be frozen, the giblets should be frozen separately to keep them from spoiling. A whole bird purchased frozen should be kept in its wrapper until ready to use; flash-frozen by the processor to lock in flavour, the bird can be kept for as long as a year at −18°C (0°F) or below.

Dealing with frozen poultry

The safest way to thaw frozen poultry is gradually in the refrigerator, where the cold slows the growth of bacteria. But it takes time: 12 to 16 hours for a whole 2 kg (4 lb) bird, 4 to 9 hours for pieces. Fresh poultry frozen at home should be used before six months have elapsed in order to guard against a deterioration in the taste and texture of the meat.

Some of the recipes presented here may be prepared in advance and frozen, but this practice is not recommended unless schedules demand it. The success of the dishes depends on fresh ingredients, and critical flavours will inevitably be lost or distorted when the food is frozen. Certain herbs, for example, seem to relinquish much of their character; such seasonings as garlic, onions, pepper, nutmeg and cloves become more intense. Furthermore, there is little point in freezing the book's many sautés, grills and stir-fries, since they take so little time to cook in the first place. As for the other recipes, most of them have been developed with the exigencies of time in mind, and the dishes themselves are meant to be served immediately, full of aroma and goodness. If, however, any of the dishes are to be frozen, their vegetables should be undercooked, since they will cook still further when they are defrosted and reheated. The dishes should be cooled thoroughly in the refrigerator before being wrapped, labelled, dated and placed in the freezer. And they should be eaten as soon afterwards as possible, preferably within the month.

When is the bird done?

How long to cook poultry is, in the end, a matter of personal choice, but the adventurous eater will want to experiment a bit. Too much poultry is rendered dry, tough and tasteless by careless cooking — the "rubber chicken" of the big fund-raising dinner being a case in point. In this book, poultry is cooked respectfully. Chicken and turkey come out moist and tender. Duck breast skinned and sautéed emerges a rosy pink, rich in flavour not unlike that of the best beef, but without beef's calories.

One simple test for doneness is to poke the meat with a finger; it should feel firm but springy to the touch. Another test is to pierce a thigh with the tip of a sharp knife; the juices should run clear (when they are pink, the meat needs further cooking).

For whole birds, the most reliable method is to insert a quick-reading meat thermometer in the thickest part of the thigh muscle, taking

The Key to Better Eating

This book, like others in the Healthy Home Cooking series, presents an analysis of nutrients contained in a single serving of each dish, listed beside the recipe itself, as on the right. Approximate counts for calories, protein, cholesterol, total fat, saturated fat (the kind that increases the body's blood cholesterol) and sodium are given.

Healthy Home Cooking addresses the concerns of today's weight-conscious, health-minded cooks by providing recipes that take into account guidelines set by nutritionists. The secret of eating well, of course, has to do with maintaining a balance of foods in the diet; most of us consume too much sugar and salt, too much fat and too many calories, even too much protein.

Interpreting the chart

The chart below gives dietary guidelines for healthy men, women and children. Recommended figures vary from country to country, but the principles are the same everywhere. Here, the average daily amounts of calories and protein are from a report by the U.K. Department of Health and Social Security; the maximum advisable daily intake of fat is based on guidelines given by the National Advisory Committee on Nutrition Education (NACNE); those for cholesterol and sodium on upper limits suggested by the World Health Organisation.

The volumes in the Healthy Home Cooking series do not purport to be diet books, nor do they focus on health foods. Rather, they express a commonsense approach to cooking that uses salt, sugar, cream, butter and oil in moderation while employing other ingredients that also provide flavour and satisfaction. Herbs, spices, aromatic vegetables, fruits, peels, and juices, wines and vinegars are all used towards this end.

The recipes make few unusual demands. Naturally they call for fresh ingredients, offering substitutes when these are unavailable. (The substitute is not calculated in the nutrient analysis, however.) Most of the ingredients can be found in any well-stocked supermarket;

Calories **245**
Protein **24g**
Cholesterol **45mg**
Total fat **8g**
Saturated fat **2g**
Sodium **340mg**

---

the occasional exception can be bought in speciality or ethnic shops.

In Healthy Home Cooking's test kitchens, heavy-bottomed pots and pans are used to guard against burning the food whenever a small amount of oil is used, but nonstick pans could be utilized as well. Both safflower oil and virgin olive oil are favoured for sautéing. Safflower was chosen because it is the most highly polyunsaturated vegetable fat available in supermarkets, and polyunsaturated fats reduce blood cholesterol; if unobtainable, use sunflower oil, also high in polyunsaturated fats. Virgin olive oil is used because it has a fine fruity flavour lacking in the lesser grade known as "pure". In addition, it is — like all olive oil — high in monounsaturated fats, which are thought not to increase blood cholesterol. Sometimes both virgin and safflower oils are combined, with the olive oil contributing its fruitiness to the safflower oil. When virgin olive oil is unavailable, "pure" may be substituted.

About cooking times

To help the cook plan ahead effectively, Healthy Home Cooking takes time into account in all of its recipes. While recognizing that everyone cooks at a different speed, and that stoves and ovens differ in temperatures, the series provides approximate "working" and "total" times for every dish. Working time stands for the actual minutes spent on preparation; total time includes unattended cooking time, as well as time devoted to marinating, steeping or soaking. Since the recipes emphasize fresh foods, they may take a bit longer to prepare than "quick and easy" dishes that call for canned or packaged products, but the payoff in flavour and often in nutrition should compensate for the little extra time involved.

In order to simplify meal planning, most recipes list accompaniments. These are intended only as suggestions, however; cooks should let their imaginations be their guide and come up with their own ideas to achieve an appealing and sensible balance of foods.

Recommended Dietary Guidelines

		Average Daily Intake		Maximum Daily Intake			
		CALORIES	PROTEIN grams	CHOLESTEROL milligrams	TOTAL FAT grams	SATURATED FAT grams	SODIUM milligrams
Females	7-8	1900	47	300	80	32	2000*
	9-11	2050	51	300	77	35	2000
	12-17	2150	53	300	81	36	2000
	18-54	2150	54	300	81	36	2000
	54-74	1900	47	300	72	32	2000
Males	7-8	1980	49	300	80	33	2000
	9-11	2280	57	300	77	38	2000
	12-14	2640	66	300	99	44	2000
	15-17	2880	72	300	108	48	2000
	18-34	2900	72	300	109	48	2000
	35-64	2750	69	300	104	35	2000
	65-74	2400	60	300	91	40	2000

*(or 5g salt)

care that the thermometer does not come into contact with the bone. Turkey, for example, is done when its internal temperature reaches 83° to 85°C (180° to 185°F). Allowing a large bird to stand at room temperature for about 20 minutes after it finishes roasting will make the meat easier to carve.

Choosing a wine accompaniment

What to drink with poultry is, like the cooking of it, largely a matter of preference. Wine is a pleasant accompaniment to any bird, although beer seems to better complement dishes with a spicy Asian accent, such as the turkey satays on page 99 or the yogurt-baked chicken thighs on page 58. Picking an appropriate wine is harder today than it was a dozen years ago. For one thing, there are more wines to choose from. For another, dishes have become more varied and complex, making the old rule — red wine with red meat, white wine with poultry or fish — obsolete. The new cooking audaciously combines varied foods and flavours and borrows freely from foreign cuisines. The recipes in this book are typical of the new cooking. For interest and flavour, they draw upon a full repertoire of herbs and spices and other savoury ingredients, and the finished dishes often are served with light sauces or dressings. Someone seeking to heighten his or her pleasure in the food has an obligation to give careful thought to the selection of a wine to drink with it.

Although there can be no strict rules, the following considerations should be borne in mind when choosing the wine: take into account the nature of the dish and try to match like with like. If the dish is, for example, the duck breasts with sour apples on page 115, the pink, rich-tasting meat automatically suggests a red wine, while the tart apple seems to call for a tart or slightly acid wine that can hold its own against the fruit's assertiveness. A young Bordeaux or a big Beaujolais such as a Juliénas or a Morgon would make a perfect companion.

The turkey escalopes on page 97 contrast white breast meat with red and green peppers. A white wine seems in order, but the sweet, somewhat acid flavour of the peppers requires that the wine share these qualities to complement the dish properly. Thus a good choice here would be a Vouvray from the Loire or a crisp Alsatian Pinot Gris.

The hearty roast goose with apple and red cabbage stuffing on page 121 demands a full-bodied red wine — perhaps a mature Burgundy or Côtes du Rhône. A simple roast chicken stuffed under the skin with fresh thyme *(page 78)* can be consumed with any good wine — a white Burgundy, a Chianti Classico or a Rioja would all go well. The beauty of poultry is that it encourages such experimentation.

A Basic Chicken Stock

Makes 2 to 3 litres (3½ to 5¼ pints)
Working time: about 20 minutes
Total time: about 3 hours

2 to 2.5 kg	uncooked chicken trimmings and bones (preferably wings, necks and backs), the bones cracked with a heavy knife	4 to 5 lb
2	carrots cut into 1 cm (½ inch) rounds	2
2	celery sticks cut into 2.5 cm (1 inch) pieces	2
2	large onions, cut in half, one half stuck with 2 cloves	2
2	sprigs fresh thyme, or ½ tsp dried thyme	2
1 or 2	bay leaves	1 or 2
10 to 15	parsley stems	10 to 15
5	black peppercorns	5

Put the trimmings and bones in a heavy stockpot with enough water to cover them by 5 cm (2 inches). Bring the liquid to the boil, skimming off the scum that rises to the surface. Simmer for 10 minutes, skimming and adding a little cold water to help precipitate the scum. Add the vegetables, herbs and peppercorns, and submerge them in the liquid. If necessary, add enough additional water to cover the vegetables or bones. Return to the boil, then lower the heat and simmer for 2 to 3 hours, skimming once more.

Strain the stock and allow it to stand until tepid, then refrigerate it overnight or freeze it long enough for the fat to congeal. Spoon off and discard the layer of fat.

Tightly covered, the stock may safely be kept for three to four days in the refrigerator. Stored in small, well-covered freezer containers, the stock may be kept frozen for up to six months.

EDITOR'S NOTE: *The chicken gizzard and heart may be added to the stock, along with the bird's uncooked skin. Wings and necks — rich in natural gelatine — produce a particularly gelatinous stock, ideal for sauces and jellied dishes.*

Since the recipes in this book contain little salt, cooks may wish to prepare a stock with a more complex flavour. Unpeeled, lightly crushed garlic cloves, dried basil, leeks, and additional bay leaves or parsley stems may be used to heighten the flavour of the stock without overwhelming it. Turkey, duck or goose stock may be prepared in the same way, but the fatty skin of duck or goose should not be used.

1 *Two spatchcocked chickens, topped with Parmesan cheese and garnished with basil, are served with a basil-yogurt sauce and stewed tomatoes (recipe, page 81).*

Chicken: Today's Perfect Meat

Chicken has something to offer everyone — dark and white meat, multiple cooking options, and the ability to marry the flavours of most herbs and spices. Its nutritional credentials are no less compelling: chicken has fewer calories and is easier to digest than beef, yet a 90 g (3 oz) serving of boneless grilled chicken breast contains about the same amount of protein as lean beef — 25 g. With its skin removed and any excess visible fat scraped away, chicken becomes even more healthy: it loses at least 40 calories per 90 g (3 oz) serving. No wonder that chicken is such a popular choice of meat.

Success in preparing the chicken dishes in this book depends partly on choosing the right kind of bird for the recipe at hand. Birds weighing 1.25 to 1.50 kg (2½ to 3 lb), usually called spring chickens, are about six weeks old when slaughtered. Their age and size makes them especially tender. They can be grilled as well as sautéed and roasted. Broilers — young roasting chickens — weigh 1.75 to 2 kg (3½ to 4 lb) and are seven to eight weeks old. Older roasting chickens weigh 2 to 2.5 kg (4 to 5 lb) but, particularly round the festive seasons, larger birds are also available.

As chickens grow older and bigger, they develop more fat in and under their skin. Since they cannot be roasted easily without skin, the fat can be reduced by first steaming the bird and then putting it immediately into a hot oven; this also helps tenderize the meat. Cut into pieces and skinned, roasters may also be sautéed, grilled or braised. The largest roasting birds are often called capons, though the true capon — a male chicken that has been castrated and is allowed to grow to about 4.5 kg (10 lb): a procedure that renders it meatier, more tender and tastier, but gives it more fat — is no longer generally available.

The old-fashioned boiling fowl, that for centuries has imparted rich flavour to hearty soups and stews the world over, may be eight months in age when marketed, and its flesh will inevitably be stringier than that of younger birds. At the opposite extreme in age and size is the poussin, the baby of the chicken family, which is specified for a number of recipes in the section that follows. Poussins are a mere four to five weeks old at slaughtering and usually weigh about 500 g (1 lb). They may be sautéed, roasted or grilled; each bird is often a single portion in itself.

Determining how much chicken to buy for a meal depends on how it is to be cooked and how many people it is supposed to feed. For a whole bird, 250 g (8 oz) works out to about 90 g (3 oz) after cooking and the removal of the skin and bones. As for chicken parts, one breast, a whole leg, two drumsticks, two thighs or three wings usually constitute a 90 g (3 oz) serving, considered an ideal adult portion by nutritionists.

Stir-Fried Chopped Chicken on Lettuce Leaves

Serves 6
Working time: about 30 minutes
Total time: about 45 minutes

Calories **275**
Protein **27g**
Cholesterol **65mg**
Total fat **13g**
Saturated fat **2g**
Sodium **590mg**

600 g	chicken breast meat, finely chopped	1¼ lb
15 g	dried Chinese mushrooms	½ oz
1 tbsp	cornflour	1 tbsp
2 tbsp	dry sherry	2 tbsp
¼ tsp	salt	¼ tsp
1 tsp	Sichuan peppercorns, or ½ tsp freshly ground black pepper	1 tsp
2	iceberg lettuces	2
3 tbsp	safflower oil	3 tbsp
1 tbsp	finely chopped fresh ginger root	1 tbsp
2	garlic cloves, finely chopped	2
2	spring onions, finely chopped	2
90 g	water chestnuts, chopped	3 oz
250 g	bamboo shoots, chopped	8 oz
60 g	lean ham, finely chopped	2 oz
3 tbsp	low-sodium soy sauce, or naturally fermented shoyu	3 tbsp
2 tsp	dark sesame oil	2 tsp

Soak the mushrooms in a bowl of hot water for 10 minutes. Stir to release any sand, then let them stand in the water for another 20 minutes before draining them. Cut off and discard the stems, slice the mushrooms thinly, and set them aside.

In a bowl, mix the cornflour and the sherry. Add the salt and the chicken. Combine well and set aside to marinate for at least 15 minutes.

Meanwhile, in a small, heavy frying pan, toast the peppercorns over medium heat for 3 to 4 minutes, shaking the pan frequently. Remove the peppercorns from the pan and crush them with the flat of a knife. Set aside.

Carefully separate the lettuce leaves. Trim them with a sharp knife or scissors to produce 12 cuplike leaves of comparable size. Set aside.

Heat a wok or a large, heavy frying pan over high heat. Add 2 tablespoons of the safflower oil and swirl the pan to coat its surface. Add the chicken and stir-fry until the meat loses its pink hue — 2 to 3 minutes. Remove the chicken and set it aside.

Heat the remaining tablespoon of safflower oil over high heat. Add the ginger, garlic, spring onions, water chestnuts and bamboo shoots, and stir-fry for 2 minutes. Then add the ham, mushrooms and peppercorns or black pepper, and stir-fry for another minute. Toss in the chicken and stir-fry until it is heated through.

Remove the wok or pan from the heat and stir in the soy sauce and the sesame oil. Arrange the lettuce leaves on a platter, spoon the mixture on to them and serve. The chicken-filled leaves are all the more delicious eaten with the hands.

SUGGESTED ACCOMPANIMENTS: *steamed rice; bean sprouts.*

EDITOR'S NOTE: *Stir-frying is designed to sear meats and cook vegetables quickly, without sacrificing their colour, texture or flavour. It must be executed speedily so that the meats will not toughen and the vegetables will not wilt.*

Sautéed Chicken Breasts with Liver and Grapes

Serves 4
Working (and total) time: about 40 minutes

Calories **295**
Protein **32g**
Cholesterol **210mg**
Total fat **11g**
Saturated fat **3g**
Sodium **215mg**

4	chicken breasts, skinned and boned (about 500 g/1 lb)	4
5 g	unsalted butter	⅙ oz
1 tbsp	safflower oil	1 tbsp
¼ tsp	salt	¼ tsp
	freshly ground black pepper	
12.5 cl	Madeira	4 fl oz
45 g	shallots, finely chopped	45 g
½ tsp	crushed mustard seeds	½ tsp
1 tsp	fresh thyme, or ¼ tsp dried thyme	1 tsp
125 g	chicken livers	4 oz
125 g	seedless grapes, cut in half	4 oz
2 tbsp	soured cream	2 tbsp
2 tsp	plain low-fat yogurt	2 tsp
1 tsp	cornflour, mixed with 1 tbsp fresh lime juice	1 tsp
1 tbsp	chopped parsley	1 tbsp

Heat the butter and 1 teaspoon of the oil in a heavy frying pan over medium-high heat. Cook the chicken breasts on one side until they are lightly browned — about 4 minutes. Turn the pieces over and sprinkle them with the salt and pepper. Cook for 3 minutes on the second side, then remove the breasts, place on a heated platter, and set aside.

Pour the Madeira into the pan and simmer to reduce it by half — about 3 minutes. Add the shallots, mustard seeds and thyme, and simmer for 2 or 3 minutes more. Pour the sauce over the chicken, scraping out the pan deposits along with it.

Wipe the pan with a paper towel. Heat the remaining 2 teaspoons of oil in the pan over medium-high heat, and sauté the chicken livers, turning occasionally, until they brown — about 6 minutes. Reduce the heat to low, return the chicken breasts and their sauce to the pan, and add the grapes. Stir the soured cream and yogurt into the cornflour-lime juice mixture, then pour it into the pan. Simmer until the chicken is cooked through — about 5 minutes. Garnish the chicken with the chopped parsley and serve immediately.

SUGGESTED ACCOMPANIMENTS: *rice pilaff; green beans.*

Chicken Cutlets with Summer Herbs and Tomato Sauce

Serves 4
Working time: about 30 minutes
Total time: about 30 minutes

Calories **280**
Protein **30g**
Cholesterol **70mg**
Total fat **10g**
Saturated fat **2g**
Sodium **325mg**

4	chicken breasts, skinned and boned (about 500 g/1 lb), pounded to about 1 cm (½ inch) thickness	4
1	garlic clove, finely chopped	1
2	large tomatoes, skinned, seeded and coarsely chopped	2
1 tbsp	virgin olive oil	1 tbsp
12.5 cl	unsalted chicken stock	4 fl oz
¾ tsp	tarragon vinegar	¾ tsp
1 tbsp each	finely chopped fresh tarragon, basil and parsley, mixed, plus a few sprigs for garnish	1 tbsp each
¼ tsp	salt	¼ tsp
¼ tsp	freshly ground white pepper	¼ tsp
45 g	dry breadcrumbs	1½ oz
2	egg whites	2
1 tbsp	safflower oil	1 tbsp

To prepare the sauce, cook the garlic and tomatoes in the olive oil over medium-high heat in a small saucepan, stirring occasionally, until soft — about 5 minutes. Add the stock, the vinegar and 2 tablespoons of the herb mixture, and bring to the boil. Reduce the heat, cover and simmer for 5 minutes. Purée the sauce in a food processor or blender and return to the pan to keep warm.

Meanwhile, sprinkle the salt and pepper over the breasts. Mix the remaining tablespoon of herbs with the breadcrumbs on a large plate. In a small bowl, whisk the egg whites vigorously and dip the breasts in the whites, then in the breadcrumb mixture.

Heat the safflower oil in a large, heavy frying pan over medium-high heat and sauté the chicken on one side until lightly brown — about 3 minutes. Turn the breasts, cover the pan loosely, and sauté until they feel firm but springy to the touch — about 4 minutes more. Transfer the breasts to a heated platter and spoon the sauce over them. Garnish with sprigs of herbs.

SUGGESTED ACCOMPANIMENT: *corn on the cob.*

Chicken Breasts Sautéed with Coriander

Serves 4
Working time: about 30 minutes
Total time: about 30 minutes

Calories **205**
Protein **29g**
Cholesterol **75mg**
Total fat **7g**
Saturated fat **2g**
Sodium **235mg**

4	chicken breasts, skinned and boned (about 500 g/1 lb)	4
1 tbsp	safflower oil	1 tbsp
	freshly ground black pepper	
¼ tsp	salt	¼ tsp
8 cl	plain low-fat yogurt	3 fl oz
2 tbsp	single cream	2 tbsp
1 tsp	cornflour, mixed with 1 tbsp water	1 tsp
17.5 cl	unsalted chicken stock	6 fl oz
2 tbsp	fresh lemon juice	2 tbsp
2	garlic cloves, finely chopped	2
2 tbsp	finely chopped shallot	2 tbsp
1	small tomato, skinned, seeded and chopped	1
20 g	fresh coriander leaves, coarsely chopped, 4 leaves reserved for garnish	¾ oz

In a heavy frying pan, heat the oil over medium-high heat. Sauté the chicken breasts on one side for 5 minutes, then turn them and sprinkle with the pepper and half of the salt. Sauté on the second side until they are firm but springy to the touch — about 4 minutes. Transfer the chicken to a heated platter and keep it warm.

In a small bowl, stir the yogurt and cream into the cornflour mixture. Put the stock and lemon juice in the pan; add the garlic and shallot, reduce the heat to low, and simmer for 30 seconds. Stir in the tomato, the yogurt mixture and the remaining salt. Cook over low heat for 1 minute, then add the chopped coriander. Pour the sauce over the chicken and garnish each breast with a fresh coriander leaf, if desired.

SUGGESTED ACCOMPANIMENT: *sautéed courgettes.*

Sautéed Chicken Breasts with Raspberry Sauce

Serves 4
Working time: about 30 minutes
Total time: about 40 minutes

Calories **225**
Protein **27g**
Cholesterol **80mg**
Total fat **7g**
Saturated fat **3g**
Sodium **155mg**

4	chicken breasts, skinned and boned (about 500 g/1 lb)	4
⅛ tsp	salt	⅛ tsp
	freshly ground black pepper	
1 tsp	honey	1 tsp
1 tbsp	raspberry vinegar	1 tbsp
15 g	unsalted butter	½ oz
12.5 cl	dry white wine	4 fl oz
1	shallot, finely chopped	1
125 g	fresh raspberries	4 oz
¼ litre	unsalted chicken stock	8 fl oz
	mint sprigs, for garnish (optional)	

Sprinkle the chicken breasts with the salt and pepper and put them on a plate. Stir the honey into the raspberry vinegar and mix well. Dribble this mixture over the breasts and allow them to marinate for 15 minutes.

Preheat the oven to 100°C (200°F or Mark ¼). In a heavy frying pan, melt the butter over medium-high heat, and sauté the breasts until golden — about 4 minutes on each side. Transfer the chicken to a serving platter and put the platter in the oven to keep warm. Add the wine and shallot to the pan. Reduce the liquid until it barely coats the pan — there should be about 2 tablespoons. Reserve 12 of the raspberries for a garnish. Add the stock and the remaining raspberries and reduce by half. Purée the mixture in a food processor or blender, then strain it through a fine sieve.

Return the sauce to the pan and bring it to the boil. Spoon it over the chicken and garnish with the reserved raspberries and the mint sprigs, if desired.

SUGGESTED ACCOMPANIMENTS: *peas; steamed rice.*

Chicken with Peanuts and Ginger Sauce

Serves 6
Working time: about 20 minutes
Total time: about 2 hours and 20 minutes

Calories **260**					
Protein **30g**	750 g	chicken breast meat, cut into 1 cm	1½ lb	45 g	peanuts, crushed with a rolling pin	1½ oz
Cholesterol **70mg**		(½ inch) cubes		1 tbsp	safflower oil	1 tbsp
Total fat **12g**	12.5 cl	dry white wine	4 fl oz			
Saturated fat **3g**	45 g	fresh ginger, finely chopped	1½ oz			
Sodium **200mg**	1	garlic clove, crushed	1			
	¼ tsp	salt	¼ tsp			
		freshly ground black pepper				
	¼ litre	unsalted chicken stock	8 fl oz			
	2 tbsp	peanut butter	2 tbsp			
	1 tsp	tomato paste (optional)	1 tsp			
	2	spring onions, julienned	2			

Make a marinade of the wine, ginger, garlic, salt and pepper, and let the chicken stand in it for 2 hours.

Near the end of the marinating time, prepare the sauce. Pour the stock into a small saucepan and whisk in the peanut butter and the tomato paste, if used. Add the spring onions and simmer the sauce over low heat, uncovered, for 2 minutes. Remove the saucepan from the heat and set it aside.

Remove the cubes from the marinade and set them aside. Strain the marinade and add it to the sauce. Return the mixture to a simmer and cook over low heat, stirring occasionally, until the sauce is thick enough to coat the back of a spoon — about 4 minutes. Remove the pan from the heat.

Roll the chicken cubes in the crushed peanuts, sparsely coating the cubes. Heat the oil in a heavy frying pan over high heat. When the oil is hot but not smoking, add the chicken cubes and lightly brown them, stirring gently to keep intact as much of the peanut coating as possible — about 3 minutes. Remove the frying pan from the heat and allow the chicken to finish cooking as it rests in the hot pan — about 2 minutes more. Transfer the chicken to a warmed platter and pour the sauce over it just before serving.

SUGGESTED ACCOMPANIMENTS: *steamed rice; fried bananas; cucumber salad.*

Sautéed Chicken with Mustard, Caraway Seeds and Chervil

Serves 4
Working time: about 1 hour
Total time: about 1 hour

Calories **440**
Protein **30g**
Cholesterol **105mg**
Total fat **18g**
Saturated fat **8g**
Sodium **375mg**

4	chicken breasts, skinned and boned (about 500 g/1 lb), pounded to 1 cm (½ inch) thickness	4
⅛ tsp	salt	⅛ tsp
	freshly ground black pepper	
3 tbsp	Dijon mustard	3 tbsp
8 cl	plain low-fat yogurt	3 fl oz
2 tsp	caraway seeds	2 tsp
5 tbsp	chopped fresh chervil or parsley	5 tbsp
90 g	dry breadcrumbs	3 oz
30 g	unsalted butter	1 oz
1 tbsp	safflower oil	1 tbsp
3	tart green apples, cored and cut into 5 mm (¼ inch) slices	3
2 tbsp	aquavit or kümmel (optional)	2 tbsp
12.5 cl	unsweetened apple juice	4 fl oz
1 tbsp	fresh lemon juice	1 tbsp
4 tbsp	double cream	4 tbsp

Sprinkle the pounded breasts with the salt and pepper.

In a small bowl, whisk together the mustard, yogurt, caraway seeds and 4 tablespoons of the chervil or parsley. Generously coat the breasts with the mixture, then place them in the breadcrumbs and pat on the crumbs evenly. Chill for at least 10 minutes, or for up to an hour.

Once the breasts have been chilled, heat 15 g (½ oz) of the butter and the oil in a large heavy frying pan over medium heat. Place the breasts in the pan and sauté, turning once, until the crumbs are golden — 6 to 8 minutes.

Heat the remaining butter in a heavy frying pan over medium heat. Toss in the apple slices and cook them for 4 to 5 minutes, turning the slices occasionally. Add the aquavit or kümmel, if using, and simmer to evaporate — 1 to 2 minutes. Add the apple juice, the lemon juice and more pepper, and simmer for 3 to 4 minutes. Push the apples to one side of the pan and whisk in the cream. Cook for 2 minutes more.

To serve, place the chicken on a heated platter and, using a slotted spoon to lift the apple slices from the pan, arrange the slices around the breasts. Continue simmering the sauce until it thickens slightly — 2 to 3 minutes. Pour the sauce over the chicken and apples, and garnish with the remaining tablespoon of chervil or parsley. Serve immediately.

SUGGESTED ACCOMPANIMENT: *mashed turnips or swedes.*

Chicken Breasts Stuffed with Garlic and Carrots

Serves 4
Working time: about 45 minutes
Total time: about 1 hour

Calories **245**			
Protein **28g**	4	chicken breasts, skinned and boned (about 500 g/1 lb)	4
Cholesterol **75mg**	1 tbsp	virgin olive oil	1 tbsp
Total fat **9g**	24 to 32	garlic cloves, peeled	24 to 32
Saturated fat **2g**	½ tsp	salt	½ tsp
Sodium **360mg**	1	large carrot, cut into 12 strips 5mm (¼ inch) thick and 10 cm (4 inches) long	1
	2 tbsp	fresh rosemary leaves	2 tbsp
	1 tsp	safflower oil	1 tsp
		freshly ground black pepper	
	12.5 cl	unsalted chicken stock	4 fl oz
	4 tbsp	dry white wine	4 tbsp
	1	shallot, finely chopped	1

Heat the olive oil in a heavy frying pan over low heat. Slowly cook the garlic cloves in the olive oil, stirring occasionally, for 20 minutes.

Sprinkle the garlic cloves with ⅛ teaspoon of the salt and continue cooking until they turn golden-brown all over — about 10 minutes more. Remove the cloves with a slotted spoon and set them aside. Do not discard the oil in the frying pan.

While the garlic is browning, prepare the carrots and the chicken. Blanch the carrot strips in boiling water until tender — about 4 minutes — then drain them and set them aside. Lay the chicken breasts on a cutting board, their smooth sides facing down. Along the thinner long edge of each breast, make a horizontal slit and cut nearly through to the opposite side. Open each breast so that it forms two flaps hinged at the centre. Sprinkle the rosemary and ¼ teaspoon of the salt over the flaps. Arrange three carrot strips on the larger flap of each breast, and distribute the garlic cloves between the carrot strips. Fold the top flaps over the bottoms, align their edges, and press the breasts as nearly closed as possible.

Add the safflower oil to the oil in the pan and turn the heat to medium high. When the oil is hot, put the stuffed breasts in the pan and sauté them on one side until they are browned — about 5 minutes. Turn the breasts gently and sprinkle them with the remaining salt and the pepper. Cook the breasts on the second side until they feel firm but springy to the touch — 5 to 7 minutes more. Carefully remove the breasts from the frying pan and place them on a warmed serving platter.

Prepare the sauce by stirring the stock, wine and shallot into the pan juices to deglaze it. Stir frequently until the sauce is reduced by half. Pour some sauce over each breast and serve immediately.

SUGGESTED ACCOMPANIMENT: *mange-tout with lemon butter.*

Chicken Riesling

Serves 4
Working time: about 30 minutes
Total time: about 1 hour

Calories **310**			
Protein **27g**	4	chicken breasts, skinned and boned (about 500 g/1 lb)	4
Cholesterol **80mg**		freshly ground black pepper	
Total fat **11g**	½ tsp	salt	½ tsp
Saturated fat **3g**	1 tbsp	safflower oil	1 tbsp
Sodium **365mg**	15 g	unsalted butter	½ oz
	2 tbsp	finely chopped shallots	2 tbsp
	90 g	mushrooms, thinly sliced	3 oz
	35 cl	Riesling wine	12 fl oz
	1 tbsp	chopped fresh tarragon or 1 tsp dried tarragon	1 tbsp
	30 cl	unsalted chicken stock	½ pint
	2 tsp	cornflour	2 tsp
	125 g	red grapes, halved and seeded	4 oz

Preheat the oven to 100°C (200°F or Mark ¼).

Sprinkle the chicken with the pepper and ¼ teaspoon of the salt. Heat the oil over medium-high heat in a large, heavy frying pan. Sauté the pieces in the oil until brown — about 5 minutes on each side. Transfer the chicken to a platter and cover it with foil.

Add the butter, shallots and mushrooms to the pan, sprinkle with half of the remaining salt, and sauté until the shallots soften — 2 to 3 minutes. With a slotted spoon, transfer the mushrooms to the platter with the chicken, and keep it warm in the oven. Add all but 4 tablespoons of the Riesling to the pan along with the tarragon, and reduce the liquid to about 4 tablespoons. Pour in the stock and reduce by half. Mix the cornflour with the remaining wine. Reduce the heat so that the sauce simmers, and stir in the cornflour mixture and the remaining salt. Add the halved grapes and cook for 2 minutes. Arrange some of the mushroom mixture on each breast, and pour the sauce over all.

SUGGESTED ACCOMPANIMENTS: *garlic bread; oak leaf lettuce salad.*

Chicken, Aubergine and Tomato Sauté

Serves 4
Working time: about 45 minutes
Total time: about 1 hour

Calories **370**
Protein **30g**
Cholesterol **75mg**
Total fat **19g**
Saturated fat **4g**
Sodium **205mg**

4	chicken breasts, skinned and boned (about 500 g/1 lb)	4
2	small aubergines, sliced in 5 mm (¼ inch) thick rounds	2
5 g	unsalted butter	⅙ oz
4 tbsp	virgin olive oil	4 tbsp
	freshly ground black pepper	
¼ tsp	salt	¼ tsp
4 tbsp	dry sherry	4 tbsp
2 tbsp	fresh lemon juice	2 tbsp
1 tsp	fresh thyme, or ¼ tsp dried thyme	1 tsp
30 g	dried mushrooms, rinsed and soaked for 1 hour in ¼ litre (8 fl oz) warm water, the remaining water strained through doubled muslin to remove grit and reserved	1 oz
3	large ripe tomatoes, skinned, sliced in 2 cm (¾ inch) thick rounds, drained on paper towels	3
1 tbsp	red wine vinegar	1 tbsp
2	garlic cloves, finely chopped	2
2	spring onions, trimmed and finely chopped	2

In a large saucepan, bring 2 litres (3½ pints) of water to the boil. Blanch the aubergine slices a few at a time in the boiling water for 30 seconds. Remove them with a slotted spoon and drain them on paper towels.

Heat the butter and 1 tablespoon of the oil in a heavy frying pan over medium-high heat. Sauté the chicken breasts on one side until they brown — about 4 minutes.

Turn them over and sprinkle them with the pepper and half the salt. Reduce the heat to low and cook for 2 minutes. Then add the sherry, lemon juice, thyme and 4 tablespoons of the water in which the mushrooms soaked. Simmer, covered, until the pieces feel firm but springy to the touch — about 5 minutes. Remove the pan from the heat and set it aside.

Preheat the oven to 100°C (200°F or Mark ¼). Heat 1 tablespoon of the remaining oil in a large frying pan over medium-high heat. Sauté one third of the aubergine slices in a single layer until golden-brown, turning them once. Repeat the process twice more with the remaining aubergine, adding ½ tablespoon of the oil to the pan before each batch. Cover the bottom of an ovenproof serving dish with the slices.

Heat the remaining tablespoon of oil in the pan over medium-high heat. Sprinkle the tomato slices with the remaining salt and sauté them until softened— about 2 minutes on the first side and 1 to 2 minutes on the second, depending on the ripeness of the tomatoes.

Arrange the tomatoes on top of the aubergine. Remove the chicken pieces from their liquid and layer them on top. Put the dish in the oven to keep warm while you make the sauce.

Bring the liquid in the frying pan to a simmer over medium heat, then add the mushrooms and the remaining mushroom liquid along with the vinegar, garlic and half of the chopped spring onions. Simmer the mixture over low heat until it is reduced by half — about 10 minutes. Spoon this sauce over the chicken, then sprinkle with the remaining chopped spring onions and serve at once.

SUGGESTED ACCOMPANIMENT: *lettuce salad.*

Chicken Paprika with Yogurt

Serves 4
Working time: about 45 minutes
Total time: about 1 hour

Calories **475**
Protein **46g**
Cholesterol **145mg**
Total fat **26g**
Saturated fat **9g**
Sodium **330mg**

1.5 kg	chicken, cut into serving pieces, the legs and breasts skinned	3 lb
2 tbsp	safflower oil	2 tbsp
¼ tsp	salt	¼ tsp
275 g	onions, finely chopped	9 oz
1	garlic clove, finely chopped	1
¼ litre	unsalted chicken stock	8 fl oz
2 tbsp	paprika	2 tbsp
17.5 cl	plain low-fat yogurt	6 fl oz
17.5 cl	soured cream	6 fl oz

In a large, heavy frying pan, heat the oil over medium-high heat. Add as many chicken pieces as will fit without crowding, and sauté them on one side until brown — about 4 minutes. Turn the pieces, sprinkle them with the salt, and sauté until the second sides brown — 3 to 4 minutes more. Transfer the chicken to a plate. Repeat with the remaining pieces.

Reduce the heat to medium low and add the onions and garlic to the oil remaining in the pan. Cook, stirring occasionally, until the onions turn translucent — about 10 minutes. Stir in the chicken stock and the paprika, and bring the liquid to a simmer.

Return all of the chicken pieces to the pan, reduce the heat to low, and cover. Simmer until the juices run clear when a thigh is pierced with the tip of a sharp knife — about 25 minutes. Transfer the chicken to a heated

platter and cover with foil to keep warm.

Skim any fat from the liquid in the pan. Bring the liquid to the boil over medium-high heat and reduce the stock to about half — 3 to 4 minutes. In a small bowl, whisk together the yogurt and soured cream. Stir in a little of the cooking liquid, then reduce the heat to low and whisk the yogurt mixture into the pan. Cook for 1 minute, then pour the sauce over the chicken and serve immediately.

SUGGESTED ACCOMPANIMENTS: *egg noodles; peas.*

Chicken Breasts with Tarragon and Tomato

Serves 4
Working time: about 30 minutes
Total time: about 2 hours and 30 minutes

Calories **225**
Protein **27g**
Cholesterol **90mg**
Total fat **10g**
Saturated fat **5g**
Sodium **215mg**

4	chicken breasts, skinned and boned (about 500 g/1 lb)	4
12.5 cl	buttermilk	4 fl oz
1 tbsp	fresh lime or lemon juice	1 tbsp
1 tbsp	fresh tarragon leaves or 1 tsp dried tarragon	1 tbsp
15 g	unsalted butter	½ oz
¼ tsp	salt	¼ tsp
2	tomatoes, skinned, seeded, finely chopped	2
1	shallot, finely chopped	1
	finely ground black pepper	
12.5 cl	single cream	4 fl oz

In a wide, shallow bowl, combine the buttermilk, lime or lemon juice, and half of the tarragon. Marinate the chicken in this mixture for 2 hours or overnight. Remove the chicken from the marinade, gently wiping off as much liquid as possible with your fingers.

In a heavy frying pan, heat the butter over medium heat. Cook the chicken breasts on one side for 5 minutes. Turn the pieces over, sprinkle them with the salt, and cook for 5 minutes more. Remove them from the pan and keep them warm.

In the same pan, cook the tomatoes, shallot, pepper and the remaining tarragon over medium heat until the tomato liquid evaporates — about 3 minutes. Stir in the cream, reduce the heat to low, and simmer for 1 minute, stirring. Cut the breasts into slices and arrange them on a serving platter. Pour the sauce over just before serving.

SUGGESTED ACCOMPANIMENTS: *julienned carrots; steamed courgettes.*

Stir-Fried Chicken with Broccoli, Red Onions and Cashew Nuts

Serves 4
Working time: about 25 minutes
Total time: about 35 minutes

Calories **350**
Protein **27g**
Cholesterol **55mg**
Total fat **20g**
Saturated fat **3g**
Sodium **520mg**

3	chicken breasts (about 350 g/12 oz), skinned, boned and sliced into 7.5 cm (3 inch) strips about 1 cm (⅓ inch) wide	3
½ tsp	salt	½ tsp
¾ tsp	freshly ground white pepper	¾ tsp
1¼ tbsp	peanut oil	1¼ tbsp
3 tbsp	safflower oil	3 tbsp
5	slices fresh ginger root, crushed with the flat of a large knife blade or lightly pounded to just loosen the fibres	5
5	large garlic cloves, peeled and crushed lightly so they remain whole	5
250 g	broccoli, florets separated, stems trimmed and thinly sliced diagonally	8 oz
2	carrots, thinly sliced diagonally	2
4 to 6	water chestnuts, sliced (optional)	4 to 6
1	small red onion, chopped into 2.5 cm (1 inch) squares	1
2 tbsp	unsalted cashew nuts	2 tbsp
3	spring onions, sliced diagonally	3
12.5 cl	unsalted chicken stock	4 fl oz
2 tbsp	cornflour, mixed with 1 tbsp low-sodium soy sauce, or naturally fermented shoyu, and 1 tbsp dry sherry	2 tbsp
¼ tsp	dark sesame oil	¼ tsp

In a bowl, sprinkle the chicken strips with ¼ teaspoon of the salt and ½ teaspoon of the pepper; stir well.

Heat a wok or a large, deep, heavy frying pan over ▶

medium-high heat. Meanwhile, blend the peanut oil and the safflower oil in a small bowl. When the wok or pan is hot to the touch, slowly pour in 2 tablespoons of the blended oil so that it evenly coats the entire cooking surface.

To flavour the oil, stir-fry the ginger and garlic for about 30 seconds. Then add the chicken strips and stir-fry them in the flavoured oil, tossing frequently, until the meat turns white — about 3 minutes.

Discard the ginger and garlic. Transfer the chicken to a plate and set it aside; do not discard the oil.

Pour an additional tablespoon of the blended oil into the wok or pan. Add the broccoli and carrot pieces, sprinkle them with the remaining salt and pepper, and stir-fry until the oil has coated all the pieces — 1 to 2 minutes. Pour in the remaining tablespoon of blended oil, then add the water chestnuts, if you are using them, the onion, cashews and two thirds of the spring onions. Stir-fry these with the other vegetables for 1 to 2 minutes more.

Return the chicken to the wok or pan and stir-fry the chicken and vegetables together. Push the contents to the sides and pour the stock into the centre. Stir the cornflour mixture into the stock and heat until the liquid boils and thickens. Redistribute the chicken and vegetables in the sauce and stir to coat all the pieces evenly — 1 to 2 minutes. Add the sesame oil and stir well.

Serve the dish with the remaining sliced spring onions sprinkled over the top.

SUGGESTED ACCOMPANIMENT: *Chinese noodles.*

EDITOR'S NOTE: *Stir-frying is designed to sear meats and cook vegetables quickly, without sacrificing their colour, texture or flavour. It must be executed speedily so the meats will not toughen and the vegetables will not wilt.*

Sautéed Chicken Breasts with Apricots, Bourbon and Pecans

Serves 4
Working time: about 30 minutes
Total time: about 8 hours

Calories **405**
Protein **29g**
Cholesterol **75mg**
Total fat **11g**
Saturated fat **2g**
Sodium **250mg**

4	chicken breasts, skinned and boned (about 500 g/1 lb)	4
250 g	dried apricots	8 oz
8 cl	bourbon whiskey	3 fl oz
17.5 cl	unsalted chicken stock	6 fl oz
5 g	unsalted butter	⅙ oz
1 tsp	safflower oil	1 tsp
¼ tsp	salt	¼ tsp
	freshly ground black pepper	
1	shallot, finely chopped	1
1 tsp	tomato paste	1 tsp
2 tsp	grainy mustard	2 tsp
30 g	pecans, toasted in a 180°C (350°F or Mark 4) oven, then crushed with a rolling pin	1 oz
1	spring onion, cut into 5 cm (2 inch) long pieces and thinly sliced	1

Marinate the apricots in the bourbon and a third of the stock for 8 hours or overnight. Alternatively, bring the bourbon and a third of the stock to the boil, then turn off the heat and steep the apricots in the liquid until they soften — about 10 minutes.

Heat the butter and the oil in a heavy frying pan over medium-high heat. Sauté the chicken breasts on one side until lightly coloured — about 4 minutes. Turn them over and sprinkle with the salt and pepper. Sauté them on the second side for 4 minutes. Drain the bourbon and stock from the apricots, and pour it over the chicken. Add the remaining stock, reduce the heat to low and cook until the chicken feels firm but springy to the touch — about 5 minutes. Transfer the chicken to a plate and cover with aluminium foil to keep it warm.

Add the apricots and shallot to the pan and simmer for 2 minutes. Whisk in the tomato paste and mustard and simmer for 3 minutes, stirring occasionally. Return the breasts to the pan for 1 or 2 minutes to heat through.

Arrange the chicken and the apricots on a warmed serving platter. Spoon the sauce over the chicken and sprinkle with the pecans and spring onion.

SUGGESTED ACCOMPANIMENT: *steamed Swiss chard.*

Stir-Fried Chicken with Red Cabbage and Chilies

Serves 4
Working (and total) time: about 45 minutes

Calories **265**
Protein **23g**
Cholesterol **55mg**
Total fat **10g**
Saturated fat **1g**
Sodium **355mg**

3	chicken breasts, skinned and boned (about 350 g/12 oz) cut into 1cm (½ inch) wide strips	3
4 tbsp	finely chopped stoned prunes	4 tbsp
2	garlic cloves, finely chopped	2
1 to 2	large dried red chili peppers, seeded, cut into very thin strips, or ½ to 1 tsp crushed red pepper flakes	1 to 2
2 tbsp	safflower oil	2 tbsp
150 g	French beans	5 oz
1 tbsp	low-sodium soy sauce, or naturally fermented shoyu	1 tbsp
1	small red cabbage, cored and cut into 5 cm (2 inch) strips	1
¼ tsp	salt	¼ tsp
7	spring onions, trimmed, halved lengthwise and cut into 5 cm (2 inch) strips	7

Combine the prunes, garlic, chilies or crushed red pepper flakes, and ½ tablespoon of the oil in a large, shallow dish. Add the chicken and marinate for at least 30 minutes, turning occasionally to coat the meat. Blanch the French beans for 1 minute in ½ litre (16 fl oz) of boiling water. Refresh the beans under cold running water, place them in a bowl, and add the soy sauce. Set aside to marinate, turning occasionally to coat the beans.

Heat a wok or large, heavy frying pan over high heat. Pour in an additional tablespoon of oil and stir-fry the cabbage with the salt until the cabbage wilts — about 3 minutes. Add the beans with the soy sauce and half the spring onions. Continue stir-frying for 3 minutes, stirring and tossing. Empty the wok or pan into a large bowl.

Return the pan to the heat. Pour in the remaining oil and immediately add the chicken and its marinade along with the rest of the spring onions. Reduce the heat to medium high and stir and toss until the chicken is cooked — about 4 minutes. Add the cabbage mixture, mix well, and serve immediately.

SUGGESTED ACCOMPANIMENTS: *saffron rice; firm tofu sautéed with soy sauce.*

EDITOR'S NOTE: *Stir-frying is designed to sear meats and cook vegetables quickly, without sacrificing their colour, texture or flavour. It must be executed speedily so the meats will not toughen and the vegetables will not wilt.*

Chili Peppers — A Cautionary Note

Both dried and fresh hot chili peppers should be handled with care. Their flesh and seeds contain volatile oils that can make skin tingle and cause eyes to burn. Rubber gloves offer protection —but the cook should still be careful not to touch the face, lips or eyes when working with chilies.

Soaking fresh chilies in cold, salted water for an hour will remove some of their fire. If canned chilies are substituted for fresh ones, they should be rinsed in cold water in order to eliminate as much of the brine used to preserve them as possible.

Poached Chicken
with Fennel

Serves 6
Working time: about 30 minutes
Total time: about 1 hour

Calories **340**
Protein **29g**
Cholesterol **95mg**
Total fat **11g**
Saturated fat **4g**
Sodium **515mg**

6	chicken legs, skinned	6
1 tsp	black peppercorns	1 tsp
2	garlic cloves, peeled	2
¼ litre	anise-flavoured liqueur	8 fl oz
¾ litre	unsalted chicken stock	1¼ pints
1	onion, thinly sliced	1
½ tsp	fennel seeds	½ tsp
1 tsp	salt	1 tsp
2	large fennel bulbs, the tough outer layer and feathery green tops trimmed and reserved, the bulbs cut lengthwise into 6 pieces	2
1	stick celery, trimmed, cut into 7.5 cm (3 inch) strips about 5 mm (¼ inch) wide	1
1	bay leaf	1
2	large lettuce leaves, preferably cos	2
250 g	baby carrots, tops removed, peeled	8 oz
15 g	unsalted butter	½ oz
	freshly ground black pepper	

Crush the peppercorns and the garlic with a mortar and pestle and mash them into a paste. Spread the paste over each chicken leg.

Bring the liqueur to the boil in a large, heavy fireproof casserole. Add the chicken legs and turn them to coat them with the liqueur. Add the stock, onion, fennel seeds and salt; if necessary, pour in enough water or additional stock to just cover the chicken. Return the liquid to the boil. Reduce the heat to medium low and simmer the chicken legs for 15 minutes.

Meanwhile, make a bouquet garni: wrap the tough outer layer and trimmings from the fennel, the celery strips and the bay leaf in the lettuce leaves, and tie the bundle with string. Add the bouquet garni to the casserole, submerging it in the poaching liquid.

At the end of the 15 minutes, add the fennel pieces, pressing them into the liquid. Cover the casserole and simmer for 5 minutes more. Add the carrots and continue cooking, uncovered, until the juices run clear when a thigh is pierced with the tip of a sharp knife — 7 to 10 minutes. Transfer the chicken legs and the vegetables to a warmed serving platter.

To make the sauce, reduce the poaching liquid over high heat to about 30 cl (½ pint). Remove and discard the bouquet garni. Whisk the butter and some pepper into

the sauce and pour it over the legs and vegetables; garnish them, if you like, with the feathery fennel tops.

SUGGESTED ACCOMPANIMENT: *sautéed onions and potatoes.*

Poached Chicken Strips in Gingered Orange Sauce

Serves 6
Working time: about 45 minutes
Total time: 1 hour and 30 minutes

Calories **180**
Protein **20g**
Cholesterol **55mg**
Total fat **5g**
Saturated fat **2g**
Sodium **185mg**

4	chicken breasts, skinned and boned (about 500 g/1 lb), cut into 1 cm (½ inch) wide strips	4
¼ tsp	salt	¼ tsp
	freshly ground black pepper	
¼ litre	fresh orange juice	8 fl oz
¾ litre	unsalted chicken stock	1¼ pints
4 to 5 cm	fresh ginger root (25 to 30 g/¾ to 1 oz), peeled and cut into chunks	1½ to 2 inches
2	navel oranges, the rind julienned and the flesh segmented	2
¼ tsp	aromatic bitters	¼ tsp
1 tsp	whisky	1 tsp
30 g	cream cheese	1 oz
1 tbsp	cornflour	1 tbsp

Put the chicken strips in a shallow dish and sprinkle them with half of the salt and some pepper. Pour in the orange juice. Turn the pieces to coat them with the juice. Cover the dish with plastic film and refrigerate for 1 hour.

Lift the chicken strips out of the marinade and set them aside. To make the poaching liquid, pour the marinade into a large saucepan. Add ½ litre (16 fl oz) of the stock, the remaining salt and some pepper. Squeeze each ginger chunk through a garlic press into the pan, scraping the paste from the outside bottom of the press into the pot and then turning the press over to add the juices. Bring the liquid to the boil, reduce the heat, cover the pan, and simmer for 4 minutes. Remove the pan from the heat and let the ginger steep in the poaching liquid for 15 minutes.

While the ginger is steeping, put the orange rind in a small saucepan. Cover the rind with 12.5 cl (4 fl oz) of the stock, the bitters and the whisky. Cook briskly over medium-high heat until almost all the liquid has evaporated, and set the pan aside. In another small saucepan, pour the remaining stock over the orange segments; cover and set aside.

Return the poaching liquid to the boil. Add the chicken strips and reduce the heat to medium. Simmer the liquid until the chicken feels firm but springy to the touch — about 1 minute. Remove the chicken strips with a slotted spoon and set them in the centre of a warmed serving platter.

In a small bowl, soften the cream cheese with the back of a spoon. Stir in the cornflour. Pour about 12.5 cl (4 fl oz) of the hot poaching liquid into the bowl and whisk well. Add the same amount again of poaching liquid, then pour the contents of the bowl back into the pan and cook over medium heat, whisking, until the sauce thickens slightly — 2 or 3 minutes.

Heat the orange segments in the chicken stock. Spoon some sauce over the chicken strips and garnish them with the orange rind. Lift the orange segments out of the stock and arrange them around the chicken. Pass the remaining sauce separately.

SUGGESTED ACCOMPANIMENT: *buckwheat groats (kasha) cooked in chicken stock with sliced mushrooms.*

strips to fit inside the breasts. Arrange some spring onions, 2 or 3 cucumber strips, and 2 or 3 pepper strips across the grain of the meat at the wide edge of each breast. Roll the chicken round the vegetables and fasten each roll lengthwise with a small skewer.

Heat the oil in a heavy frying pan over medium heat and gentle sauté the rolls, turning them, until golden — about 4 minutes. Remove the chicken and pour the sauce into the pan, stirring, being sure to scrape up any brown bits from the bottom. Return the chicken to the pan, cover loosely, and simmer for 8 minutes, turning once.

Transfer the chicken to a heated platter, remove the skewers, and cut the chicken into slices. Pour the sauce over the slices and serve immediately.

SUGGESTED ACCOMPANIMENT: *rice with peas and mushrooms.*

Poached Chicken with Black Bean Onion Sauce

THE FERMENTED BLACK BEANS CALLED FOR IN THIS RECIPE ARE
AVAILABLE WHERE ASIAN FOODS ARE SOLD

Serves 4
Working time: about 30 minutes
Total time: about 1 hour and 30 minutes

Calories **485**
Protein **45g**
Cholesterol **125mg**
Total fat **18g**
Saturated fat **4g**
Sodium **235g**

1.5 kg	chicken, trussed	3 lb
2 tbsp	safflower oil	2 tbsp
3	onions, sliced	3
1 tbsp	flour	1 tbsp
2 tsp	fermented black beans, rinsed well	2 tsp
2	garlic cloves, finely chopped	2
¼ litre	dry white wine	8 fl oz
¾ litre	unsalted beef stock	1 ¼ pints
2 tbsp	brandy	2 tbsp
1	small potato, peeled and cut into chunks	1
	freshly ground black pepper	
15 g	unsalted butter, cut into pieces (optional)	½ oz

Red Pepper and Chicken Spirals

Serves 4
Working time: about 30 minutes
Total time: about 45 minutes

Calories **250**
Protein **28g**
Cholesterol **70mg**
Total fat **11g**
Saturated fat **2g**
Sodium **535mg**

4	chicken breasts, skinned, boned, the long triangular fillets removed and reserved for another use, lightly pounded to 5mm (¼ inch) thickness	4
¼ tsp	salt	¼ tsp
½ tsp	crushed Sichuan peppercorns, or ¼ tsp crushed black peppercorns	½ tsp
3	spring onions, blanched for 30 seconds, drained, cooled, patted dry, and halved lengthwise	3
1	cucumber, peeled, halved lengthwise, seeded, cut into 5 mm (¼ inch) wide strips, blanched for 30 seconds, drained, cooled and patted dry	1
1	sweet red pepper, seeded, deribbed, cut into 1 cm (½ inch) strips, blanched for 2 minutes, drained and patted dry	1
2 tbsp	safflower oil	2 tbsp
Mirin sauce		
3 tbsp	low-sodium soy sauce, or naturally fermented shoyu	3 tbsp
1 tbsp	sugar	1 tbsp
2 tbsp	mirin, or dry sherry	2 tbsp
2 tsp	rice vinegar	2 tsp
½ tsp	crushed Sichuan peppercorns, or ¼ tsp crushed black peppercorns	½ tsp

To prepare the sauce, combine the soy sauce, sugar, *mirin* or sherry, vinegar, crushed peppercorns and 3 tablespoons of water in a small bowl. Set aside.

Sprinkle the chicken with the salt and crushed peppercorns. Cut the spring onions, cucumber strips and pepper

Pour the oil into a deep, fireproof casserole set over medium-low heat, and stir in the sliced onions. Cover the casserole and cook, stirring occasionally, until the onions are greatly reduced in bulk and quite limp — about 30 minutes.

Uncover the casserole and stir in the flour, black beans and garlic. Cook, stirring, for 1 minute. Add the wine, ¾ litre (1¼ pints) of the stock, the brandy, potato and some pepper. Lower the chicken into the casserole. If necessary, pour in enough additional stock or water to almost cover the bird.

Place a sheet of aluminium foil over the chicken and cover the casserole. Poach gently over medium-low heat, turning the bird several times, until the juices run clear when a thigh is pierced with the tip of a sharp knife — about 45 minutes. Transfer the chicken to a carving board and cover it with the foil to keep it warm.

To prepare the sauce, first skim the fat off the cooking liquid. Set a strainer or colander over a bowl and pour the liquid through it. Reserve 4 tablespoons of the onions. Transfer the drained potato pieces and the remaining onions to a food processor or blender, add 12.5 cl (4 fl oz) of the strained cooking liquid, and purée the mixture until smooth. Pour in an additional ¼ litre (8 fl oz) of the cooking liquid and purée again until smooth.

Pour the sauce into a small pan and warm it over low heat. Remove the sauce from the heat and, if desired, swirl in the butter. (The butter lends richness and gloss to the sauce.)

Carve the chicken into serving pieces. Spoon some sauce over the pieces and scatter the reserved onions over them. Pass the remaining sauce separately.

SUGGESTED ACCOMPANIMENTS: *polenta; green beans.*

Cranberried Chicken

Serves 4
Working time: about 20 minutes
Total time: about 3 hours

Calories **610**		
Protein **42g**		
Cholesterol **133mg**		
Total fat **13g**		
Saturated fat **5g**		
Sodium **133mg**		

1.5 kg	chicken, cut into serving pieces, skinned	3 lb
1.75 litres	cranberry or apple juice	3 pints
30 g	basil, lightly crushed to bruise the leaves, or 1½ tbsp dried basil	1 oz
1	onion, sliced	1
250 g	cranberries	8 oz
125 g	sugar	4 oz
2 tbsp	raspberry vinegar	2 tbsp
1 tsp	cornflour, mixed with 2 tbsp water	1 tsp
15 g	unsalted butter, cut into pieces	½ oz

In a large, non-reactive saucepan, simmer 1.25 litres (2 pints) of the cranberry juice with the basil and onion for 10 minutes. Let the liquid cool, then add the chicken pieces. Marinate for 2 hours at room temperature or overnight in the refrigerator, turning the pieces occasionally.

If needed, pour in enough water to cover the chicken pieces. Bring the liquid to a simmer and reduce the heat. Partially cover the pan. Poach the chicken gently, skimming the foam from the surface, until the juices run clear when a thigh is pierced with the tip of a sharp knife —15 to 20 minutes.

Simmer the cranberries in the rest of the juice with the sugar until they almost burst — about 7 minutes. Drain the cranberries and discard the liquid.

Transfer the chicken to a heated serving platter and cover it to keep it warm. Strain the poaching liquid and return it to the pot. Add the vinegar and bring the liquid to the boil. Cook over medium-high heat until the liquid

is reduced to about 35 cl (12 fl oz) — 15 to 25 minutes. Stir in the cornflour mixture and the cooked cranberries, and simmer until the sauce has thickened slightly — 2 or 3 minutes. Remove the pot from the heat and swirl in the butter. Spoon some of the sauce over the chicken and pass the rest separately.

SUGGESTED ACCOMPANIMENTS: *wild rice; braised fennel.*

Chicken Poached
in Milk and Curry

Serves 4
Working time: about 15 minutes
Total time: about 1 hour and 15 minutes

Calories **450**
Protein **52g**
Cholesterol **160mg**
Total fat **20g**
Saturated fat **10g**
Sodium **490mg**

1.5 kg	chicken, wings reserved for another use, the rest skinned and cut into serving pieces	3 lb
¾ litre	milk	1 ¼ pints
2	large onions, thinly sliced	2
4 or 5	bay leaves	4 or 5
2 tsp	fresh thyme, or ½ tsp dried thyme	2 tsp
3	garlic cloves, crushed	3
1 tsp	curry powder	1 tsp
½ tsp	salt	½ tsp
	freshly ground black pepper	
150 g	shelled peas	5 oz
15 g	unsalted butter	½ oz

In a large, heavy-bottomed saucepan over medium heat, combine the milk, onions, bay leaves, thyme, garlic, curry powder, salt and two or three generous grindings of pepper. Bring the liquid just to a simmer, then immediately remove the pan from the heat. Allow the mixture to stand for 30 minutes so that the milk can pick up the flavours; after 15 minutes, preheat the oven to 175°C (325° F or Mark 3).

Arrange the chicken pieces in a baking dish just large enough to hold them snugly — no larger than 23 by 33 cm (9 by 13 inches). Bring the milk-and-onion mixture to a simmer again and pour it over the chicken pieces. Set the saucepan aside; do not wash it. Drape the onion slices over any chicken pieces that protrude from the liquid so that the chicken will not dry out during cooking. Put the dish in the oven and poach the chicken until the juices run clear when a thigh is pierced with the tip of a sharp knife — 35 to 40 minutes.

Take the dish from the oven and turn the oven off Remove the chicken pieces from their poaching liquid

and distribute them among four shallow serving bowls or soup plates. Strain the poaching liquid into the saucepan, and use some of the drained onion slices to garnish each piece of chicken. Discard the remaining onions. Place the bowls in the oven to keep the chicken warm while you finish preparing the sauce.

Cook the liquid in the saucepan over medium heat until it is reduced by about one quarter; there should be approximately 55 cl (18 fl oz) of liquid left. Add the peas and cook them until they are tender — about 5 minutes. Remove the pan from the heat and whisk in the butter. Pour some of the sauce and peas over the chicken in each bowl and serve immediately.

SUGGESTED ACCOMPANIMENT: *crusty French bread to dunk in the sauce.*

Chicken Fan with Basil-Tomato Sauce

Serves 4
Working time: about 30 minutes
Total time: about 30 minutes

Calories **210**
Protein **29g**
Cholesterol **75mg**
Total fat **6g**
Saturated fat **1g**
Sodium **90mg**

4	chicken breasts, skinned and boned (about 500 g/1 lb)	4
½ litre	unsalted chicken stock	16 fl oz
125 g	fresh basil leaves	4 oz
1	garlic clove	1
2 tsp	mayonnaise	2 tsp
1	tomato, skinned, seeded and chopped	1

In a pot large enough to hold the chicken breasts snugly, simmer the stock with 30 g (1 oz) of the basil leaves over medium-low heat for 5 minutes. Add the breasts to the stock, cover, and poach gently for 8 minutes.

Turn the breasts over and poach until they feel firm but springy to the touch — about 4 minutes more.

Meanwhile, chop the garlic in a food processor or blender. Add the remaining basil along with 12.5 cl (4 fl oz) of water, and purée the mixture. Pour the purée into a sieve and lightly press it with a spoon to remove excess water. To prepare the sauce, scrape the purée into a small bowl and stir in the mayonnaise and half of the chopped tomato.

Lift the chicken breasts from their liquid and pat dry. Cut each piece diagonally into slices and spread them in a fan pattern on individual serving plates. Spoon about 1½ tablespoons of the sauce at the base of each fan. Scatter the remaining chopped tomato over the sauce.

SUGGESTED ACCOMPANIMENT: *spaghetti squash or vegetable marrow with Parmesan cheese.*

Braised Chicken Legs with Celery, Shallots and Red Onion

Serves 4
Working time: about 20 minutes
Total time: about 50 minutes

Calories **300**
Protein **28g**
Cholesterol **100mg**
Total fat **17g**
Saturated fat **5g**
Sodium **345mg**

4	whole chicken legs, skinned	4
¼ tsp	salt	¼ tsp
	freshly ground white pepper	
2 tbsp	safflower oil	2 tbsp
4	celery sticks, sliced diagonally into 5mm (¼ inch) wide slices	4
2 tbsp	shallots, halved lengthwise, thinly sliced	2 tbsp
¼ litre	unsalted chicken stock	8 fl oz
½ tsp	celery seeds	½ tsp
15 g	unsalted butter	½ oz
½	large red onion, thinly sliced	½
2 tsp	cornflour, mixed with 1 tbsp water	2 tsp

Preheat the oven to 180°C (350° F or Mark 4). Sprinkle the chicken legs with the salt and pepper. Heat 1 tablespoon of the oil in a large, fireproof casserole over medium-high heat. Brown the legs in the oil for about 2 minutes on each side. Transfer the legs to a plate and set them aside.

Add the remaining tablespoon of oil to the casserole and sauté the celery, stirring frequently, for about 1 minute. Add the shallots and sauté them for another minute, taking care not to brown them. Deglaze the casserole with the stock and stir in the celery seeds. Return the legs to the casserole, bring the liquid to a simmer, and cover. Cook the chicken in the oven until the juices run clear when a thigh is pierced with the tip of a sharp knife — about 25 minutes.

Meanwhile, melt the butter in a heavy frying pan over medium-low heat, and sauté the onion until translucent — about 10 minutes. Set aside.

Remove the legs from the casserole, strain the liquid into a saucepan, and reserve the celery. To finish the sauce, bring the liquid to a simmer over low heat, stir in the cornflour mixture, and simmer, stirring constantly, until the sauce thickens — about 2 minutes. Spread the celery on a warmed serving platter, pour the sauce over the celery and lay the legs on top. Strew the sautéed onions over the chicken and serve at once.

SUGGESTED ACCOMPANIMENT: *puréed carrots and parsnips.*

Spanish-Style Chicken and Saffron Rice

THIS DISH DEPARTS FROM THE TRADITIONAL ARROZ CON POLLO
BY CALLING FOR BROWN RICE RATHER THAN WHITE. THE RESULT IS
A DEEPER, HEARTIER FLAVOUR.

Serves 4
Working time: about 30 minutes
Total time: about 1 hour and 30 minutes

Calories **570**
Protein **41g**
Cholesterol **105mg**
Total fat **20g**
Saturated fat **4g**
Sodium **410mg**

1.25 kg	chicken, skinned, cut into serving pieces	2½ lb
	freshly ground black pepper	
½ tsp	salt	½ tsp
3 tbsp	virgin olive oil	3 tbsp
2	medium onions, thinly sliced	2
175 g	long-grain brown rice	6 oz
12.5 cl	dry white wine	4 fl oz
⅛ tsp	crushed saffron threads	⅛ tsp
35 cl	unsalted chicken stock	12 fl oz
2 tbsp	mildly hot chilies	2 tbsp
⅛ tsp	crushed cumin seeds	⅛ tsp
2	garlic cloves, finely chopped	2
2	large ripe tomatoes, skinned, seeded and chopped	2
1 each	red and yellow sweet pepper, grilled, skinned, seeded and cut into 2.5 cm (1 inch) strips	1 each
	fresh coriander for garnish (optional)	

Sprinkle the chicken pieces with pepper and ¼ teaspoon of salt. In a lidded fireproof 4 litre (7 pint) casserole, heat 2 tablespoons of the olive oil over medium-high heat. Sauté the chicken until golden-brown — about 4 minutes on each side — and remove to a plate.

Add the remaining tablespoon of oil to the casserole and cook the onions over medium heat until translucent — about 10 minutes. Add the brown rice and cook 2 minutes, stirring constantly to coat the grains thoroughly; pour in the white wine, bring to the boil, then reduce the heat, cover, and simmer until all the liquid has been absorbed — about 8 minutes. Add the saffron to the stock and pour over the rice. Stir in the chilies, cumin seeds, the remaining salt and the garlic. Simmer 15 minutes more and add the tomatoes and chicken, pushing them down into the rice. Cook until the juices run clear when a thigh is pierced with the tip of a sharp knife — about 25 minutes more. Garnish with the pepper strips and coriander.

flour mixture and the grated orange rind, and simmer for 5 minutes.

Brush the chicken pieces with the glaze and place them under the grill for a few minutes to brown. Garnish the chicken with the orange segments and pour the sauce over them.

SUGGESTED ACCOMPANIMENT: *sugar snap peas.*

Saffron Chicken Stew

Serves 4
Working time: about 20 minutes
Total time: about 1 hour and 10 minutes

Calories **595**
Protein **37g**
Cholesterol **90mg**
Total fat **17g**
Saturated fat **3g**
Sodium **685mg**

4	chicken legs, skinned, cut into thighs and drumsticks	4
1	garlic clove, halved	1
¼ tsp	freshly ground black pepper	¼ tsp
½ tsp	salt	½ tsp
2 tbsp	safflower oil	2 tbsp
1	aubergine (about 350 g/12 oz), cut into 2.5 cm (1 inch) cubes	1
250 g	yellow squash, cut into 5cm (2 inch) cubes	8 oz
6	spring onions	6
3	celery sticks, trimmed and cut into 1 cm (½ inch) pieces	3
125 g	baby carrots	4 oz
1	large ripe tomato, skinned, seeded and coarsely chopped	1
½ tsp	fennel seeds	½ tsp
⅛ tsp	saffron threads, crumbled	⅛ tsp
1	bay leaf	1
1 tsp	fresh thyme, or ¼ tsp dried thyme	1 tsp
¼ litre	dry vermouth	8 fl oz
8	red potatoes (about 750 g/1 ½ lb), with a band peeled from the middle of each	8
4 tbsp	coarsely chopped parsley	4 tbsp
8	slices French bread, toasted	8

Rub the chicken pieces with the garlic and reserve it; sprinkle the chicken with the pepper and ¼ teaspoon of the salt. Heat 1 tablespoon of the oil in a 6 litre (10 pint) saucepan over medium heat. Brown the pieces in the oil for about 3 minutes on each side. Remove the chicken and set it on paper towels to drain.

Add the remaining tablespoon of oil to the pan. Add the garlic, aubergine, squash and the remaining salt, and sauté lightly over high heat for about 1 minute. Pour in 1.5 litres (2½ pints) of water. Return the chicken pieces to the pan. Add the spring onions, celery, carrots, tomato, fennel seeds, saffron, bay leaf, thyme and vermouth, and bring the mixture to the boil. Reduce the heat and simmer gently for about 30 minutes, skimming off the fat from time to time. Add the potatoes and simmer for 15 minutes more. The vegetables should be tender but not soft. Remove the bay leaf and garlic. Add the parsley a few minutes before serving.

Serve the stew in soup bowls, accompanied by the slices of toasted French bread.

Orange-Glazed Chicken

Serves 4
Working time: about 20 minutes
Total time: about 1 hour

Calories **455**
Protein **40g**
Cholesterol **125mg**
Total fat **23g**
Saturated fat **6g**
Sodium **420mg**

1.5 kg	chicken, quartered	3 lb
½ tsp	salt	½ tsp
	freshly ground black pepper	
1 tbsp	safflower oil	1 tbsp
1	garlic clove, crushed	1
¼ litre	unsalted chicken stock	8 fl oz
1 tsp	cornflour, mixed with 1 tbsp water	1 tsp
1	navel orange, peeled and segmented, the rind grated	1
Orange glaze		
4 tbsp	orange juice	4 tbsp
4 tbsp	brown sugar	4 tbsp
2 tbsp	cider vinegar	2 tbsp
1 tsp	Dijon mustard	1 tsp

Sprinkle the chicken with the salt and pepper. Heat the oil in large, heavy frying pan over medium-high heat. Add the chicken pieces and brown them lightly — about 4 minutes on each side. Push the chicken to one side of the pan, add the garlic, and sauté for 15 seconds. Stir in the stock and allow it to come to a simmer. Redistribute the chicken pieces in the pan. Reduce the heat to low and braise until the juices run clear when a thigh is pierced with the tip of a sharp knife — about 25 minutes.

Meanwhile, make the glaze. In a small saucepan over medium-low heat, combine the orange juice, brown sugar, vinegar and mustard. Bring the mixture to a simmer and cook it for 3 minutes.

When the chicken is cooked, transfer it to a grill pan. Skim off and discard the fat from the braising liquid in the frying pan. Bring the liquid to a simmer, stir in the corn-

Braised Chicken with Plums and Lemons

Serves 4
Working time: about 20 minutes
Total time: about 45 minutes

Calories **260**
Protein **28g**
Cholesterol **90mg**
Total fat **11g**
Saturated fat **5g**
Sodium **170mg**

4	chicken breasts, skinned and boned (about 500 g/1 lb)	4
½ litre	unsalted chicken stock	16 fl oz
4	red plums, blanched in the stock for 1 minute, peeled (skins reserved), halved and stoned	4
2 tsp	sugar	2 tsp
30 g	unsalted butter	1 oz
⅛ tsp	salt	⅛ tsp
	freshly ground black pepper	
2 tbsp	chopped shallots	2 tbsp
8	paper-thin lemon slices	8

In a saucepan over medium heat, cook the plum skins in the chicken stock until the liquid is reduced to 12.5 cl (4 fl oz). Strain the stock and return it to the pan. Reduce the heat to low, and add the plum halves and sugar. Simmer the mixture for 1 minute, then remove it from the heat and set aside. Preheat the oven to 190°C (375°F or Mark 5).

In a shallow fireproof casserole over medium heat, melt the butter. Lay the breasts in the casserole and sauté them lightly on one side for about 2 minutes. Turn them over, salt and pepper the cooked side, and add the shallots. Place the plum halves cut side down between the breasts. Pour the stock into the casserole and arrange two lemon slices on each breast.

Put the uncovered casserole in the oven. Cook until the chicken feels firm but springy to the touch — about 10 minutes. Remove the casserole from the oven and lift out the plums and breasts with a slotted spoon. Place them on a warmed platter and return the lemon slices to the sauce. Cover the chicken and plums with foil to keep them warm. Simmer the sauce over medium-high heat until it is reduced to about 4 tablespoons — 5 to 7 minutes. Put the lemon slices back on top of the breasts and arrange the plums around them. Pour the sauce over all and serve.

SUGGESTED ACCOMPANIMENT: *mashed swedes and potatoes.*

Chicken with Orange and Onion

Serves 8
Working time: about 30 minutes
Total time: about 1 hour and 15 minutes

Calories **370**
Protein **42g**
Cholesterol **125mg**
Total fat **14g**
Saturated fat **3g**
Sodium **255mg**

Two	chickens, wings removed, quartered	Two
1.5 kg	and skinned	3 lb
2 tbsp	flour	2 tbsp
½ tsp	salt	½ tsp
	freshly ground black pepper	
2 tbsp	safflower oil	2 tbsp
1	orange, rind only, julienned	1
3	onions, thinly sliced	3
2 tsp	fresh thyme, or ½ tsp dried thyme	2 tsp
30 cl	fresh orange juice	½ pint
2 tbsp	fresh lemon juice	2 tbsp
1 tbsp	honey	1 tbsp
17.5 cl	dry white wine	6 fl oz

Dust the chicken pieces with the flour. Sprinkle them with ¼ teaspoon of the salt and some of the pepper.

In a large, heavy frying pan, heat the oil over medium-high heat and sauté the chicken in several batches until golden-brown — about 5 minutes on each side. Transfer the pieces to a 23 by 33 cm (9 by 13 inch) baking dish and scatter the orange rind over them.

Preheat the oven to 180°C (350°F or Mark 4). Over medium-low heat, cook the onions in the oil in the pan, stirring occasionally, until they are translucent — about 10 minutes. Stir in the thyme and the remaining salt and spread the mixture over the chicken pieces.

Pour the orange and lemon juice, honey and wine into the pan. Bring the liquid to the boil and reduce it to about ¼ litre (8 fl oz). Pour the liquid over the chicken. Cook the pieces uncovered in the oven, basting once with the liquid, until the juices run clear when a thigh is pierced with the tip of a sharp knife — about 35 minutes.

SUGGESTED ACCOMPANIMENTS: *new potatoes cooked in their jackets; steamed celery.*

Braised Chicken with Red and Green Apples

Serves 4
Working time: about 30 minutes
Total time: about 1 hour and 15 minutes

Calories **535**
Protein **40g**
Cholesterol **135mg**
Total fat **27g**
Saturated fat **8g**
Sodium **560mg**

1.5 kg	chicken, cut into serving pieces	3 lb
¼ tsp	freshly ground black pepper	¼ tsp
¾ tsp	salt	¾ tsp
5 g	unsalted butter	⅙ oz
1 tbsp	safflower oil	1 tbsp
1	small onion, coarsely chopped	1
1	celery stick, trimmed, coarsely chopped	1
½	carrot, coarsely chopped	½
1	garlic clove, crushed	1
1½	cooking apples, peeled, thinly sliced	1½
1 tbsp	chopped fresh tarragon, or 1 tsp dried tarragon, with some whole leaves reserved for a garnish if fresh tarragon is used	1 tbsp
¼ litre	dry vermouth	8 fl oz
¼ litre	unsalted chicken stock	8 fl oz
2 tsp	plain low-fat yogurt	2 tsp
2 tbsp	double cream	2 tbsp

	Apple garnish	
1 tbsp	sugar	1 tbsp
1 tsp	tarragon vinegar	1 tsp
3 tbsp	unsalted chicken stock	3 tbsp
½ each	unpeeled firm red and tart green apple, quartered and cut into 5mm (¼ inch) slices	½ each

Sprinkle the chicken pieces with the pepper and ½ teaspoon of the salt. Melt the butter with the oil in a large, heavy-bottomed sauté pan over medium-high heat and sauté the pieces on both sides until golden — about 4 minutes on each side. Put the sautéed pieces on paper towels and leave them to drain.

Pour off all but 1 tablespoon of the fat. Add the onion, celery, carrot, garlic, apples and tarragon, and cook, stirring occasionally, until the onions are translucent — about 5 minutes.

Add the vermouth and reduce the liquid by two thirds. Return the chicken to the pan, add the stock, and bring the liquid to the boil. Reduce the heat, cover tightly and simmer until the juices run clear when a thigh is pierced with the tip of a sharp knife — about 20 minutes. With a slotted spoon, transfer the contents of the pan to a heated serving platter and keep warm.

To make a sauce, pour 35 cl (12 fl oz) of the braising liquid into a small saucepan. Skim off the fat, then bring the liquid to a simmer and reduce it by half. Add the remaining ¼ teaspoon of salt, the yogurt and the cream. Whisk until well blended.

To prepare the apple garnish, melt the sugar in a heavy-bottomed saucepan over low heat, stirring with a wooden spoon until the sugar caramelizes — it will turn a honey-brown. Standing back from the stove to avoid being splattered, add the vinegar and the stock all at once; the caramelized sugar will solidify. Continue cooking until the sugar melts once more and the liquid becomes syrupy. Add the apple slices and toss them in the liquid for about 1 minute. Arrange them round the chicken and sprinkle with the fresh tarragon leaves. Pass the sauce separately.

SUGGESTED ACCOMPANIMENT: *braised leeks or stewed onions.*

Chicken Braised with Haricot Beans and Tomatoes

THIS IS A LOW-FAT VARIATION ON THE CASSOULET OF SOUTH-WESTERN FRANCE.

Serves 6
Working time: about 1 hour
Total time: about 1 day

Calories **505**			
Protein **42g**	1.75 kg	chicken, skin and wing tips removed, cut into serving pieces	3½ lb
Cholesterol **100mg**	500 g	dried haricot beans, soaked overnight in water and drained	1 lb
Total fat **19g**	½ tsp	salt	½ tsp
Saturated fat **4g**		freshly ground black pepper	
Sodium **520mg**	1 tbsp	fresh thyme, or ¾ tsp dried thyme	1 tbsp
	2 tbsp	safflower oil	2 tbsp
	12.5 cl	dry white wine	4 fl oz
	2	leeks, trimmed, halved lengthwise and cut into 1 cm (½ inch) pieces	2
	400 g	canned peeled tomatoes, the tomatoes halved and the liquid reserved	14 oz
	1 tbsp	fresh rosemary, or ¾ tsp dried rosemary	1 tbsp
	6	garlic cloves, finely chopped	6
	3	bay leaves	3
	60 cl	unsalted chicken stock	1 pint
	90 g	dry breadcrumbs	3 oz
	2 tbsp	virgin olive oil	2 tbsp
	2 tsp	chopped fresh parsley	2 tsp

Place the beans in a large saucepan or casserole and cover them with 5 cm (2 inches) of water. Bring to the boil over high heat. Boil the beans for 10 minutes, skimming off any foam as it accumulates. Reduce the heat to low. Gently stir in the pepper and one third of the thyme. Cover the pan and simmer the beans for about 35 minutes. Drain the beans. Preheat the oven to 190°C (375°F or Mark 5).

In a large, heavy frying pan, heat the safflower oil over medium-high heat. Add the chicken pieces and brown them lightly — about 3 minutes on each side. With a slotted spoon, transfer the chicken pieces to a plate. Pour off any accumulated fat from the pan and reserve it. Pour the wine into the pan and deglaze over medium-high heat, scraping up any brown bits with a wooden spoon.

When the wine boils, add the leeks, the tomatoes and their liquid, the rosemary, the remaining thyme, the salt and half of the garlic. Reduce the heat to low and simmer the mixture, stirring frequently, until the vegetables are tender — about 10 minutes. Then remove the frying pan from the heat.

Spread the remaining garlic evenly over the bottom of a large, deep casserole. Add half of the cooked beans in an even layer, then distribute the chicken pieces on the beans and top with the bay leaves. Spoon half of the tomato-and-leek mixture over the chicken, then add the remaining beans in another even layer, and spoon the remaining tomato-and-leek mixture over them. Pour in 35 cl (12 fl oz) of the stock and sprinkle the breadcrumbs over all. Dribble the reserved fat and the olive oil on to the breadcrumbs.

Bake the casserole for 45 minutes. Carefully pour in the remaining stock around the edges of the dish so as not to soak the breadcrumb topping. Bake for about 30 minutes more, or until a golden-brown crust has formed and the beans are tender.

Scatter the parsley over the top and serve.

SUGGESTED ACCOMPANIMENT: *lettuce salad.*

EDITOR'S NOTE: *This dish can be prepared a day in advance and refrigerated overnight, further melding the flavours. Before serving, warm the dish in a moderate oven for 35 minutes.*

Jellied Chicken
with Lemon and Dill

Serves 8
Working time: about 30 minutes
Total time: about 1 day

Calories **340**
Protein **43g**
Cholesterol **125mg**
Total fat **14g**
Saturated fat **3g**
Sodium **235mg**

Two 1.5 kg	chickens, skinned, and cut into serving pieces	Two 3 lb
¼ tsp	salt	¼ tsp
	freshly ground black pepper	
2 tbsp	virgin olive oil	2 tbsp
1	large onion, finely chopped	1
5 tbsp	chopped fresh dill	5 tbsp
1 litre	unsalted chicken stock	1¾ pints
3	large carrots, thinly sliced	3
125 g	shelled peas	4 oz
8 cl	fresh lemon juice	3 fl oz

Sprinkle the chicken pieces with the salt and pepper. Heat the olive oil in a large, heavy frying pan and sauté as many pieces as will fit without crowding over medium-high heat until golden — about 5 minutes on each side. Arrange the pieces in a large casserole.

In the remaining oil, cook the onion over medium-low heat until translucent — about 10 minutes; stir in half the dill. Spoon the onion mixture on to the chicken pieces. Pour the stock over all and bring to a simmer on top of the stove. After 20 minutes, turn the pieces, add the carrots and peas, and continue cooking until the juices run clear when a thigh is pierced with the tip of a sharp knife — about 10 minutes more.

Pour the lemon juice over the chicken and vegetables, and cool to room temperature. Sprinkle the remaining dill on top. Refrigerate for 6 hours or overnight to allow the natural gelatine to set. Serve cold.

SUGGESTED ACCOMPANIMENTS: *rice salad; sliced tomatoes.*
EDITOR'S NOTE: *If fresh dill is unavailable, parsley, tarragon or chervil may be substituted.*

Chicken Mole

THIS IS A VARIATION ON THE MEXICAN DISH *MOLE POBLANO,*
HERE MADE WITH CHICKEN RATHER THAN TURKEY.

Serves 6
Working time: about 1 hour
Total time: about 2 hours

Calories **295**
Protein **28g**
Cholesterol **100mg**
Total fat **17g**
Saturated fat **4g**
Sodium **240mg**

12	chicken thighs, skinned and boned	12
1 tsp	coriander seeds	1 tsp
¼ tsp	aniseeds	¼ tsp
2	garlic cloves, coarsely chopped	2
¼ tsp	cinnamon	¼ tsp
¼ tsp	salt	¼ tsp
¼ tsp	freshly ground black pepper	¼ tsp
2 tbsp	safflower oil	2 tbsp
2	hot chili peppers, halved lengthwise, seeded and finely chopped (see caution, page 25)	2
1	onion, chopped	1
2	small ripe tomatoes, skinned, seeded and chopped	2
30 cl	unsalted chicken stock	½ pint
15 g	plain chocolate, grated	½ oz
2 tsp	cornflour, mixed with 2 tbsp red wine	2 tsp

In a small, heavy-bottomed saucepan, toast the coriander and aniseeds over medium heat for 3 to 4 minutes, shaking the pan frequently. Put the seeds along with the garlic, cinnamon, salt and pepper in a mortar; using a pestle, grind the seasonings to a paste.

Heat 1 tablespoon of the oil in a large, heavy frying pan over medium heat. Sauté the chilies in the oil, stirring constantly until they begin to brown — about 3 minutes. Then add the onion, tomatoes and seasoning paste. Cook until almost all the liquid evaporates — about 10 minutes. Transfer the mixture to a bowl and set aside.

Clean the pan and set it over medium-high heat. Add the remaining tablespoon of oil. Sauté the chicken thighs, in two batches if necessary, so that the pieces do not touch, until they are brown — about 4 minutes on each side. Pour off the fat. Add the stock, onion-and-tomato mixture, and chocolate. Bring the sauce to the boil and stir well to melt the chocolate. Reduce the heat to low, cover, and simmer until the juices run clear when a thigh is pierced with the tip of a sharp knife — about 20 minutes.

Transfer the pieces to a serving platter and keep them warm. Stir the cornflour-and-wine mixture into the sauce and simmer, stirring frequently, until the sauce is reduced to approximately 35 cl (12 fl oz) — about 7 minutes. Pour the sauce over the chicken.

SUGGESTED ACCOMPANIMENTS: *yellow rice; black or red kidney beans; orange and onion salad.*

Curried Chicken with Chutney and Raisins

Serves 4
Working time: about 30 minutes
Total time: about 1 hour

Calories **475**
Protein **45g**
Cholesterol **125mg**
Total fat **22g**
Saturated fat **4g**
Sodium **435mg**

1.5 kg	chicken, skinned, cut into serving pieces	3 lb
½ tsp	salt	½ tsp
½ tsp	freshly ground black pepper	½ tsp
30 g	cornmeal	1 oz
3 tbsp	safflower oil	3 tbsp
1	onion, finely chopped	1
1	carrot, finely chopped	1
½	small green pepper, finely chopped	½
3	garlic cloves, finely chopped	3
350 g	tomatoes, preferably the Italian plum variety, skinned, seeded and coarsely chopped, with juice reserved	12 oz

35 cl	unsalted chicken stock	12 fl oz
1 tbsp	curry powder	1 tbsp
2 tsp	mango chutney	2 tsp
1	bay leaf	1
1½ tbsp	raisins	1½ tbsp
1½ tbsp	sultanas	1½ tbsp
1 tbsp	sesame seeds	1 tbsp

Sprinkle the chicken pieces with the salt and pepper, and dredge them lightly in the cornmeal. In a fireproof casserole large enough to hold the chicken in a single layer, heat 2 tablespoons of the oil over medium heat. Brown the chicken for 2 minutes on each side. Remove the chicken and set it aside. Preheat the oven to 180°C (350°F or Mark 4).

Put the remaining tablespoon of oil into the casserole. Add the onion, carrot and green pepper, and sauté lightly for about 1 minute. Add the garlic and sauté for 30 seconds more. Pour in the tomatoes, their reserved

juice and the stock. Stir in the curry powder, chutney, bay leaf, and 1 tablespoon each of raisins and sultanas. Return the chicken to the casserole and bring the liquid to a simmer. Bake the casserole, covered, for 10 minutes. While it is baking, brown the sesame seeds in a pie tin in the oven — about 10 minutes.

When the breasts feel firm but springy to the touch, remove them from the oven and set them aside on a plate, leaving the other chicken pieces in the casserole. Cover the breasts with aluminium foil to keep them warm. Bake the other pieces until the juices run clear when a thigh is pierced with the tip of a sharp knife — about 5 minutes more. Serve the chicken straight from the casserole or arranged on a platter, with the toasted sesame seeds and the remaining raisins and sultanas scattered across the top.

SUGGESTED ACCOMPANIMENTS: *steamed rice; side dishes of yogurt, unsalted peanuts and sliced banana.*

Chicken Legs with Dark Rum, Papaya, Mango and Banana

Serves 4
Working time: about 30 minutes
Total time: about 50 minutes

Calories **540**
Protein **30g**
Cholesterol **110mg**
Total fat **18g**
Saturated fat **6g**
Sodium **395mg**

4	whole chicken legs, skinned, cut into thighs and drumsticks	4
½ tsp	salt	½ tsp
	freshly ground white pepper	
1 tbsp	safflower oil	1 tbsp
1	large onion, cut into eighths, layers separated	1
2	garlic cloves, finely chopped	2
2 tsp	finely chopped fresh ginger root	2 tsp
¼ litre	dark rum	8 fl oz
½ litre	unsalted chicken stock	16 fl oz
4 tbsp	double cream	4 tbsp
1	large tomato, skinned, cored, seeded and cut into large chunks	1
1	medium papaya, scooped into balls with a melon-baller or cut into cubes, with the extra flesh chopped and reserved	1
1	small mango, peeled and cut into cubes	1
1	small banana, cut into 1 cm (½ inch) slices	1
⅛ tsp	freshly grated nutmeg	⅛ tsp

Sprinkle the chicken with ¼ teaspoon of the salt and some pepper. In a large fireproof casserole, heat the oil over medium heat. Brown the chicken pieces lightly — about 4 minutes on each side.

Add the onion and cook it with the chicken, stirring frequently, until the onion is translucent — about 5 minutes. Add the garlic and ginger, and cook for 1 minute more. Remove the casserole from the heat and allow it to cool for 1 minute. Reserve 1 teaspoon of the rum and set it aside, and pour the rest into the casserole. Return the casserole to the heat and simmer until the liquid is reduced by half — about 5 minutes.

Add the stock to the casserole and bring it to the boil. Reduce the heat to low, and simmer until the juices run clear when a thigh is pierced with a sharp knife — about 5 minutes more. Transfer the chicken pieces to a heated serving platter and cover them with foil.

In a saucepan, bring the cream, tomato and extra papaya flesh to a simmer. Pour in the braising liquid from the casserole and simmer until the sauce thickens slightly — about 3 minutes. Purée the mixture in a food processor or blender, and return it to the pan.

Add the papaya balls or cubes, mango, banana, nutmeg, the reserved teaspoon of rum and the remaining salt, and cook just until the fruit is heated through — about 1 minute. Remove the foil from the chicken and pour the sauce over the pieces. Serve immediately.

SUGGESTED ACCOMPANIMENT: *yellow rice.*

Add the chopped tomato to the casserole and raise the heat to medium high, stirring until the excess liquid evaporates — about 7 minutes. Pour in the wine and the reserved tomato juice. Simmer until the liquid is reduced by one third — about 10 minutes. Return the drumsticks to the casserole, immersing them in the sauce. Season with the remaining salt and some additional pepper.

Cover the casserole and braise the chicken in the oven until the meat is tender and clings loosely to the bone — about 30 minutes. Arrange it on a deep platter.

Place the uncovered casserole over high heat. Add the parsley, then further reduce the sauce by one third — about 5 minutes. Spoon this thickened sauce over the drumsticks and serve.

SUGGESTED ACCOMPANIMENT: *pasta tossed with extra cacciatore sauce.*

Chicken Drumsticks Cacciatore

Serves 6
Working time: about 40 minutes
Total time: about 1 hour and 30 minutes

Calories **305**
Protein **30g**
Cholesterol **95mg**
Total fat **14g**
Saturated fat **3g**
Sodium **365mg**

12	chicken drumsticks	12
¼ tsp	salt	¼ tsp
	freshly ground black pepper	
1 tbsp	virgin olive oil	1 tbsp
1	onion, finely chopped	1
1	small carrot, cut into 3 mm (⅛ inch) slices	1
1	small stick celery, cut into 3 mm (⅛ inch) slices	1
1	large green pepper, seeded, deribbed and cut into 1 cm (½ inch) squares	1
1	small sweet red pepper, seeded, deribbed and cut into 1 cm (½ inch) squares	1
5	garlic cloves, finely chopped	5
2 tsp	fresh oregano leaves, chopped, or ¾ tsp dried oregano	2 tsp
1 tsp	fresh thyme, or ¼ tsp dried thyme	1 tsp
800 g	canned plum tomatoes, drained and chopped, with the juice reserved	1 lb 12 oz
12.5 cl	dry white wine	4 fl oz
2 tbsp	chopped parsley	2 tbsp

Rub the chicken with half the salt and the pepper. In a shallow fireproof casserole with a lid, heat the oil over medium-high heat. Add the drumsticks and brown them on all sides — about 12 minutes. Transfer the pieces to a plate.

Reduce the heat to medium. Combine the onion, carrot, celery, green and red peppers, and garlic in the casserole. Sprinkle the oregano and thyme over the vegetables and stir. Sauté until the peppers are softened — about 5 minutes. Preheat the oven to 170°C (325°F or Mark 3).

Chicken Breasts with Courgettes in Red Wine Sauce

Serves 6
Working time: about 35 minutes
Total time: about 50 minutes

Calories **385**
Protein **29g**
Cholesterol **85mg**
Total fat **16g**
Saturated fat **5g**
Sodium **250mg**

4	chicken breasts, skinned and boned (about 500 g/1 lb)	4
¼ tsp	salt	¼ tsp
½ tsp	freshly ground black pepper	½ tsp
2	large yellow or green courgettes, sliced into 1 cm (½ inch) rounds	2
2 tbsp	safflower oil	2 tbsp
1	garlic clove, finely chopped	1
35 cl	unsalted chicken stock	12 fl oz
1 tbsp	finely chopped shallots	1 tbsp
90 g	onions, finely chopped	3 oz
30 g	celery, finely chopped	1 oz
30 g	carrots, finely chopped	1 oz
½ litre	red wine	16 fl oz
1 tbsp	double cream	1 tbsp
½ tsp	finely chopped fresh sage, or ¼ tsp dried sage	½ tsp
15 g	unsalted butter	½ oz

Sprinkle the chicken breasts with half of the salt and ¼ teaspoon of the pepper. Sprinkle the courgettes with the remaining salt and pepper. Heat 1 tablespoon of the oil in a heavy frying pan over medium-high heat. Lightly brown the breasts in the pan — about 2 minutes on each side. Remove the breasts and sauté the courgettes and garlic for about 1 minute in the oil remaining in the pan. Remove the courgettes and deglaze the pan with 12.5 cl (4 fl oz) of the stock. Reduce the heat to low and return the breasts to the pan. Simmer, partly covered, until the meat feels firm but springy to the touch — 10 to 12 minutes.

While the breasts are cooking, prepare the sauce. Heat the remaining tablespoon of oil over medium-low heat in a heavy-bottomed saucepan. Add the shallots, onions, celery and carrots, and cook until the onions are translucent — about 10 minutes. Pour in the wine, increase the heat to medium, and cook until reduced by half — about 7 minutes. Add the cream, sage and the remaining stock. Again reduce by half. Purée the sauce in a food processor or blender and strain it. When the chicken breasts are done, move them to the side of the pan and pour in the sauce. Stir the sauce to mix it thoroughly, then whisk in the butter. Return the courgettes to the pan to heat through, and serve.

SUGGESTED ACCOMPANIMENT: *sautéed green peppers and onions*.

Chicken Legs Stewed
with Prunes

Serves 4
Working time: about 40 minutes
Total time: about 3 hours and 45 minutes

Calories **500**
Protein **30g**
Cholesterol **100mg**
Total fat **12g**
Saturated fat **4g**
Sodium **265mg**

4	large chicken legs, skinned	4
¼ litre	brandy	8 fl oz
20	stoned prunes (about 150 g/5 oz)	20
15 g	unsalted butter	½ oz
¼ tsp	salt	¼ tsp
	freshly ground black pepper	
1	large onion, cut in half and thinly sliced	1
1	large carrot, cut diagonally into 5 mm (¼ inch) slices	1
4	garlic cloves, finely chopped	4
1 tsp	dry mustard	1 tsp
1 tsp	fresh thyme, or ¼ tsp dried thyme	1 tsp
40 cl	unsalted chicken stock	14 fl oz
10	parsley stems, tied in a bunch with string	10
3 tbsp	fresh lemon juice	3 tbsp
1 tbsp	chopped fresh parsley	1 tbsp

Pour the brandy over the prunes and marinate them for at least 2 hours at room temperature, or alternatively leave them to stand overnight in the refrigerator.

Heat the butter in a large, heavy frying pan over medium-high heat. Lightly brown the chicken legs for about 5 minutes on each side. Sprinkle the salt and pepper over the legs and transfer them to a large, fireproof casserole, and set them aside. In the pan used to brown the legs, combine the onion, carrot, garlic, mustard and thyme, and reduce the heat to medium. Sauté, stirring frequently, until the onion is translucent — 5 to 7 minutes.

Preheat the oven to 170°C (325°F or Mark 3).

Add the prunes, brandy and stock to the onion-and-carrot mixture. Let the liquid come to a simmer and continue cooking for 3 minutes, then empty the pan into the casserole; the mixture should nearly cover the legs. Drop in the bunch of parsley stalks.

Cover the casserole and cook in the oven for 1 hour. Reduce the oven temperature to 100°C (200°F or Mark ¼). Transfer the legs to a serving platter and cover them with foil. Open the oven door to partially vent the heat, and put the platter inside. Add the lemon juice to the sauce, remove the bunch of parsley and reduce the liquid by half over medium heat — 15 to 20 minutes. Pour the sauce over the chicken legs and serve immediately, garnished with the chopped parsley.

SUGGESTED ACCOMPANIMENT: *steamed cauliflower.*

Lemon-Mustard Chicken with Root Vegetables

Serves 6
Working time: about 20 minutes
Total time: about 45 minutes

Calories **265**
Protein **29g**
Cholesterol **80mg**
Total fat **9g**
Saturated fat **3g**
Sodium **260mg**

6	large chicken breasts, skinned, fat removed	6
1 tbsp	safflower oil	1 tbsp
30 g	unsalted butter	1 oz
1	onion, cut into 12 pieces	1
1	garlic clove, finely chopped	1
12.5 cl	dry sherry	4 fl oz
¼ tsp	salt	¼ tsp
	freshly ground black pepper	
2 tbsp	fresh lemon juice	2 tbsp
2 tbsp	Dijon mustard	2 tbsp
½ litre	unsalted chicken stock	16 fl oz
2	carrots, cut into 1 cm (½ inch) rounds	2
2	parsnips, cut into 1 cm (½ inch) rounds	2
1	small swede, or 2 medium turnips, peeled and cut into 1 cm (½ inch) cubes	1
1	lemon, grated rind only	1
4 tbsp	chopped parsley	4 tbsp

Heat the oil and butter in a large, heavy frying pan or fireproof casserole over medium-high heat. Sauté the chicken, bone side up, until the pieces turn golden — about 4 minutes. Remove the chicken and set it aside. Add the onion pieces to the pan, and sauté for 2 minutes. Add the garlic and sauté for about 15 seconds. Pour off the fat. Add the sherry to deglaze the pan, and stir. Lower the heat and simmer until the liquid is reduced by half — about 4 minutes.

Return the chicken breasts, bone side down, to the simmering mixture and sprinkle them with the salt and pepper. Stir in the lemon juice, mustard and stock; then add the carrots, parsnips and swede or turnips. Bring the sauce to the boil, stirring. Reduce the heat to low, partially cover the pan, and simmer until the vegetables are tender — about 20 minutes. Arrange the chicken and vegetables in a serving dish. Pour the sauce over the chicken, and garnish with the lemon and parsley before serving.

SUGGESTED ACCOMPANIMENTS: *curly endive salad; dark rye bread.*

flour with the salt and pepper, and dust the chicken pieces all over. Sauté them in the olive oil in a large heavy frying pan over medium-high heat until they are nicely browned — about 5 minutes on each side. Remove the pieces from the pan and arrange them on top of the chick-peas and almonds.

In the same pan, cook the onion over medium-low heat until translucent — about 10 minutes. Add the garlic, ginger, turmeric, cinnamon, cumin and currants, and mix well. Cook another 2 to 3 minutes. Spoon the mixture on to the chicken.

Add ¼ litre (8 fl oz) of the stock and the lemon juice and bring to a simmer on top of the stove, then cover the casserole and place it in the oven. Cook until the chicken juices run clear when a thigh is pierced with the tip of a sharp knife — about 45 minutes.

Shortly before the chicken is done, bring the remaining chicken stock to the boil in a saucepan and slowly pour in the couscous, stirring continuously. Remove from the heat and allow to stand 5 minutes, then fluff with a fork.

Spoon the couscous on to a serving platter and arrange the chicken pieces, chick-peas and almonds on top. Pour the juices over all.

SUGGESTED ACCOMPANIMENTS: *yogurt; steamed Swiss chard.*

Braised Chicken, Almonds and Chick-Peas

IN THE MOROCCAN ORIGINAL, THE SKIN IS LEFT ON. IN THIS SKINLESS VERSION, WHOLEMEAL FLOUR ADDS COLOUR AND FLAVOUR TO THE CHICKEN.

Serves 4
Working time: about 20 minutes
Total time: about 1 day

Calories **680**
Protein **51g**
Cholesterol **105mg**
Total fat **25g**
Saturated fat **4g**
Sodium **615mg**

1.25 kg	chicken, skinned and cut into quarters	2½ lb
200 g	dried chick-peas, soaked overnight in water and drained	7 oz
75 g	blanched almonds, toasted and coarsely chopped	2½ oz
1 tsp	wholemeal flour	1 tsp
¼ tsp	salt	¼ tsp
¼ tsp	freshly ground black pepper	¼ tsp
2 tbsp	virgin olive oil	2 tbsp
1	large onion, chopped	1
4	garlic cloves, finely chopped	4
½ tsp	ground ginger	½ tsp
⅛ tsp	ground turmeric	⅛ tsp
⅛ tsp	ground cinnamon	⅛ tsp
⅛ tsp	ground cumin	⅛ tsp
2 tbsp	currants	2 tbsp
60 cl	unsalted chicken stock	1 pint
2 tbsp	fresh lemon juice	2 tbsp
200 g	couscous	7 oz

Put the soaked chick-peas in a large saucepan, covering with cold water to a level 2.5 cm (1 inch) above them. Bring to the boil, then lower the heat and simmer for 60 minutes. Drain the chick-peas and place them in an ovenproof casserole with the almonds.

Preheat the oven to 180°C (350°F or Mark 4). Mix the

Chicken Casserole with Dried Fruits and Caramelized Onions

Serves 4
Working time: about 30 minutes
Total time: about 1 hour and 45 minutes

Calories **585**
Protein **34g**
Cholesterol **110mg**
Total fat **20g**
Saturated fat **6g**
Sodium **470mg**

8	chicken thighs, skinned	8
1 tbsp	safflower oil	1 tbsp
15 g	unsalted butter, plus ½ tsp	½ oz
½ tsp	salt	½ tsp
	freshly ground black pepper	
175 g	long-grain brown rice	6 oz
1	small onion, chopped	1
60 cl	unsalted chicken stock	1 pint
1	bouquet garni, made by tying together 2 sprigs fresh thyme, several parsley stems and 1 bay leaf	1
45 g	dried apricots, cut in half	1½ oz
45 g	sultanas	1½ oz
45 g	currants	1½ oz
1 tbsp	grainy mustard	1 tbsp
¼ tsp	grated orange rind (optional)	¼ tsp
125 g	pearl or pickling onions, blanched for 30 seconds and peeled	4 oz
⅛ tsp	sugar	⅛ tsp

In a 4 litre (7 pint) fireproof casserole, heat the oil and the 15 g (½ oz) butter over medium-high heat. Cook four of the chicken thighs on one side until lightly browned — about 4 minutes. Turn the thighs and sprinkle them with ⅛ teaspoon of the salt and some pepper. Sauté them on the second side for 3 minutes more. Remove the thighs from the casserole and set them aside. Repeat the process with the remaining thighs and set them aside.

Reduce the heat to medium. Add the rice and chopped onion to the casserole and cook until the grains of rice are translucent — about 5 minutes. Add 35 cl (12 fl oz) of the stock, the remaining salt and the bouquet garni. Bring the liquid to the boil. Lower the heat, cover the casserole, and simmer for 20 minutes. Preheat the oven to 180°C (350°F or Mark 4).

Stir the apricots, sultanas, currants, mustard and orange rind, if using, into the casserole. Return the chicken pieces to the casserole, pressing them down into

the rice. Pour the remaining stock over the top. Cover and bake in the oven for 35 minutes.

Meanwhile, to caramelize the onions, put them in a small pan with the sugar and the ½ teaspoon of butter. Pour in just enough water to cover the onions. Boil rapidly until no water remains — 10 to 15 minutes. Watching the onions carefully lest they burn, shake the pan until they are evenly browned all over.

Add the caramelized onions to the casserole and bake until the rice is tender — about 15 minutes more. Remove the bouquet garni and serve the chicken from the casserole accompanied by the rice, fruit and onion.

SUGGESTED ACCOMPANIMENT: *chicory salad*.

Chicken Fricassee with Watercress

Serves 4
Working time: about 45 minutes
Total time: about 45 minutes

Calories **250**
Protein **18g**
Cholesterol **60mg**
Total fat **10g**
Saturated fat **4g**
Sodium **250mg**

4	large chicken thighs, skinned, boned, excess fat removed, meat cut into 2.5 cm (1 inch) cubes	4
12.5 cl	plain low-fat yogurt	4 fl oz
2 tbsp	single cream	2 tbsp
2 tbsp	cornflour, mixed with 4 tbsp water	2 tbsp
2 tsp	fresh thyme, or ½ tsp dried thyme	2 tsp
1 tsp	fresh rosemary, or ¼ tsp dried rosemary	1 tsp
15 g	unsalted butter	½ oz
2	carrots, julienned	2
250 g	mushrooms, thickly sliced	8 oz
3 tbsp	finely chopped shallots	3 tbsp
12.5 cl	dry white wine	4 fl oz
12.5 cl	unsalted chicken stock	4 fl oz
4	garlic cloves, finely chopped	4
¼ tsp	salt	¼ tsp
2	bunches watercress, thick stems removed	2

In a small bowl, combine the yogurt, cream, cornflour mixture, thyme and rosemary. Set aside.

Melt the butter over medium heat in a large, heavy frying pan. Add the carrots and cook for 2 minutes, stirring once. Stir in the chicken, mushrooms, shallots, wine, stock, garlic, salt and the yogurt mixture. Reduce the heat to medium low, cover, and cook for 5 minutes.

Uncover the pan and stir well. Scatter the watercress over the top but do not stir it in; the watercress should be allowed to steam. Cover again and cook until the chicken pieces are done — about 5 minutes more. Drain the contents of the pan in a large colander or strainer, catching the sauce in a bowl. Put the contents of the colander on a platter and set aside to keep warm.

Return the sauce to the pan. Over medium heat, whisking occasionally to keep the sauce from burning, reduce it by approximately half. This should take 10 to 15 minutes. Return the chicken mixture to the pan, and stir to coat the chicken with the sauce. Serve at once.

SUGGESTED ACCOMPANIMENT: *pasta with tomato and Parmesan cheese.*

Braised Chicken with Potatoes, Leeks and Kale

Serves 4
Working time: about 30 minutes
Total time: about 1 hour and 15 minutes

Calories **440**
Protein **42g**
Cholesterol **125mg**
Total fat **23g**
Saturated fat **6g**
Sodium **540mg**

1.75 kg	chicken	3½ lb
	freshly ground black pepper	
¾ tsp	salt	¾ tsp
1 tbsp	safflower oil	1 tbsp
1	leek, halved lengthwise, cleaned thoroughly and cut into 1 cm (½ inch) slices	1
2 tbsp	thinly sliced shallots	2 tbsp
125 g	fresh kale, stemmed, washed and coarsely chopped	4 oz
2 tsp	fresh thyme, or ½ tsp dried thyme	2 tsp
½ tsp	cayenne pepper	½ tsp
3	red potatoes, unpeeled, cut into 4 cm (1½ inch) pieces	3

Rub the inside of the chicken with pepper and ¼ teaspoon of the salt, and truss the bird.

In a large, fireproof casserole, heat the oil over medium-high heat. Add the leek, shallots and kale, and sauté until the kale begins to wilt. Pour in 1 litre (1¾ pints) of water, then add the remaining salt, some more pepper and the thyme. Place the chicken in the casserole and sprinkle the cayenne pepper over it. Bring the liquid to the boil, reduce the heat to low, partially cover and simmer for 50 minutes.

Transfer the chicken from the casserole to a warmed platter. Cover it with foil to keep it warm. Skim off any fat in the casserole. Add the potatoes and simmer until they are tender — about 10 minutes. Arrange the vegetables round the chicken and pour the braising liquid over it.

Chicken Rolled in Vine Leaves

Serves 4
Working time: about 30 minutes
Total time: about 1 day

Calories **465**
Protein **36g**
Cholesterol **60mg**
Total fat **19g**
Saturated fat **4g**
Sodium **550mg**

350 g	chicken breast meat, cut into 1 cm (½ inch) cubes	12 oz
½ litre	unsalted chicken stock	16 fl oz
250 g	yellow split peas, soaked overnight and drained	8 oz
1 tsp	chopped fresh mint	1 tsp
2 tbsp	chopped fresh coriander	2 tbsp
¾ tsp	salt	¾ tsp
	freshly ground black pepper	
1	medium aubergine, peeled and cut into 1 cm (½ inch) cubes	1
2 tbsp	safflower oil	2 tbsp
5	garlic cloves, peeled and crushed lightly so that they remain whole	5
2 tbsp	tahini	2 tbsp
4	black olives, stoned	4
2 tsp	fresh lemon juice	2 tsp
8	vine leaves, preserved in brine	8
4	tomatoes, halved	4
15 g	unsalted butter, melted	½ oz

Put the stock, peas, mint, half the coriander, ¼ teaspoon of the salt and some pepper in a saucepan and bring to the boil. Reduce the heat, cover, and simmer until the peas are cooked — about 45 minutes.

Meanwhile, toss the aubergine cubes with ¼ teaspoon of the salt and drain them on paper towels.

Season the chicken cubes with the remaining ¼ teaspoon of salt and some pepper. Heat 1 tablespoon of the oil in a heavy frying pan over medium-high heat. Sauté the chicken cubes until lightly browned — about 4 minutes. Transfer to a mixing bowl.

Add the remaining oil to the pan and sauté the garlic cloves for 2 minutes. Transfer them to a food processor or blender. Sauté the aubergine cubes in the oil remaining in the pan until they brown — about 5 minutes. Add the aubergine, tahini, the remaining coriander, the olives, lemon juice and some black pepper to the processor or blender, and purée. Reserve 2 tablespoons of the mixture for garnish and mix the remaining purée with the chicken to make a filling. Preheat the oven to

180°C (350°F or Mark 4).

Rinse the vine leaves and lay them flat. Place 2 tablespoons of the filling on each leaf. Fold the sides of a leaf in to encase the filling, and roll it up. Repeat with the remaining leaves. Spread the cooked split peas in the bottom of a baking dish and place the rolled vine leaves on top. Top each tomato half with a little of the reserved aubergine mixture and arrange the tomatoes between the rolled leaves. Bake for 15 minutes. Brush the vine leaves with the melted butter just before serving.

Plum-Coated Chicken with Chinese Cabbage

Serves 8
Working time: about 1 hour and 30 minutes
Total time: about 2 hours

Calories **270**
Protein **23g**
Cholesterol **70mg**
Total fat **13g**
Saturated fat **4g**
Sodium **315mg**

Two	chickens, skinned and cut into serving	Two
1.5 kg	pieces, wings reserved for later use	3 lb
2	Chinese cabbages, about 750 g (1½ lb) each	2
1 litre	unsalted chicken stock	1¾ pints
5	large ripe red plums	5
2 tbsp	honey	2 tbsp
12.5 cl	red wine vinegar	4 fl oz
30 g	unsalted butter	1 oz
2 tbsp	fresh lemon juice	2 tbsp
1 tbsp	safflower oil	1 tbsp
¾ tsp	salt	¾ tsp
1 tbsp	virgin olive oil	1 tbsp

Discard any brown outer leaves of the cabbages. Cut 5 cm (2 inches) off the base of each cabbage; rinse the leaves and pat them dry. Cut out and discard the white core at the base of each leaf. Slice the leaves into 5 cm (2 inch) squares and set them aside.

Bring the stock to the boil in a saucepan. Cut a shallow cross on the bottom of each plum, and boil the plums in the stock until the skin begins to peel away from the cross — about 2 minutes. Peel the plums over the stock, letting their skins and juice fall into the hot liquid, and set the plums aside. Stir 1 tablespoon of the honey and half of the vinegar into the stock. Reduce the liquid over medium-high heat to approximately half — about 15 minutes — and set it aside.

Meanwhile, prepare the plum sauce. Cut the plums in half, remove their stones and cut the halves into cubes. Melt the butter in a large heavy-bottomed saucepan over medium heat. Add the plums and the remaining tablespoon of honey and the remaining vinegar. Cook, stirring often, until the plums are reduced to a dense, pasty consistency — 45 to 60 minutes. Stir in 12.5 cl (4 fl oz) of the stock and the lemon juice. Transfer the plum sauce to a food processor or blender. Process until smooth — about 30 seconds — stopping once to scrape down the sides.

Simmer the remaining stock to reduce it to about 17.5 cl (6 fl oz) — 10 to 15 minutes. Strain and set aside.

While the stock is simmering, heat the safflower oil in a large heavy frying pan over medium-high heat. Sauté half of the chicken pieces on one side until brown — about 4 minutes. Turn the pieces, sprinkle them with ¼ teaspoon of the salt, and cook on the second side till brown — 3 to 4 minutes more. Transfer the pieces to a platter. Repeat the procedure with the remaining chicken pieces. Reserve the pan for the cabbage. Preheat the oven to 200°C (400°F or Mark 6).

Arrange the chicken pieces, smooth side up, in a large ovenproof serving dish. Brush a thick coat of plum sauce over each piece. Whisk the remaining sauce into the reduced stock. Bake the chicken until the juices run clear when a thigh is pierced with the tip of a sharp knife — about 30 minutes.

While the chicken is baking, cook the cabbage. Cover the bottom of a large pot with 2.5 cm (1 inch) of water, lower a vegetable steamer into the pot and bring the water to the boil. Add the cabbage squares, cover tightly and steam until the leaves are wilted, stirring once — about 6 minutes. Drain the cabbage well.

Heat the olive oil in the pan over medium heat. Add the cabbage and sprinkle it with the remaining salt. Toss well to coat the cabbage with the hot oil, and immediately remove it from the heat.

Remove the chicken pieces from the serving dish, leaving the juices in the dish. Arrange the cabbage on top of the juices, and place the chicken on the cabbage. Warm the sauce and spoon it over the chicken.

SUGGESTED ACCOMPANIMENT: *baked potatoes with chives and yogurt.*

Honey-Basil Chicken

Serves 4
Working time: about 20 minutes
Total time: about 1 hour

Calories **260**
Protein **27g**
Cholesterol **90mg**
Total fat **12g**
Saturated fat **3g**
Sodium **215mg**

4	whole chicken legs, skinned	4
¼ tsp	salt	¼ tsp
	freshly ground black pepper	
1 tbsp	safflower oil	1 tbsp
7.5 g	unsalted butter	¼ oz
2 tbsp	honey	2 tbsp
2 tbsp	unsalted chicken stock	2 tbsp
2	garlic cloves, thinly sliced	2
30 to 40	fresh basil leaves	30 to 40

Preheat the oven to 200°C (400°F or Mark 6). Cut a piece of aluminium foil 30 cm (1 ft) square for each leg. Sprinkle the legs with the salt and pepper. Heat the oil and butter in a frying pan over medium heat, then brown the legs for about 2 minutes on each side. Put a leg in the middle of each foil square, and dribble 1½ teaspoons of the honey and 1½ teaspoons of the stock over each one. Lay one quarter of the garlic slices on each piece, cover with a loose layer of the basil leaves, and wrap the foil snugly over the top. Put the foil packages on a baking sheet and set it in the oven.

After 30 minutes, remove a foil package from the oven and unwrap it carefully to preserve the juices. Test for doneness by piercing the thigh with the tip of a sharp knife; if the juices run clear, it is done. If necessary, return the leg to the oven and bake about 5 minutes more.

To serve, undo each package and transfer the legs to a platter. Remove any garlic or basil that sticks to the foil and put them back on the chicken. Pour the collected juices from the foil packages over the legs.

SUGGESTED ACCOMPANIMENTS: *steamed carrots; cos lettuce salad.*

Baked Chicken Breasts Stuffed with Tahini

TAHINI (SESAME PASTE) IS MADE FROM ROASTED
OR UNROASTED GROUND SESAME SEEDS.

Serves 4
Working time: about 30 minutes
Total time: about 45 minutes

Calories **360**
Protein **32g**
Cholesterol **75mg**
Total fat **17g**
Saturated fat **3g**
Sodium **455mg**

4	chicken breasts, skinned and boned (about 500 g/1 lb)	4
2 tbsp	tahini, or 2 tbsp toasted sesame seeds pulverized with a mortar and pestle	2 tbsp
2 tbsp	chopped parsley	2 tbsp
2	garlic cloves, finely chopped	2
1 tsp	fresh lemon juice	1 tsp
⅛ tsp	cayenne pepper	⅛ tsp
½ tsp	salt	½ tsp
	freshly ground black pepper	
2 tbsp	plain low-fat yogurt	2 tbsp
2 tbsp	sesame seeds	2 tbsp
45 g	dry breadcrumbs	1½ oz
1½ tbsp	safflower oil	1½ tbsp
1	shallot, thinly sliced	1
4 tbsp	sherry	4 tbsp
¼ litre	unsalted chicken stock	8 fl oz
2 tsp	cornflour, mixed with 1 tbsp water	2 tsp
1	tomato, skinned, seeded and cut into strips	1

To make the stuffing, combine the tahini or pulverized sesame seeds, parsley, garlic, lemon juice and cayenne pepper in a small bowl. Cut a pocket in each breast half: make a horizontal slit along the thicker long edge, beginning 1 cm (½ inch) from one end and stopping 1 cm from the other. Then slice horizontally into the breast, cutting to within 1 cm of the opposite edge to form a cavity bordered by 1 cm of uncut flesh. Stuff one quarter of the tahini and herb mixture into each breast pocket. Sprinkle the chicken pieces with ¼ teaspoon of the salt and some pepper.

Preheat the oven to 180°C (350°F or Mark 4). To breadcrumb the pieces, first coat them with the yogurt. Mix the sesame seeds with the breadcrumbs, and dredge the breasts in this mixture to coat them. Heat 1 tablespoon of the oil in a fireproof casserole over medium heat. Cook the chicken breasts until golden-brown — about 3 minutes per side.

Place the casserole in the oven and bake the breasts, turning them once, until they feel firm but springy to the touch — about 15 minutes. Transfer the chicken to a serving platter and keep it warm.

For the sauce, heat the remaining oil in a small saucepan over medium-high heat. Sauté the sliced shallot in the oil for 1 minute, then add the sherry and reduce the mixture to about 1 tablespoon. Pour in the stock and bring the liquid to a simmer. Stir in the cornflour mixture and cook for 2 minutes more. Incorporate the tomato strips, the remaining salt and some pepper. Pour the sauce over the stuffed breasts and serve.

SUGGESTED ACCOMPANIMENT: *tomato or cucumber salad with fresh mint.*

Baked Chicken Legs Stuffed with Millet

Serves 4
Working time: about 45 minutes
Total time: about 2 hours

Calories **405**
Protein **36g**
Cholesterol **125mg**
Total fat **24g**
Saturated fat **8g**
Sodium **345mg**

4	chicken legs	4
15 g	unsalted butter	½ oz
1	onion, chopped	1
4 tbsp	millet	4 tbsp
½ tsp	fresh rosemary, or ⅛ tsp dried rosemary	½ tsp
¾ tsp	chopped fresh sage, or ¼ tsp dried sage	¾ tsp
12.5 cl	unsalted chicken stock	4 fl oz
⅛ tsp	salt	⅛ tsp
	freshly ground black pepper	
30 g	prosciutto, cut in thin strips	1 oz
60 g	low-fat mozzarella, diced	2 oz
2 tsp	safflower oil	2 tsp
2 tbsp	dry white wine	2 tbsp

To make the stuffing, heat the butter over medium-low heat in a small, heavy-bottomed saucepan. Add the onion and cook until translucent — about 5 minutes. Add the millet, rosemary and sage, and cook for 4 minutes. Stir in the stock, salt and pepper, and bring to the boil. Reduce the heat to low, cover the pan, and simmer until the liquid is gone — about 20 minutes. The millet should be tender but not mushy. Empty this mixture into a small bowl and let it cool slightly before stirring in the prosciutto and mozzarella.

Meanwhile, place the legs skin side down on a work surface. Remove the thigh bone from each leg: beginning at the end of the bone, gently scrape and cut the flesh away with the tip of a small, sharp knife, until you reach the joint. Prise the bone away from the joint and remove the bone. To make a pocket for the stuffing, start a cut at the channel left by the bone and work outwards towards the edge of the thigh, stopping just short of slicing through to the skin. Repeat the process on the other side of the channel.

Mound stuffing on to the centre of each thigh. Close

the meat back over the stuffing, wrapping the skin over the openings. Mould each thigh into a log shape and sew it up with a needle and thick thread. Preheat the oven to 180°C (350°F or Mark 4).

Heat the oil in a large, heavy frying pan over medium-high heat. Sauté the legs, skin side down, until they turn golden — about 4 minutes. Turn the pieces over and sauté them 2 minutes more. Transfer the legs to an oven-proof dish. Discard the fat and deglaze the pan with the wine; pour the liquid over the chicken. Bake until the legs feel firm but springy to the touch — about 20 minutes. Serve immediately.

SUGGESTED ACCOMPANIMENT: *grilled tomatoes.*

Chicken Pillows

Serves 6
Working time: about 1 hour
Total time: about 1 hour and 30 minutes

Calories **350**
Protein **34g**
Cholesterol **80mg**
Total fat **16g**
Saturated fat **4g**
Sodium **350mg**

6	chicken breasts, skinned and boned, long triangular fillets removed and reserved for another use, lightly pounded	6
2 tbsp	fresh lemon juice	2 tbsp
3 tbsp	virgin olive oil	3 tbsp
90 g	low-fat mozzarella, cut into 6 slices	3 oz
2	carrots, trimmed to 12.5 cm (5 inches) in length, cut into 5 mm (¼ inch) wide strips, blanched for 3 minutes	2
1	yellow or green courgette, trimmed to 12.5 cm (5 inches) in length, cut into 5 mm (¼ inch) strips, blanched for 30 seconds	1
6	thin asparagus spears (optional), trimmed to 12.5 cm (5 inches) in length, blanched for 1 minute	6
6	spring onions trimmed to 12.5 cm (5 inches) in length, blanched for 1 minute	6
30 g	fresh breadcrumbs	1 oz
1	garlic clove, finely chopped	1
⅛ tsp	salt	⅛ tsp
2 tbsp	finely chopped mixed fresh herbs, such as basil, parsley and chives	2 tbsp
Tomato-garlic sauce		
3	ripe tomatoes, skinned, seeded and coarsely chopped	3
2	garlic cloves, finely chopped	2
2	spring onions, finely chopped	2
1 tbsp	virgin olive oil	1 tbsp
¼ tsp	salt	¼ tsp
	freshly ground black pepper	
4 tbsp	finely chopped fresh basil or parsley	4 tbsp

Marinate the chicken breasts in the lemon juice and 1 tablespoon of the oil for 1 hour at room temperature, turning the pieces occasionally.

While the chicken is marinating, prepare the sauce. In a small, heavy-bottomed saucepan, combine the tomatoes, garlic, spring onions, oil, salt and pepper. Bring the mixture to the boil over medium heat, then reduce the heat to medium low. Simmer the sauce until it

thickens slightly — about 30 minutes. Remove the sauce from the heat and stir in the basil or parsley. Preheat the oven to 190°C (375°F or Mark 5).

Remove the breasts from the marinade and place them smooth side down on a work surface. Reserve the marinade. Lay a slice of the mozzarella on each breast. Put one strip of each vegetable across the top. Roll up the breasts in loose packages and secure them with wooden picks. Arrange the chicken pillows in a baking dish. Brush them with the marinade and cover the dish with foil. Bake the chicken until it feels firm but springy to the touch — about 20 minutes.

While the breasts are baking, heat the remaining oil in a small pan over low heat and lightly brown the bread-crumbs. Add the garlic, salt and mixed herbs.

Remove the chicken pillows from the oven and sprinkle them with the breadcrumb mixture. Grill until golden — 2 to 3 minutes. If necessary, reheat the sauce. Remove the picks, arrange the pillows on a warmed platter, and serve with the tomato sauce.

SUGGESTED ACCOMPANIMENT: *small pasta shapes.*

Spicy Yogurt-Baked Chicken Thighs

Serves 4
Working time: about 25 minutes
Total time: about 2 hours and 30 minutes

Calories **275**
Protein **31g**
Cholesterol **100mg**
Total fat **13g**
Saturated fat **4g**
Sodium **135mg**

8	chicken thighs, skinned, fat removed	8
¼ litre	plain low-fat yogurt	8 fl oz
2 tbsp	fresh lime juice	2 tbsp
2 tsp	grated fresh ginger root	2 tsp
4	garlic cloves, finely chopped	4
1 tsp	ground cumin	1 tsp
1 tsp	turmeric	1 tsp
½ tsp	cayenne pepper	½ tsp
1 tsp	aniseeds or fennel seeds, ground coarsely in a mortar and pestle	1 tsp
1 tsp	cornflour, mixed with 2 tsp water	1 tsp
1	lime, cut into slices, for garnish	1

To prepare the marinade, combine the yogurt, lime juice, ginger, garlic and spices in a bowl and mix well. Place the chicken thighs in the marinade and stir to coat them. Cover the bowl and refrigerate it for 2 to 8 hours. (The yogurt will tenderize as well as flavour the meat.) Preheat the oven to 180°C (350°F or Mark 4).

Arrange the thighs in a large, shallow baking dish, leaving no more than 2.5 cm (1 inch) of space between them; reserve the marinade. Bake for 10 minutes. Stir the cornflour mixture into the marinade, then spread the mixture over the chicken pieces. Bake until the meat feels firm but springy to the touch — 10 to 15 minutes more. Transfer to a serving platter, arrange the lime slices around the thighs, and serve.

SUGGESTED ACCOMPANIMENTS: *rice with raisins; chutney.*

Spinach-Stuffed Chicken Breasts

Serves 4
Working time: about 45 minutes
Total time: about 1 hour

Calories **430**
Protein **44g**
Cholesterol **110mg**
Total fat **22g**
Saturated fat **9g**
Sodium **685mg**

4	chicken breasts, boned, skin left on (about 500 g/1 lb)	4
1 tsp	fresh thyme, or ¼ tsp dried thyme	1 tsp
¼ tsp	salt	¼ tsp
1 tsp	virgin olive oil	1 tsp
Spinach and cheese stuffing		
1	onion, finely chopped	1
15 g	unsalted butter	½ oz
1 tbsp	virgin olive oil	1 tbsp
500 g	spinach, washed, stemmed and coarsely chopped	1 lb
125 g	low-fat ricotta cheese	4 oz
60 g	Parmesan cheese, freshly grated	2 oz
1 tsp	finely chopped fresh basil, or ½ tsp dried basil	1 tsp
	freshly ground black pepper	
Yogurt-tomato sauce		
¼ litre	plain low-fat yogurt	8 fl oz
1 tbsp	red wine vinegar	1 tbsp
¼ tsp	salt	¼ tsp
1	ripe tomato, skinned, seeded and finely chopped	1
4	large basil leaves, thinly sliced	4
	freshly ground black pepper	

To prepare the stuffing, cook the onion in the butter and oil in a large, heavy frying pan over medium heat until translucent — about 5 minutes. Add the spinach to the pan and cook until it is wilted and the moisture has evaporated — about 6 minutes more. Transfer to a bowl and let it cool. Stir in the cheeses, basil and some pepper.

To make the sauce, mix the yogurt, vinegar and salt in a bowl. Reserve 1 teaspoon of the tomato and 1 teaspoon of the basil, and stir the rest into the yogurt. Add pepper to taste. Transfer the sauce to a serving bowl, garnish it with the reserved tomato and basil, and set it aside. Preheat the oven to 190°C (375°F or Mark 5).

To make pockets for the stuffing, loosen the skin of each breast by running a finger between the flesh and skin on one long side. Rub the thyme and salt into the flesh. Dribble ¼ teaspoon of the olive oil on to the skin of each breast. Neatly fill each pocket between skin and flesh with one quarter of the stuffing. Place the breasts skin side up in an oiled baking dish just large enough to hold them, and bake until the skin turns golden-brown — about 25 minutes.

Remove the dish from the oven. Put the chicken breasts on a cutting board and allow them to cool for a few minutes. Cut each breast into 1 cm (½ inch) wide slices and arrange them on a warmed serving platter or on individual plates. Serve with the yogurt sauce.

Cajun Chicken Wings

Serves 4
Working time: about 20 minutes
Total time: about 1 hour

Calories **335**
Protein **28g**
Cholesterol **85mg**
Total fat **21g**
Saturated fat **6g**
Sodium **355mg**

12	chicken wings, tips removed	12
5	dried bay leaves, crumbled into small bits	5
¾ tsp	caraway seeds	¾ tsp
½ to ¾ tsp	cayenne pepper	½ to ¾ tsp
¾ tsp	ground coriander	¾ tsp
¾ tsp	ground cumin	¾ tsp
4	garlic cloves, finely chopped	4
1½ tsp	dry mustard	1½ tsp
2 tsp	paprika	2 tsp
¾ tsp	dried thyme	¾ tsp
½ tsp	salt	½ tsp
2 tbsp	brandy	2 tbsp
2 tbsp	fresh lemon or lime juice	2 tbsp

Defat the chicken wings by cooking them in boiling water for 10 minutes. Drain, and set aside to cool. Preheat the oven to 190°C (375°F or Mark 5).

Using a large mortar and pestle, grind the bay leaf bits to a fine powder, then add the caraway seeds, cayenne pepper, coriander, cumin, garlic, mustard, paprika, thyme and salt and grind together for about 10 minutes. Add the brandy and lemon or lime juice to the pulverized herbs and stir into a thick paste.

With a pastry brush, cover both sides of each wing with the herb paste. When no more paste remains in the mortar, squeeze the last few drops from the brush. Arrange the chicken wings on a baking sheet.

Bake until the skin turns a deep brown and is quite crisp — 30 to 35 minutes.

SUGGESTED ACCOMPANIMENTS: *steamed vegetable marrow; sautéed mushrooms.*

Chicken Wrapped in Crisp Phyllo

Serves 6
Working time: about 1 hour
Total time: about 1 day

Calories **500**
Protein **37g**
Cholesterol **95mg**
Total fat **27g**
Saturated fat **7g**
Sodium **545mg**

6	chicken breasts, skinned and boned (about 750 g/1½ lb)	6
250 g	phyllo pastry (18 sheets)	8 oz
¾ tsp	salt	¾ tsp
¾ tsp	freshly ground black pepper	¾ tsp
4 tbsp	safflower oil	4 tbsp
1	garlic clove, finely chopped	1
1	shallot, finely chopped	1
350 g	fresh spinach, washed and stemmed	12 oz
4 tbsp	dry white wine	4 tbsp
¼ litre	unsalted chicken stock	8 fl oz
1 tbsp	double cream	1 tbsp
60 g	pistachio nuts, shelled, peeled and coarsely chopped	2 oz
250 g	low-fat ricotta cheese	8 oz

Slice each breast diagonally into three medallions. Sprinkle the pieces with ½ teaspoon each of the salt and pepper. Heat 1 tablespoon of the oil in a heavy frying pan over medium-high heat. Sear the chicken pieces for about 30 seconds on each side in several batches, adding as much as 2 additional tablespoons of oil as necessary between batches. Set the chicken aside on a plate.

Immediately add the garlic and shallot to the pan, and sauté them for about 30 seconds, stirring. Add the spinach, reduce the heat to low, and cover. Cook until the spinach is wilted — about 2 minutes. Remove the pan from the heat and take out half of the spinach mixture. Chop this finely and reserve it for the filling.

Heat the pan again over medium heat. Pour in the wine and stock, and stir to deglaze the pan. Stir in the remaining salt and pepper and the cream, and cook until the liquid is reduced by half. Purée the sauce in a blender. Pour it into a small saucepan and set it aside.

Preheat the oven to 170°C (325°F or Mark 3). To make the filling, combine the pistachios, ricotta and chopped spinach mixture. Gently blot the chicken medallions with paper towels to remove any excess juice. Unwrap the phyllo. Peel off a stack of three sheets — about 30 by 45 cm (12 by 18 inches) and place them on a dry work surface. Cover the remaining sheets with a damp — not wet — paper towel to prevent them from drying out.

Centre a piece of chicken near an edge of the dough. ▶

Spread a thin layer of filling over the chicken, then top it with another medallion, a second layer of filling and a third chicken slice. Fold the sides of the dough over the chicken and roll it up. Place the roll seam side down in an oiled baking dish. Repeat with the remaining chicken pieces and phyllo sheets to make six rolls in all. Brush the rolls with the remaining tablespoon of oil.

Bake the rolls for 45 minutes. If additional baking is required to brown the phyllo, raise the temperature to 230°C (450°F or Mark 8) and keep the rolls in the oven a few minutes more. Warm the sauce and serve the rolls on top of it, as shown here, or pass it separately.

SUGGESTED ACCOMPANIMENTS: *sautéed mushrooms and mange-tout; mixed green salad.*

EDITOR'S NOTE: *Phyllo pastry sheets may be made at home (see page 83) or bought fresh or frozen.*

Chicken-and-Cheese-Filled Calzones

THIS RECIPE WAS INSPIRED BY THE ITALIAN *CALZONE,* A KIND OF PIE MADE WITH PIZZA DOUGH.

Serves 4
Working time: about 1 hour
Total time: about 3 hours

Calories **625**
Protein **37g**
Cholesterol **70mg**
Total fat **22g**
Saturated fat **6g**
Sodium **590mg**

Two	chicken breasts, skinned, boned and	Two
175 g	halved	6 oz
1 tbsp	virgin olive oil	1 tbsp
1 tbsp	cornmeal	1 tbsp
Dough		
15 g	dried yeast	½ oz
¼ tsp	sugar	¼ tsp
325 g	strong plain flour	11 oz
½ tsp	salt	½ tsp
¼ tsp	fennel seeds, crushed	¼ tsp
3 tbsp	virgin olive oil	3 tbsp
Tomato and red pepper sauce		
3	ripe tomatoes, skinned, seeded, chopped	3
1	sweet red pepper, seeded, deribbed, chopped	1
1	onion, chopped	1
2	garlic cloves, finely chopped	2
¼ tsp	fennel seeds, crushed	¼ tsp
1 tsp	fresh thyme, or ¼ tsp dried thyme	1 tsp
¾ tsp	chopped fresh oregano, or ¼ tsp dried oregano	¾ tsp
¼ tsp	salt	¼ tsp
	freshly ground black pepper	
Cheese filling		
175 g	low-fat ricotta cheese	6 oz
3 tbsp	freshly grated Parmesan cheese	3 tbsp

To make the dough, pour ¼ litre (8 fl oz) of lukewarm water into a small bowl and sprinkle the yeast and sugar

into it. Let stand for 2 to 3 minutes, then whisk the mixture with a fork until the yeast and sugar are completely dissolved. Allow the mixture to sit in a warm place until the yeast bubbles up — 10 to 15 minutes.

Sift 300 g (10 oz) of the flour and the salt into a large bowl. Stir in the fennel seeds. Make a well in the centre and pour in the yeast mixture and the oil. Mix the dough by hand; as soon as it can be gathered into a ball, place it on a floured board and add as much as needed of the remaining flour if the mixture is too soft and sticky. Knead the dough until it is smooth and elastic — about 10 minutes.

To make the dough in a food processor, put the flour, salt and fennel seeds into the bowl of the processor and pulse twice to mix. Combine the frothy yeast mixture with the oil. With the motor running, pour in the mixture as fast as the flour will absorb it; process until a ball of dough forms. Then process until the dough comes away from the sides of the bowl — about 40 seconds more.

Put the dough in a clean bowl and cover it with a towel. Set the bowl in a warm, draught-free place until the dough has doubled in size — about 1 to 1½ hours.

To make the sauce, place the tomatoes, red pepper, onion, garlic, fennel seeds, thyme, oregano, salt and pepper in a large, heavy-bottomed saucepan. Simmer the mixture over medium heat, stirring frequently, until the liquid is absorbed — about 30 minutes. Remove from the heat and set aside.

Meanwhile, in a small bowl, mix the ricotta and Parmesan cheeses. Set aside. Preheat the oven to 240°C (475°F or Mark 9).

In a large, heavy frying pan, heat the oil over medium-high heat. Place the breasts in the pan and sauté them for about 2 minutes on one side; turn and cook them on the other side — about 2 minutes more. (The meat should not be cooked through.) Remove the chicken from the heat and set aside.

Knock back the dough. Cut it into four equal pieces. Flatten each piece with the palm of the hand to produce a circle about 2.5 cm (1 inch) thick. Carefully stretch the dough by holding each round by its edge and rotating it with the fingers to obtain circles 15 cm (6 inches) in diameter. Alternatively, the dough can be stretched by patting it into a circle with the fingertips.

To assemble the calzones, place half a chicken breast on each round of dough, a little off-centre. Spread one quarter of the sauce on each breast and top with one quarter of the cheese filling. Moisten the inside edges of the dough with water and bring them up over the cheese to form a seal, and overlap the dough by 1 cm (½ inch). Crimp the dough to close the calzones.

Place a baking sheet in the preheated oven for 2 minutes. Remove it from the oven and sprinkle the cornmeal on the areas on which the calzones will bake. Place the calzones on the cornmeal and brush the dough with the excess oil from the pan. Bake until golden — 15 to 20 minutes.

SUGGESTED ACCOMPANIMENT: *spinach salad.*

Yogurt-Baked Chicken with Pimientos and Chives

Serves 4
Working time: about 20 minutes
Total time: about 2 hours and 30 minutes

Calories **320**
Protein **45g**
Cholesterol **130mg**
Total fat **11g**
Saturated fat **4g**
Sodium **320mg**

1.5 kg	chicken, quartered, skinned and fat removed	3 lb
¼ litre	plain low-fat yogurt	8 fl oz
2 tbsp	finely cut fresh chives	2 tbsp
¼ tsp	salt	¼ tsp
¼ tsp	white pepper	¼ tsp
1 tbsp	plain flour	1 tbsp
35 cl	unsalted chicken stock	12 fl oz
1 tbsp	very finely chopped pimiento	1 tbsp

To prepare the marinade, combine the yogurt, chives, salt and pepper in a shallow dish. Add the chicken and marinate it in the refrigerator for at least 2 hours.

Preheat the oven to 170°C (325°F or Mark 3). Transfer the chicken to a baking dish and reserve the marinade. Bake the chicken until the juices run clear when a thigh is pierced with the tip of a sharp knife — 25 to 30 minutes.

While the chicken is cooking, put the stock in a saucepan and bring it to the boil. Reduce the heat to maintain a slow simmer. Thoroughly mix the flour into the reserved marinade. Stir a few tablespoons of the hot stock into the marinade, then add the marinade to the stock, and simmer for 3 minutes. Add the pimiento and stir the sauce well.

Transfer the chicken from the baking dish to individual serving plates, and spoon the sauce over the pieces just before serving.

SUGGESTED ACCOMPANIMENTS: *broad beans; cornbread.*

Crêpes Filled with Chicken and Sweetcorn

Serves 4
Working time: about 30 minutes
Total time: about 1 hour

Calories **385**
Protein **26g**
Cholesterol **120mg**
Total fat **17g**
Saturated fat **5g**
Sodium **415mg**

250 g	chicken breasts, skinned and boned, cut into 1 cm (½ inch) cubes	8 oz
¼ tsp	salt	¼ tsp
	freshly ground black pepper	
½ tsp	safflower oil	½ tsp
Crêpe batter		
¼ litre	semi-skimmed milk	8 fl oz
1	egg yolk (reserve white for filling)	1
90 g	plain flour	3 oz
15 g	unsalted butter, melted	½ oz
½ tsp	turmeric	½ tsp
⅛ tsp	salt	⅛ tsp
	freshly ground black pepper	
1 tsp	fresh thyme or ¼ tsp dried thyme	1 tsp
½ tsp	chopped parsley	½ tsp
½ tsp	chopped fresh tarragon or ¼ tsp dried tarragon	½ tsp
½ tsp	chopped fresh mint	½ tsp
½ tsp	safflower oil for the crêpe pan, if necessary	½ tsp
Sweetcorn filling and sauce		
2 tbsp	safflower oil	2 tbsp
1	shallot, chopped	1
165 g	uncooked sweetcorn kernels	5½ oz
¼ litre	unsalted chicken stock	8 fl oz
1 tbsp	double cream	1 tbsp
125 g	low-fat cottage cheese	4 oz
2 tbsp	finely cut fresh chives	2 tbsp
1	egg white	1

To make the crêpe batter, whisk together the milk and the egg yolk in a mixing bowl. Add the flour in small amounts, whisking continuously until all the flour has been incorporated and there are no lumps. Stir in the butter, turmeric, salt, pepper and herbs.

To make the crêpes, heat a crêpe pan or a 15 cm (6 inch) non-stick frying pan over medium-high heat. If you are using a crêpe pan, pour in ½ teaspoon of oil and wipe with a paper towel. Pour 2 to 3 tablespoons of the crêpe batter into the hot pan and swirl it to just coat the bottom of the pan. Pour any excess back into the mixing bowl. Cook until brown — about 30 seconds — then lift the edge of the crêpe and turn it over. Cook on the second side until brown — about 15 seconds more. Slide the crêpe on to a plate. The crêpe should be paper-thin; if it is not, add up to 5 cl (2 fl oz) additional milk to the batter. Repeat the process with the remaining batter to make at least eight crêpes, and set them aside. Preheat the oven to 170°C (325°F or Mark 3).

To prepare the crêpe filling, sprinkle the chicken cubes with the salt and pepper. Heat 1 tablespoon of the oil in a heavy frying pan over medium-high heat. Sauté the chicken for 4 minutes and transfer it to a mixing bowl. ▶

Add the remaining tablespoon of oil to the pan and sauté the shallot for 30 seconds. Add the sweetcorn and sauté for 3 minutes more. Remove one third of the sweetcorn and add it to the chicken for the filling. To prepare the sauce, add the stock and the cream to the pan, and simmer for 3 minutes. Then purée the mixture in a food processor or blender.

Add the cottage cheese, 1 tablespoon of the chives, and the egg white to the bowl containing the chicken and sweetcorn, and mix well. Fill each crêpe with about 4 tablespoons of this mixture, and roll it up. Wipe the inside of a baking dish with ½ teaspoon of oil. Place the rolled crêpes seam side down in the dish and cover them with the sauce. Bake until the filling is heated through — about 20 minutes. Remove the crêpes from the oven and garnish them with the remaining chives.

SUGGESTED ACCOMPANIMENT: *oak leaf lettuce salad.*

Peach-Glazed Poussins with Ginger

Serves 4
Working time: about 20 minutes
Total time: about 50 minutes

Calories **330**
Protein **23g**
Cholesterol **45mg**
Total fat **11g**
Saturated fat **2g**
Sodium **490mg**

Two	poussins, halved, backbones	Two
750 g	removed	1½ lb
17.5 cl	orange juice	6 fl oz
125 g	dried peaches, thinly sliced	4 oz
2 tbsp	grated fresh ginger root	2 tbsp
1 tbsp	low-sodium soy sauce, or naturally fermented shoyu	1 tbsp
1 tbsp	safflower oil	1 tbsp
1	spring onion, finely sliced	1
2 tbsp	brown sugar	2 tbsp
1 tbsp	fresh lime juice	1 tbsp
½ tsp	salt	½ tsp

Preheat the grill. To make the glaze, combine the orange juice, peaches, ginger, soy sauce, safflower oil, spring onion, brown sugar and lime juice in a small saucepan over medium heat. Cook, stirring once, for 5 minutes. Set the glaze aside.

Preheat the oven to 190°C (375°F or Mark 5). Sprinkle the poussins with the salt and put them skin side up on a grill pan. To render some of their fat, place the birds under the grill, close to the heat, and grill them until light brown — 3 to 5 minutes. Remove the birds from the grill pan to an ovenproof casserole. Coat the poussins with the peach glaze and bake them for 25 minutes.

SUGGESTED ACCOMPANIMENT: *green beans with toasted almonds.*

Oven-Fried Cinnamon Chicken

Serves 4

Working time: about 15 minutes

Total time: about 1 hour

Calories **425**
Protein **47g**
Cholesterol **125mg**
Total fat **17g**
Saturated fat **3g**
Sodium **565g**

1.5 kg	chicken, quartered and skinned	3 lb
½ tsp	salt	½ tsp
½ tsp	freshly ground white pepper	½ tsp
4 tbsp	plain flour	4 tbsp
¼ tsp	turmeric	¼ tsp
1 tsp	cinnamon	1 tsp
3	egg whites	3
60 g	fresh breadcrumbs	2 oz
2 tbsp	safflower oil	2 tbsp

Preheat the oven to 170°C (325°F or Mark 3). Mix the salt, pepper and flour, and spread on a plate. In a small bowl, whisk the turmeric and cinnamon into the egg whites. Dredge the chicken pieces in the flour, then dip them in the egg whites and coat them with the breadcrumbs.

In a fireproof pan or shallow casserole large enough to hold the chicken pieces in a single layer, heat the oil over medium heat. Lay the pieces bone side up in the pan and brown them lightly on one side — about 2 minutes. Turn the pieces over, put the pan in the oven, and bake for 30 minutes.

Remove the pan and increase the oven temperature to 230°C (450°F or Mark 8). Wait about 5 minutes, then return to the oven and let the coating crisp for 4 or 5 minutes, taking care not to burn it.

SUGGESTED ACCOMPANIMENT: *sautéed cherry tomatoes.*

Chicken on a Bed of Savoy Cabbage

Serves 8
Working time: about 45 minutes
Total time: about 1 hour

Calories **395**
Protein **46g**
Cholesterol **130mg**
Total fat **16g**
Saturated fat **4g**
Sodium **365mg**

Two 1.5 kg	chickens, cut into serving pieces, all but the wings skinned	Two 3 lb
1.75 kg	Savoy cabbage	3½ lb
5 tbsp	wholemeal flour	5 tbsp
¼ tsp	cinnamon	¼ tsp
1½ tbsp	safflower oil	1½ tbsp
½ tsp	salt	½ tsp
1 tbsp	virgin olive oil	1 tbsp
3	ripe tomatoes, skinned, seeded, chopped	3
1	garlic clove, finely chopped	1
	Curry sauce	
2	carrots, thinly sliced	2
35 cl	plain low-fat yogurt	12 fl oz
1 to 3 tsp	curry powder	1 to 3 tsp
1 tbsp	virgin olive oil	1 tbsp
½ tsp	cinnamon	½ tsp
1 tbsp	honey	1 tbsp
¼ tsp	salt	¼ tsp

In order for its flavours to meld, make the sauce first. Cook the carrots in ¼ litre (8 fl oz) of water in a small covered saucepan over medium heat until they are soft — about 8 minutes. Drain the carrots and transfer them to a food processor or blender. Add 2 or 3 tablespoons of the yogurt and purée the mixture, scraping the sides down once. Add the remaining yogurt, 1 teaspoon of the curry powder, the olive oil, cinnamon, honey and salt, and purée again. Taste the sauce and blend in up to 2 teaspoons additional curry powder if desired. Transfer the sauce to a serving vessel and set it aside where it will stay lukewarm.

Discard any brown or wilted outer leaves of the cabbage. Slice it into quarters, then cut out the core. Cut each quarter crosswise into three pieces, then separate the leaves and set them aside.

Preheat the oven to 200°C (400°F or Mark 6). Mix the flour with the cinnamon and coat the chicken pieces with this mixture. Heat 1 tablespoon of the safflower oil in a large, heavy frying pan over medium-high heat. Sauté half of the pieces on one side until brown — 4 to 5 minutes. Turn the pieces over and sprinkle them with ⅛ teaspoon of the salt. Sauté the chicken on the second side until brown — about 4 minutes more.

Transfer the browned chicken pieces to an ovenproof serving dish with their smooth sides facing up. Add the remaining safflower oil to the frying pan and sauté the remaining chicken pieces the same way. Arrange the pieces smooth sides up in the dish. Reserve the pan for the tomatoes and cabbage.

Bake the chicken pieces until the juices run clear when a thigh is pierced with the tip of a sharp knife — about 25 to 30 minutes.

While the chicken is baking, cook the cabbage. Pour enough water into a large pot to cover the bottom by about 1 cm (½ inch). Set a vegetable steamer in the pot and put the cabbage in the steamer. Cover the pot tightly and bring the water to the boil. Steam the cabbage, uncovering it once to stir it, until it is wilted — 5 to 7 minutes. Drain the cabbage well.

Heat the olive oil in the frying pan over medium heat. Add the tomatoes and garlic, and cook for 1 minute. Stir in the cabbage and the remaining salt; toss well to heat the vegetables through. Set the pan aside.

When the chicken is cooked, remove the pieces, leaving the juices in the serving dish. Arrange the cabbage and tomatoes in the bottom of the dish, then place the chicken on top. Serve the sauce separately.

SUGGESTED ACCOMPANIMENT: *steamed new potatoes with freshly cut chives.*

Lime and Mint Chicken

Serves 6
Working time: about 15 minutes
Total time: about 4 hours and 15 minutes

Calories **250**
Protein **27g**
Cholesterol **100mg**
Total fat **12g**
Saturated fat **3g**
Sodium **185mg**

12	chicken thighs, skinned	12
½ tsp	sugar	½ tsp
	Lime marinade	
¼ litre	fresh lime juice	8 fl oz
8 cl	dry white wine	3 fl oz
45 g	fresh mint leaves, chopped, plus 6 whole mint sprigs reserved for garnish	1½ oz
1½ tsp	cumin seeds, crushed, or ¾ tsp ground cumin	1½ tsp
3	spring onions, thinly sliced	3
1	large dried red chili pepper, seeded and thinly sliced (see caution, page 25), or ½ to ¾ tsp crushed red pepper flakes	1
¼ tsp	salt	¼ tsp

Combine the marinade ingredients in a shallow bowl or

dish large enough to hold the chicken thighs. Put the thighs in the bowl and coat them with the marinade. Cover the bowl and refrigerate it for 4 to 6 hours.

Preheat the grill. Remove the chicken from the marinade and arrange the pieces in a grill pan. Strain the marinade into a small bowl and reserve both the strained liquid and the drained mint mixture. Grill the chicken 10 to 15 cm (4 to 6 inches) below the heat source until it is browned — 6 to 8 minutes. Remove the pan from the grill and turn the pieces over. Spoon some of the mint mixture over each thigh. Grill the thighs until the juices run clear when a piece is pierced with the tip of a sharp knife — 6 to 8 minutes more.

Meanwhile, stir the sugar into the strained marinade. Put the liquid in a small pan and boil it over high heat for 2 minutes, stirring frequently, to produce a light sauce.

To serve, spoon some of the sauce over each thigh and garnish with the mint sprigs.

SUGGESTED ACCOMPANIMENTS: *baked sweet potatoes; steamed cauliflower.*

Saffron Chicken
with Yogurt

Serves 6
Working time: about 30 minutes
Total time: about 1 day

6	whole chicken legs, skinned	6
4 tbsp	unsalted chicken stock	4 tbsp
⅛ tsp	saffron (about 20 threads)	⅛ tsp
¼ tsp	salt	¼ tsp
	freshly ground black pepper	
12.5 cl	plain low-fat yogurt	4 fl oz
90 g	onion, chopped	3 oz
2	garlic cloves, finely chopped	2
1 tsp	grated fresh ginger root	1 tsp
4 tbsp	fresh lemon juice	4 tbsp
⅛ tsp	cayenne pepper	⅛ tsp
¼ tsp	ground cumin	¼ tsp

Calories **210**
Protein **28g**
Cholesterol **90mg**
Total fat **9g**
Saturated fat **2g**
Sodium **185mg**

Combine the stock and saffron in a small saucepan over medium heat and bring them to a simmer. Remove the pan from the heat and let the saffron steep for about 5 minutes. The stock will turn golden.

Sprinkle the chicken legs with the salt and pepper. Put them in a shallow baking dish and dribble the stock-and-saffron mixture over them. Turn the legs to coat both sides and arrange them so that they do not touch.

Combine the yogurt, onion, garlic, ginger, lemon juice, cayenne pepper and cumin in a food processor or blender, and purée until smooth. Pour the mixture over the chicken legs and cover the dish with a sheet of plastic film. Refrigerate it for 8 hours or overnight.

Preheat the grill. Remove the legs from the marinade and arrange them top side down in a foil-lined grill pan. Reserve the marinade. Position the grill pan 8 to 10 cm (3½ to 4 inches) below the heat source. Grill the legs for about 8 minutes on each side, basting them with the marinade every 2 minutes. The chicken is done when the juices run clear from a thigh pierced with the tip of a sharp knife.

SUGGESTED ACCOMPANIMENTS: *toasted pitta bread; grated carrot salad.*

Grilled Chicken with Malt Vinegar and Basil

Serves 4
Working time: about 30 minutes
Total time: about 1 day

Calories **280**		
Protein **30g**		
Cholesterol **105mg**		
Total fat **15g**		
Saturated fat **4g**		
Sodium **235mg**		

4	whole chicken legs, skinned	4
17.5 cl	malt vinegar	6 fl oz
12.5 cl	dry white wine	4 fl oz
2	large shallots, thinly sliced	2
2 tsp	ground mace	2 tsp
	freshly ground black pepper	
2 tbsp	chopped fresh basil leaves, or 2 tsp dried basil	2 tbsp
¼ tsp	salt	¼ tsp

To prepare the marinade, combine the vinegar, wine, shallots, mace, pepper and basil in a saucepan. Bring the mixture to a simmer over medium heat and cook for 2 minutes. Sprinkle the chicken legs with the salt and set them in a shallow baking dish. Pour the marinade over the chicken and cover the dish with plastic film. Refrigerate for 8 hours or overnight.

Preheat the grill. Remove the legs from the marinade and arrange them on a foil-lined grill pan. Reserve the marinade. Grill the legs 8 to 10 cm (3½ to 4 inches) below the heat source for about 8 minutes on each side, brushing them with the marinade every 4 minutes. The chicken is done when the juices run clear from a thigh pierced with the tip of a sharp knife.

SUGGESTED ACCOMPANIMENTS: *boiled new potatoes; steamed red cabbage.*

Chicken Breasts with Radishes

Serves 4
Working time: about 30 minutes
Total time: about 1 day

Calories **215**
Protein **27g**
Cholesterol **70mg**
Total fat **4g**
Saturated fat **2g**
Sodium **200mg**

4	chicken breasts, skinned and boned, wings severed at the second joint from the tip	4
¼ tsp	salt	¼ tsp
6	large radishes, thinly sliced	6
¼ litre	red wine vinegar	8 fl oz
12.5 cl	dry white wine	4 fl oz
1½ tbsp	chopped fresh tarragon leaves, or ½ tbsp dried tarragon	1½ tbsp
	freshly ground black pepper	
2 tbsp	honey	2 tbsp

Sprinkle both sides of the breasts with the salt. With the knife held perpendicular to the long edge of a breast, cut diagonally into the smooth side of the flesh to make four 1 cm (½ inch) deep slits at 2 cm (¾ inch) intervals across the breast. Cut similar diagonal slits in the other breasts.

Cover the bottom of a shallow dish with the radishes and lay the breasts, cut side down, on top.

To prepare the marinade, combine the vinegar, wine, tarragon, pepper and honey in a saucepan. Bring the liquid to a simmer over medium heat, and cook for 2 minutes. Stir the marinade and pour it over the breasts. Cover the dish with plastic film and refrigerate for 8 hours or overnight.

Preheat the grill when you are ready to cook the chicken. Arrange the breasts cut side down in a foil-lined grill pan. Reserve the marinade for basting.

Grill the chicken 8 to 10 cm (3½ to 4 inches) below the heat source for 4 minutes on the first side, basting once. Turn and grill them on the second side for 2 minutes. Remove the breasts from the grill and tuck one, two or three radish slices into each of the slits, forming a fish-scale pattern. Grill the chicken for another 2 minutes. Make a small cut in the thick portion of a breast to see if the meat has turned white. If it is still pink, grill it for 1 or 2 minutes more.

Pour the accumulated cooking juices over the chicken breasts and serve.

SUGGESTED ACCOMPANIMENT: *watercress and red onion salad.*

Chicken Thighs Grilled with Sherry and Honey

Serves 4
Working (and total) time: about 25 minutes

Calories **340**		
Protein **28g**		
Cholesterol **100mg**		
Total fat **11g**		
Saturated fat **3g**		
Sodium **385mg**		

8	chicken thighs, skinned	8
¼ litre	dry sherry	8 fl oz
3 tbsp	honey	3 tbsp
4	garlic cloves, finely chopped	4
3 tbsp	red wine vinegar	3 tbsp
1 tbsp	low-sodium soy sauce, or naturally fermented shoyu	1 tbsp
1 tbsp	cornflour, mixed with 2 tbsp dry sherry	1 tbsp
¼ tsp	salt	¼ tsp

Boil the sherry in a small saucepan until it is reduced by half — about 7 minutes. Remove the pan from the stove and whisk in the honey, garlic, vinegar and soy sauce. Return the pan to the heat and whisk the cornflour mixture into the sauce. Bring the sauce to the boil and cook for 1 minute, whisking constantly. Remove the pan from the heat and let the sauce cool.

Preheat the grill. Sprinkle the salt on both sides of the thighs and lay them bone side up on a rack in a roasting pan. Brush liberally with the sauce, then grill them 10 to 15 cm (4 to 6 inches) from the heat source for 6 to 7 minutes. Turn over and brush again with sauce. Grill for 3 or 4 minutes more, then brush again with remaining sauce. Continue grilling until the juices run clear when a thigh is pierced with the tip of a sharp knife — 5 to 7 minutes more. Transfer the thighs to a platter and trickle any remaining sauce from the roasting pan over them.

SUGGESTED ACCOMPANIMENT: *mange-tout sautéed with water chestnuts and soy sauce.*

Dry Martini Poussins

Serves 4
Working time: about 30 minutes
Total time: 1 to 2 days

Calories **300**
Protein **28g**
Cholesterol **90mg**
Total fat **14g**
Saturated fat **4g**
Sodium **360mg**

Four	poussins, giblets reserved for another	Four
500 g	use, cavities washed and patted dry	1 lb
2 tbsp	juniper berries, crushed	2 tbsp
2	lemons, rind only, cut into 5 mm (¼ inch) strips	2
½ litre	unsalted chicken stock	16 fl oz
17.5 cl	gin	6 fl oz
4 tbsp	dry vermouth	4 tbsp
½ tsp	salt	½ tsp
	freshly ground black pepper	

To make the marinade, combine the juniper berries, lemon rind, 35 cl (12 fl oz) of the stock, two thirds of the gin, the vermouth, salt and pepper in a small bowl. Place the birds in a deep dish that holds them snugly, and pour the marinade over them. Swirl some of the marinade into the cavity of each bird. Cover the dish with a lid or plastic film, and refrigerate for 24 to 48 hours. Turn the birds from time to time as they marinate.

Preheat the oven to 190°C (375°F or Mark 5). Remove the birds from the marinade and put 1 tablespoon of the marinade liquid, a few of the crushed juniper berries and some of the lemon rind in the cavity of each bird. Discard the remaining marinade. Tie each pair of legs together with string. Arrange the birds breast side up on the rack of a roasting pan so that they do not touch. Roast them until they are golden-brown — 40 to 50 minutes. Pour the juices, juniper berries and lemon rind from the cavity of each poussin into the pan, and set the birds on a warmed serving platter.

To make the sauce, remove the rack and place the roasting pan over medium-high heat. Add the remaining stock and gin. Cook the sauce, stirring with a wooden spoon to dislodge any brown bits, until the liquid is reduced by about half and has thickened — 7 to 10 minutes. Strain the sauce and serve it with the birds. Garnish, if you like, with twists of fresh lemon peel.

SUGGESTED ACCOMPANIMENTS: *steamed baby carrots; new potatoes.*

Poussins with Pineapple and Mint

Serves 4
Working time: about 1 hour
Total time: about 1 hour and 30 minutes

Calories **425**
Protein **27g**
Cholesterol **50mg**
Total fat **11g**
Saturated fat **4g**
Sodium **330mg**

Two 750 g poussins, giblets reserved		Two 1 ½ lb
175 g	burghul, rinsed and drained	6 oz
1	pineapple, peeled and cored	1
2	navel oranges, the rind of one grated and reserved for the stuffing	2
2	spring onions, sliced into thin rounds	2
30 g	fresh mint, chopped, a few whole sprigs reserved for garnish	1 oz
½ tsp	salt	½ tsp
	freshly ground black pepper	
15 g	unsalted butter	½ oz
8	garlic cloves, unpeeled	8
4 tbsp	dry white wine	4 tbsp

Put the burghul in a small bowl and add enough boiling water to cover. Let the burghul soak for 10 minutes. Empty the bowl into a strainer to drain the burghul. Cut a few slices from the pineapple and reserve them for use as a garnish. Coarsely chop the rest of the pineapple in a food processor or by hand. Cook the chopped pineapple in a frying pan over medium-low heat until the juices have evaporated — 20 to 25 minutes.

Meanwhile, prepare each bird. Starting at the neck, use your fingers to separate the skin from either side of the breast. Then, with a knife, cut through the membrane attaching the skin to the breast, taking care not to puncture the skin. Remove and discard any bits of fat. Preheat the oven to 230°C (450°F or Mark 8).

To prepare the stuffing, first segment one of the oranges. Cut away the peel with a knife, cutting deep enough to remove the bitter white pith and expose the flesh. Then hold the orange over a bowl to catch its juice as you slice down to the core on either side of each segment. Dislodge the segments and let them fall into the bowl as you proceed. Cut the second orange in half and squeeze its juice into the bowl. Remove the orange segments from the juice and cut them into small pieces; reserve the juice for the sauce. Combine the orange pieces, the burghul and the chopped pineapple in a mixing bowl. Mix in the spring onions, mint, salt, some pepper and the grated orange rind.

Gently push about 30 g (1 oz) of the stuffing under the skin of each bird, moulding the skin into a smooth, round shape. Tuck the neck flap under each bird. Reserve the extra stuffing in a small ovenproof bowl or baking dish, and cover it with foil.

Melt the butter in a small pan over medium-low heat.

Place the poussins on an oiled rack in a roasting pan. Distribute the neck, gizzard, heart and garlic cloves in the bottom of the pan. Brush the birds with some of the butter and roast them in the upper third of the oven for 15 minutes. Baste them with the remaining butter and any accumulated pan juices, and return them to the oven along with the reserved stuffing. Roast until the birds are golden-brown and the juices run clear when a thigh is pierced with the tip of a sharp knife — 20 to 25 minutes more.

Remove the birds from the oven and turn it off, leaving the stuffing inside while you prepare the sauce. Remove the rack, garlic and giblets from the pan, and skim off the fat. Reserve the giblets for later use in the stockpot. Set the pan over medium heat and stir in the orange juice and wine to deglaze it. Squeeze the garlic cloves from their skins and add them to the sauce. Simmer and stir for 1 minute. Pour the sauce through a sieve set over a small bowl. Press the soft garlic through the sieve with a wooden spoon and stir the sauce well.

Cut each bird in half lengthwise, and set the halves on a platter or on individual plates. Arrange the warm stuffing around each bird and spoon the sauce over the top. Garnish with the whole mint sprigs, raw pineapple and, if you like, orange slices. Serve hot.

SUGGESTED ACCOMPANIMENT: *steamed kale.*

Roast Capon with Sage Cornbread Stuffing

Serves 8
Working time: about 45 minutes
Total time: about 2 hours and 15 minutes

Calories **445**
Protein **42g**
Cholesterol **110mg**
Total fat **21g**
Saturated fat **5g**
Sodium **345mg**

4 to 4.5 kg	capon, or roasting chicken, rinsed and patted dry	9 to 10 lb
15 g	unsalted butter	½ oz
4	large onions, thinly sliced	4
1 tbsp	safflower oil	1 tbsp
½ tsp	salt	½ tsp
45 g	lean ham, cut into small cubes	1½ oz
12.5 cl	unsalted chicken stock	4 fl oz
Sage cornbread		
125 g	cornmeal	4 oz
125 g	plain flour	4 oz
1 tbsp	baking powder	1 tbsp
¼ tsp	salt	¼ tsp
¼ tsp	freshly ground black pepper	¼ tsp
¼ litre	buttermilk	8 fl oz
1	egg, beaten	1
2 tbsp	safflower oil	2 tbsp
2 tbsp	chopped fresh sage, or 1½ tsp dried sage	2 tbsp

Preheat the oven to 220°C (425°F or Mark 7).

To prepare the cornbread, combine the cornmeal, flour, baking powder, salt and pepper. Stir in the buttermilk, egg, oil and sage. Pour the batter into a lightly oiled 20 cm (8 inch) square baking tin and bake until golden-brown — 20 to 25 minutes. Reduce the oven temperature to 190°C (375°F or Mark 5).

Meanwhile, melt the butter in a heavy-bottomed saucepan over medium-low heat. Add the onions and cook for 20 minutes, stirring occasionally. Add the tablespoon of oil and cook until the onions are caramelized — about 40 minutes more. Scrape the bottom often to avoid sticking and burning.

While the onions are cooking, truss the chicken as shown on page 138. Place a metal steamer or rack in the bottom of a large stockpot, and pour in enough water to cover the bottom by about 2.5 cm (1 inch). Bring the water to the boil, then place the bird in the pot and cover it tightly. Steam for 20 minutes over high heat. Remove the bird, sprinkle its skin immediately with ¼ teaspoon of the salt, and let it stand while you prepare the stuffing.

Crumble the cornbread into a bowl and stir in the cara-melized onions, ham and chicken stock. Pour off any juices from the cavity of the bird and sprinkle the inside with the remaining ¼ teaspoon of salt. Fill the chicken loosely with the stuffing, and cover the opening with a small piece of aluminium foil. Place any excess stuffing in a small ovenproof dish, moisten it with a little chicken stock, cover with foil and bake along with the bird during the last 20 minutes of roasting time. Put the bird breast side up on a rack in a roasting pan. Roast it until the skin is crisp and golden and the juices run clear when a thigh is pierced with the tip of a sharp knife — about 1 hour and 10 minutes.

SUGGESTED ACCOMPANIMENTS: *sautéed apples; mashed swedes.*

EDITOR'S NOTE: *The process of steaming followed by roasting helps to defat the chicken considerably, resulting in a crisp skin and fewer calories.*

Roast Chicken with Apples, Turnips and Garlic

Serves 4
Working time: about 30 minutes
Total time: about 1 hour and 30 minutes

Calories **380**	1.5 kg	chicken	3 lb
Protein **39g**	1 tbsp	paprika	1 tbsp
Cholesterol **105mg**	½ tsp	freshly ground black pepper	½ tsp
Total fat **17g**	⅛ tsp	salt	⅛ tsp
Saturated fat **5g**	5 g	unsalted butter	⅙ oz
Sodium **195mg**	2 or 3	Golden Delicious apples, peeled, cored and cut into eighths	2 or 3
	3	small turnips, peeled, quartered and thinly sliced	3
	6	garlic cloves, peeled	6
		juice of half a lemon	

Preheat the oven to 170°C (325°F or Mark 3). Mix the paprika, pepper and salt and rub the chicken inside and out with them.

Butter a roasting pan and put the chicken in it. Arrange the apples, turnips and garlic around the bird. Trickle the lemon juice over the top of the apples and tur-nips. Roast the chicken until it is golden-brown all over and a leg moves easily when it is wiggled up and down — 65 to 75 minutes. Baste the bird with the pan juices two or three times during the cooking.

When the chicken is done, skim the fat from the pan and mash the apples, turnips and garlic together with the pan juices. Serve in a separate bowl.

SUGGESTED ACCOMPANIMENT: *mange-tout or sugarsnap peas*

Thyme-Roasted Chicken

Serves 4
Working time: about 30 minutes
Total time: about 1 hour and 30 minutes

Calories **295**
Protein **38g**
Cholesterol **80mg**
Total fat **12g**
Saturated fat **4g**
Sodium **380mg**

1.75 to 2 kg	chicken, giblets reserved for another use, rinsed and patted dry	3½ to 4 lb
½ tsp	salt	½ tsp
	freshly ground black pepper	
1 tbsp	fresh thyme leaves, stems reserved for flavouring the cavity	1 tbsp
6 to 8	bay leaves, crumbled into small bits	6 to 8
12.5 cl	dry white wine	4 fl oz

Season the body cavity with ⅛ teaspoon of the salt and some pepper. Working from the edge of the cavity, gently lift the skin covering the breast, taking care not to tear it, and distribute the thyme leaves under the skin so that they evenly cover the meat. Let the skin fall back into place. Place the thyme stems and the bay leaves in the cavity. Prepare the chicken for roasting by trussing it as demonstrated on page 138. Preheat the oven to 200°C (400°F or Mark 6).

Select a stockpot that has a tight-fitting lid and is large enough to accommodate the chicken. Fill the pot 2.5 cm (1 inch) deep with water. Place the chicken in the pot on a rack high enough to hold the bird clear of the water. Set the pot over high heat, cover tightly, and steam the chicken for 15 minutes to begin to render its fat.

Carefully remove the bird from the pot and transfer it to the rack of a roasting pan. Quickly season the outside of the bird with the remaining salt and some pepper. Roast the chicken until it is a light golden-brown all over — 40 to 45 minutes.

Remove the chicken and pour the contents of its cavity into the roasting pan. Add the white wine and ¼ litre (8 fl oz) of water. Place the pan over medium heat and simmer the liquid, scraping up any pan deposits, until it is reduced by half — 7 to 10 minutes.

Carve the chicken and arrange the meat on a warmed platter. Strain the reduced sauce, and spoon it over the chicken.

SUGGESTED ACCOMPANIMENT: *julienned carrots steamed with currants.*

EDITOR'S NOTE: *The process of steaming followed by roasting helps to defat the chicken considerably, resulting in a crisp, savoury skin and fewer calories. As an alternative to the thyme leaves, 1 tablespoon of fresh rosemary or sage leaves or 4 tablespoons of chopped fresh basil leaves may be inserted between the skin and breast; the stems of these herbs may be placed in the cavity for additional aromatic flavouring.*

Emerald Chicken Roll

SO THAT THE CHICKEN WILL HAVE THE PROPER TEXTURE, ALL MEMBRANES AND CARTILAGE MUST BE REMOVED BEFORE THE MEAT IS PURÉED. CHICKEN BREASTS ARE EASIER TO USE THAN LEGS OR THIGHS.

Serves 8
Working time: about 45 minutes
Total time: about 1 hour and 15 minutes

Calories **145**
Protein **18g**
Cholesterol **50mg**
Total fat **6g**
Saturated fat **3g**
Sodium **150mg**

500 g	chicken meat, cut into 5 cm (2 inch) pieces	1 lb
7 g	dried mushrooms	¼ oz
12 to 15	large cos lettuce leaves	12 to 15
1 tbsp	chopped parsley	1 tbsp
½ tsp	chopped fresh tarragon leaves, or ½ tsp dried tarragon	½ tsp
2	spring onions, green stalks trimmed to within 5 cm (2 inches) of the white part, cut into pieces	2
½ tsp	ground coriander	½ tsp
¼ tsp	salt	¼ tsp
	freshly ground black pepper	
250 g	low-fat ricotta cheese	8 oz
12.5 cl	unsalted chicken stock	4 fl oz
1	egg white	1
½ tbsp	cornflour, mixed with 2 tbsp Madeira or port	½ tbsp
15 g	unsalted butter	½ oz
2 tbsp	finely cut fresh chives	2 tbsp

Put the mushrooms in a small bowl and pour 30 cl (½ pint) of boiling water over them. Cover, and set aside for

30 minutes. Meanwhile, place the lettuce leaves in a large pot with a tight-fitting lid and pour 12.5 cl (4 fl oz) of cold water over them. Place a piece of aluminium foil directly on top of the lettuce and cover. Bring the water to the boil and steam the leaves for 1 minute to make them limp. Remove the pan from the heat and take off the lid and foil. When the leaves are cool enough to handle, cut out the thick core at the base of each stem. Spread the leaves on paper towels to drain.

Put the chicken in the bowl of a food processor. Add the chopped parsley, tarragon, spring onion, coriander, salt and a generous grinding of pepper. Process in short bursts until the chicken is coarsely chopped. Add the ricotta cheese and the chicken stock, and purée until smooth. Scrape down the sides of the bowl; then, with the motor running, add the egg white and process until it is thoroughly incorporated — about 5 seconds more.

Remove the mushrooms from the water and squeeze them gently over the bowl to rid them of excess water; strain and reserve the soaking liquid. Chop the mushrooms into coarse pieces and add them to the processor bowl. Using a few short bursts, process just enough to incorporate the mushrooms into the chicken mixture. Poach a spoonful of the mixture in simmering water; taste and correct the seasonings, if necessary.

Spread a piece of muslin about 45 cm (18 inches) long, on a work surface. Lay the lettuce leaves one by one in a row, each long edge overlapping the next, to form a rectangle roughly 40 by 20 cm (16 by 8 inches). Spoon the chicken mixture in a row lengthwise down the ▶

centre of the lettuce rectangle. Use a rubber spatula dipped in cold water to shape the mixture into a log. Pull up the lettuce leaves on each side to cover the chicken, then roll the log in the muslin, tucking the ends of the muslin underneath or tying them with string.

Add enough water to the mushroom-soaking liquid to total 35 cl (12 fl oz). Pour the liquid into a fish kettle or wok (or other pot large enough to hold the roll) fitted with a rack or steamer. Place the chicken roll on the rack. Cover, and steam the roll until it feels firm to the touch — about 25 minutes. Lift the roll out of the steamer and set it aside. Remove the rack.

Stir the cornflour mixture into the simmering liquid. Cook until the sauce is translucent and somewhat thick — about 1 minute. Remove the pot from the heat. Add the butter, and swirl the sauce until the butter melts. Stir the chives into the sauce.

Unwrap the chicken roll, letting any accumulated juices run into the sauce. Cut the roll into diagonal slices about 2 cm (¾ inch) thick and arrange them on a serving platter. Pour the sauce into a heated sauceboat and pass it separately.

SUGGESTED ACCOMPANIMENTS: *julienned carrots; tomato salad.*

EDITOR'S NOTE: *The chicken mixture may be rolled in individual lettuce leaves, allowing about 5 to 6 tablespoons of the mixture for each roll. The steaming procedure remains the same, but the time should be reduced to 15 minutes.*

Cold Chicken and Asparagus with Lemon-Tarragon Vinaigrette

Serves 4
Working (and total) time: about 45 minutes

Calories **280**
Protein **29g**
Cholesterol **70mg**
Total fat **15g**
Saturated fat **2g**
Sodium **135mg**

4	chicken breasts, skinned and boned (about 500 g/1 lb)	4
20	asparagus spears, ends trimmed, peeled ⅓ of the way up the stalks	20
½ tsp	safflower oil	½ tsp
⅛ tsp	salt	⅛ tsp
	freshly ground black pepper	
½	sweet red pepper, julienned	½
Lemon-tarragon vinaigrette		
1 tbsp	chopped shallot, or 2 spring onions, finely chopped	1 tbsp
3 tbsp	fresh lemon juice	3 tbsp
½ tsp	fresh thyme, or ⅛ tsp dried thyme	½ tsp
1½ tsp	chopped fresh tarragon, or ½ tsp dried tarragon	1½ tsp
2 tbsp	safflower oil	2 tbsp
1 tbsp	virgin olive oil	1 tbsp
1	garlic clove, chopped	1
1 tbsp	chopped parsley	1 tbsp
1 tsp	sugar	1 tsp
	freshly ground black pepper	

To make the vinaigrette, combine the shallot or spring onions, lemon juice, thyme and tarragon. Let stand for 10 minutes, then whisk in the oils, the garlic, parsley, sugar and pepper. Allow to stand for 10 minutes more.

In a heavy frying pan, heat the safflower oil over very low heat. Sprinkle the breasts with the salt and pepper. Place the breasts in the pan and cover them with a heavy plate to weight them down and preserve their juices. Cook the breasts on one side for 5 minutes, turn, and cook for another 3 to 4 minutes. The meat should feel firm but springy to the touch, and there should be no visible pink along the edges. Remove from the pan and cool in the refrigerator for at least 10 minutes or until ready to serve.

To cook the asparagus spears, place them in a pan with a tight-fitting lid, together with 4 tablespoons of water. Cover, bring to the boil, and cook until they are tender but still crisp — about 2 minutes. Drain, rinse under cold running water, chill, and keep cool.

Slice the breasts on the diagonal and arrange each one on an individual serving plate with five asparagus spears. Garnish with the red pepper and spoon the vinaigrette over the chicken and asparagus.

SUGGESTED ACCOMPANIMENT: *French bread.*

Spatchcocked Chicken with Basil-Yogurt Sauce

THE WORD "SPATCHCOCK" COMES FROM THE IRISH TERM "DISPATCH-COCK", A DISH FOR A SUDDEN OCCASION. HERE IT REFERS TO A WHOLE CHICKEN THAT IS SPLIT OPEN AND FLATTENED FOR EVEN COOKING.

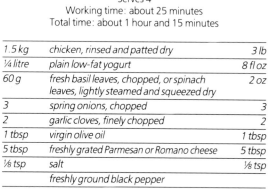

Serves 4
Working time: about 25 minutes
Total time: about 1 hour and 15 minutes

Calories **390**
Protein **45g**
Cholesterol **90mg**
Total fat **20g**
Saturated fat **6g**
Sodium **365mg**

1.5 kg	chicken, rinsed and patted dry	3 lb
¼ litre	plain low-fat yogurt	8 fl oz
60 g	fresh basil leaves, chopped, or spinach leaves, lightly steamed and squeezed dry	2 oz
3	spring onions, chopped	3
2	garlic cloves, finely chopped	2
1 tbsp	virgin olive oil	1 tbsp
5 tbsp	freshly grated Parmesan or Romano cheese	5 tbsp
⅛ tsp	salt	⅛ tsp
	freshly ground black pepper	

Prepare the bird for roasting as demonstrated in the steps below. Preheat the oven to 200°C (400°F or Mark 6). Cover the bottom of a large pot with 2.5 cm (½ inch) water. Set a steamer or rack in the pot, and bring the water to the boil. Place the chicken skin side up on the steamer. Cover tightly and steam the chicken for 15 minutes over high heat.

While the chicken is steaming, make the sauce. Combine the yogurt, basil or spinach, spring onions, garlic, oil and half the Parmesan or Romano cheese in a food processor or blender. Process until smooth, then transfer the sauce to a sauceboat and set it aside at room temperature.

Set the steamed chicken on a rack in a roasting pan.

Sprinkle it with the salt and some pepper. Roast until the skin is a crispy, light brown — about 25 minutes.

Remove the bird from the oven and sprinkle the remaining cheese over it. Return the chicken to the oven and roast until the cheese is golden-brown — 8 to 10 minutes more.

Allow the chicken to stand 10 minutes, then carve it into serving pieces. Pass the sauce separately.

SUGGESTED ACCOMPANIMENTS: *stewed tomatoes; brown rice.*

EDITOR'S NOTE: *The process of steaming followed by roasting helps to defat the chicken considerably, resulting in a crisp skin and fewer calories.*

Spatchcocking a Chicken

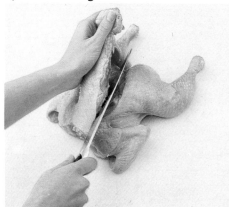

1 *REMOVING THE BACKBONE. Place a whole chicken breast side down on a work surface. With a heavy chef's knife, cut down along one side of the backbone from the tail towards the neck, using a sawing motion to cut through the rib cage. Repeat this process on the other side and pull the backbone free.*

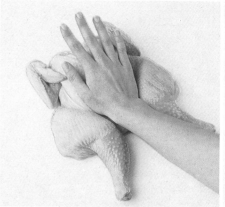

2 *FLATTENING THE BIRD. Turn the bird breast side up, with its drumsticks pointed towards you. Then, with one forceful motion, press the heel of your hand down on the breastbone to flatten out the breast. Tuck the wing tips behind the chicken's shoulders.*

3 *SECURING THE DRUMSTICKS. To keep the drumsticks from spreading out as the bird cooks, tuck them into a flap of skin: first pull the skin around the tail cavity taut, then cut a slit about 2 cm (¾ inch) long between a thigh and the tapered end of the breast. Thread the end of the drumstick through the slit. Repeat the procedure to secure the second leg.*

browned — 4 to 5 minutes. Stir in the remaining table-spoon of lime juice and a generous grinding of pepper. Using a slotted spoon, transfer the pieces to a bowl. Refrigerate them for at least 10 minutes.

Whisk the remaining 2 tablespoons of oil into the dressing mixture. Remove the couscous and the chicken from the refrigerator. Stir the dressing into the couscous. Finally, add the chicken, the remaining spring onions and the red pepper, and mix well. Serve each portion on a bed of lettuce.

SUGGESTED ACCOMPANIMENT: *sliced tomatoes.*

Chilled Chicken Couscous with Lime

Serves 4
Working time: about 30 minutes
Total time: about 40 minutes

Calories **435**
Protein **23g**
Cholesterol **55mg**
Total fat **18g**
Saturated fat **3g**
Sodium **215mg**

350 g	chicken meat, cut into 2 cm (¾ inch) pieces	12 oz
2 tbsp	finely chopped onion	2 tbsp
4 tbsp	safflower oil	4 tbsp
175 g	couscous	6 oz
¼ litre	unsalted chicken stock	8 fl oz
5 tbsp	fresh lime juice	5 tbsp
1	garlic clove, finely chopped	1
4 tsp	fresh thyme, or 1 tsp dried thyme	4 tsp
¼ tsp	salt	¼ tsp
	freshly ground black pepper	
6	spring onions, trimmed and finely chopped	6
1	sweet red pepper, seeded, deribbed and chopped into 1 cm (½ inch) squares	1
	lettuce leaves (for serving)	

In a heavy frying pan with a tight-fitting lid, sauté the onion in 1 tablespoon of the oil over medium-high heat for about 2 minutes. Stir in the couscous, the stock and ¼ litre (8 fl oz) of water, and boil rapidly for about 2 minutes. Remove the pan from the heat and cover it; let it stand for 5 minutes. Remove the lid, fluff up the cous-cous with a fork, and transfer the mixture to a large mix-ing bowl. Put the bowl in the refrigerator to cool.

For the dressing, combine 4 tablespoons of the lime juice, the garlic, thyme, salt and some pepper. Add half the spring onions and set the mixture aside.

Add another tablespoon of oil to the pan and set it over high heat. When the oil is hot, add the chicken pieces and sauté them, stirring frequently, until lightly

Sage-Flavoured Chicken Pie with Phyllo Crust

Serves 4
Working time: about 1 hour
Total time: about 1 hour and 30 minutes

Calories **440**
Protein **26g**
Cholesterol **70mg**
Total fat **17g**
Saturated fat **6g**
Sodium **370mg**

350 g	boneless chicken meat, skinned, cut into 1 cm (½ inch) cubes (from about 5 large thighs or 3 breasts)	12 o
1 tbsp	unsalted butter	1 tbs
1	potato, or turnip, peeled and cut into 5mm (¼ inch) cubes	
1	onion, chopped	
1	garlic clove, finely chopped	
125 g	mushrooms, wiped clean and quartered	4 o
1	small carrot, quartered lengthwise and cut into 5 mm (¼ inch) pieces	
¼ tsp	salt	¼ ts
	freshly ground black pepper	
1 tbsp	flour	1 tbs
1 tbsp	chopped fresh sage, or ¾ tsp dried sage	1 tbs
1	small courgette, halved lengthwise and cut into 5 mm (¼ inch) slices	
½ litre	unsalted chicken stock	16 fl o
2 tbsp	cornflour, mixed with 4 tbsp white wine	2 tbs
Phyllo crust		
125 g	plain flour	4 o
2 tbsp	virgin olive oil	2 tbs
¼ tsp	salt	¼ ts
3 tbsp	cornflour	3 tbs
15 g	unsalted butter	½ c

To prepare the pie filling, melt the butter in a large, heavy bottomed saucepan over medium heat. Add the potat or turnip, and cook, stirring, for 2 minutes. Add th onion, garlic, mushrooms, carrot, salt and pepper. Stir i the flour and mix well. Cook for 5 minutes, stirring. Ad the sage, courgette and chicken pieces. Cook for minutes, stirring. Add the sage, courgette and chicke pieces. Cook, stirring, until the courgette is soft — about 5 minutes more.

Meanwhile, heat the chicken stock in a saucepan over medium-high heat and reduce it to about 35 cl (12 fl oz). Whisk the cornflour mixture into the stock and simmer until the sauce is thickened and shiny — about 2 minutes. Pour this sauce into the chicken mixture, mix well, and set aside.

To prepare the phyllo crust, place the flour in a large bowl and make a well in the centre. Pour the oil and salt into the well. Slowly stir in lukewarm water — up to 5 tablespoons — until a soft dough results. On a board sprinkled with 1 tablespoon of the cornflour, knead the dough until it is very elastic — at least 15 minutes. Dust a large work surface with the remaining 2 tablespoons of cornflour and place the ball of dough in the centre. Roll the dough into a uniformly thin circle.

Preheat the oven to 170°C (325°F or Mark 3). Melt the butter and brush half of it over the dough. Start pulling the dough gently but steadily in every direction until it forms a circle 60 to 75 cm (2 to 2½ feet) in diameter and nearly paper thin. Fold the dough in half, then fold it again to make a quarter circle. Over the dough, fit a round 25 cm (10 inch) baking dish or quiche pan at least 4 cm (1½ inches) deep. Cut the dough into a circle 1 cm (½ inch) larger then the pan all round.

Pour the filling into the ungreased baking dish. Fold the dough exactly in half to spread it over half of the filling and pan, then unfold it over the rest of the pie. Brush the top of the pie with the remaining melted butter. Put the pie in the oven and bake it until the surface of the dough turns golden — 20 to 25 minutes.

SUGGESTED ACCOMPANIMENT: *lettuce salad.*

EDITOR'S NOTE: *Three sheets of commercially prepared phyllo dough may be substituted for the handmade phyllo called for in this recipe.*

2 *Sliced for a party, a galantine made from a whole boned turkey reveals the colourful mosaic of its fresh vegetable stuffing (recipe, page 110)..*

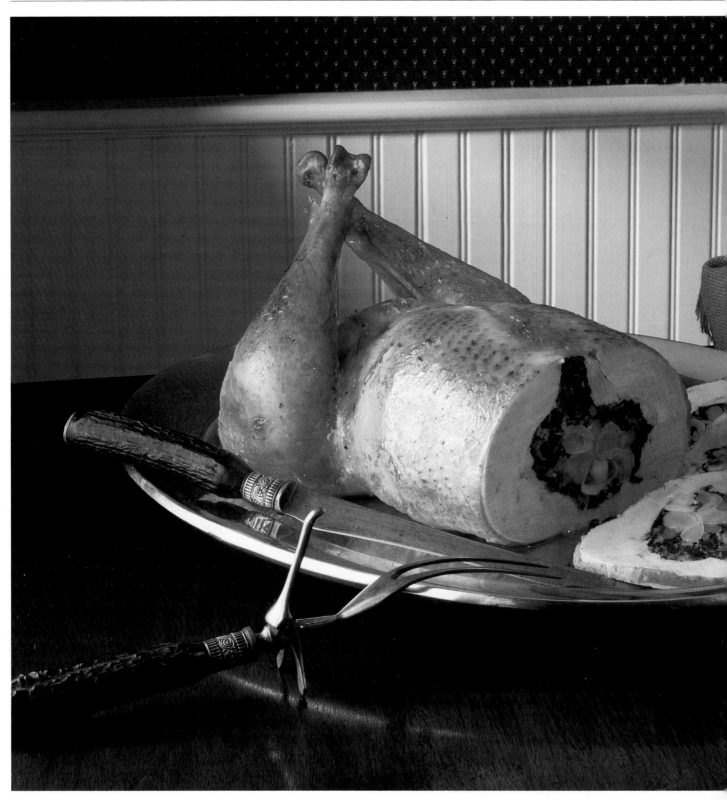

Turkey Transformed

Long a Christmas and American Thanksgiving favourite, turkey has expanded far beyond its traditional culinary horizons. It is now not only available all year but can be bought fresh or frozen, in portions, and even minced. As for cooking options, it can be sautéed, poached, stir-fried, baked, stewed, grilled or braised, as well as stuffed and roasted. And there is no better meat from the viewpoint of nutritionists: a 90 g (3 oz) serving of skinned breast, for example, contains even less saturated fat than skinned chicken, and it has fewer calories to boot. The growing popularity of turkey is reflected in the statistics: today's consumption of turkey in the U.K. is roughly double that of the 1960s, and is continuing to rise.

The mild flavour and tenderness of the white meat make turkey breast a prime substitute for veal in some dishes, while the more richly flavoured dark meat can serve as the base for other dishes normally made with lamb or pork. Yet turkey is never more interesting and exciting than when used in its own right as a "new" meat that invites fresh approaches.

The 26 recipes contained in this section demonstrate turkey's many possibilities both as family fare and as food that will surprise and please guests. Fresh, rather than frozen or cooked, meat is generally called for. Escalopes or fillets may be cut from turkey breasts at home, a moneysaving measure that also allows the cook to determine the thickness of the slices — but prepackaged escalopes can also be used. In most instances, the skin is removed; the phrase appearing in some of the recipes, "turkey breast meat", means not only raw and skinless, but boneless as well. Generally, 500 g (1 lb) of turkey breast yields about eight escalopes of about 5 cm (¼ inch) thickness. They can be pounded lightly to make them thinner; in the techniques section at the back of the book are instructions for slicing and pounding escalopes from the breast *(page 139)*, and for boning a thigh *(page 138)*.

Whatever the method of preparation, it is important to remember one thing: like chicken, turkey is best when not overcooked. Only then will all the flavour and juiciness of the bird be present.

Turkey Patties
with Beetroot Sauce

Serves 8
Working time: about 1 hour and 30 minutes
Total time: about 1 hour and 30 minutes

Calories **270**
Protein **22g**
Cholesterol **45mg**
Total fat **9g**
Saturated fat **4g**
Sodium **440mg**

500 g	turkey meat, finely chopped	1 lb
1 tbsp	virgin olive oil	1 tbsp
125 g	beet greens, Swiss chard or curly endive, finely shredded	4 oz
4	garlic cloves, finely chopped	4
3	medium potatoes, peeled, boiled, mashed and chilled	3
350 g	low-fat ricotta cheese, drained in a strainer for ½ hour	12 oz
125 g	spring onions, chopped	4 oz
1 tbsp	grainy mustard	1 tbsp
4 tbsp	chopped fresh basil, or 2 tbsp dried basil	4 tbsp
90 g	dry breadcrumbs	3 oz
½ tsp	salt	½ tsp
	freshly ground black pepper	

Beetroot sauce		
10 g	unsalted butter	⅓ oz
1	medium beetroot, peeled and julienned	1
¼ tsp	salt	¼ tsp
¼ litre	unsalted turkey or chicken stock	8 fl oz
1 tbsp	grainy mustard	1 tbsp
4 tbsp	sliced spring onions	4 tbsp
½ tsp	arrowroot or cornflour, mixed with 1 tbsp cold water	½ tsp

To make the patties, heat the olive oil in a sauté pan over medium heat. Add the greens and sprinkle the garlic on top. Reduce the heat to low, cover, and wilt the greens for about 3 minutes. Uncover, stir, and remove the pan from the heat. Allow to cool.

Preheat the oven to 190°C (375°F or Mark 5). In a large bowl, mix together the turkey, mashed potatoes, ricotta cheese, spring onions, mustard, basil, half the breadcrumbs and the cooled greens. Season with the salt and pepper. Form the mixture into 16 patties about 10 cm (4 inches) in diameter and 1 cm (½ inch) thick.

To make the sauce, melt the butter in a heavy-

Roll the turkey tightly, starting from one of the long sides and using a spatula to nudge the meat over. Tuck in the ends to keep the cheese from leaking out of the roll during cooking.

Coat the turkey with the yogurt, then the breadcrumbs. Place the roll in a large, shallow baking dish and dribble the olive oil over it. Bake the roll until firm and springy to the touch — about 20 minutes. Remove the roll from the oven and let it rest for 5 to 7 minutes as the melted cheese firms up.

While the turkey is baking, prepare the sauce. Combine the spring onions and white wine in a small saucepan and reduce the liquid to half, about 2 tablespoons. Add the tomato, sage, stock and salt and simmer for 10 minutes, stirring occasionally.

Cut the turkey into 5 mm (¼ inch) slices. Arrange the slices on a heated serving dish, ladle on the hot sauce and garnish with fresh sage or parsley.

SUGGESTED ACCOMPANIMENT: *steamed spinach*.

Turkey Legs Baked with Yams and Apples

Serves 6
Working time: about 45 minutes
Total time: about 1 hour and 15 minutes

Calories **355**
Protein **30g**
Cholesterol **105mg**
Total fat **16g**
Saturated fat **7g**
Sodium **265mg**

2	whole turkey legs, thigh bones removed	2
½ tsp	salt	½ tsp
	freshly ground black pepper	
30 g	unsalted butter	1 oz
350 g	yams or sweet potatoes, peeled and sliced into 5 mm (¼ inch) rounds	12 oz
250 g	chopped spring onions	8 oz
2	cooking apples, peeled, cored and sliced into rings 5 mm (¼ inch) thick	2
1 tsp	fresh thyme, or ¼ tsp dried thyme	1 tsp
½ tsp	safflower oil	½ tsp
12.5 cl	unsalted turkey or chicken stock	4 fl oz

Preheat the oven to 230°C (350°F or Mark 8). Season the legs inside and out with the salt and pepper. Tie the boneless thighs with string as for a roast. Spread the bottom of a baking dish with the butter. Layer the yams, spring onions and apples in the baking dish. Place the legs on top, sprinkle with the thyme, and rub with the oil.

Bake for 20 minutes, then reduce the heat to 200°C (400°F or Mark 6). Pour the stock over the legs and cook until the juices run clear when a thigh is pierced with the tip of a sharp knife — about 25 minutes more. Remove the string. Slice the thighs 5 mm (¼ inch) thick and cut the meat off the drumsticks. Arrange the meat on a heated platter with the yams and apples.

Turkey and Green Chili Enchiladas

IN MEXICAN COOKING, ENCHILADAS ARE
FILLED TORTILLAS SERVED WITH A SAUCE.

Serves 4
Working time: about 40 minutes
Total time: about 1 hour

Calories **455**
Protein **38g**
Cholesterol **70mg**
Total fat **16g**
Saturated fat **4g**
Sodium **375mg**

350 g	cooked turkey meat, shredded or slivered	12 oz
2 to 5	fresh hot green chili peppers, seeded, finely chopped (see caution, page 25)	2 to 5
1	large onion, coarsely chopped	1
1	large tomato, cored, seeded and coarsely chopped	1
2	garlic cloves, coarsely chopped	2
2 tbsp	chopped fresh coriander	2 tbsp
4 tbsp	unsalted turkey or chicken stock	4 tbsp
2 tbsp	fresh lemon juice	2 tbsp
⅛ tbsp	sugar	⅛ tbsp
350 g	tomatillos, papery husks removed, blanched 2 minutes, cored and quartered	12 oz
90 g	mild Cheddar cheese, grated	3 oz
½ tsp	ground cumin	½ tsp
1 tsp	chopped fresh oregano, or ¼ tsp. dried oregano	1 tsp
⅛ tsp	salt	⅛ tsp
8	corn tortillas (canned or freshly made)	8
12.5 cl	soured cream	4 fl oz
12.5 cl	plain low-fat yogurt	4 fl oz

Preheat the oven to 180°C (350°F or Mark 4). Scrape three quarters of the chilies into a food processor or blender. Add the onion, tomato, garlic, coriander, stock, lemon juice and sugar. Using short bursts, process the mixture into a rough purée — about 8 seconds. Add the tomatillos and process until coarsely chopped — about 5 seconds. Pour the sauce into a saucepan and simmer it over medium heat for 10 minutes.

Next, make the filling for the tortillas. In a large bowl, combine the turkey, 60 g (2 oz) of the cheese, the remaining hot chilies, the cumin, oregano, salt and half of the sauce.

Place a heavy frying pan over medium heat. Warm a tortilla in the pan for 10 seconds on each side to soften it, then place it in the hot sauce, carefully turn it over, and transfer it to a plate. Spoon about 5 tablespoons of the turkey filling down the centre of the tortilla, then roll it up to enclose the filling, and place it seam side down in a large oiled baking dish. Fill the remaining tortillas.

Pour the rest of the hot sauce over the enchiladas and sprinkle them with the remaining cheese. Bake, uncovered, for 20 minutes. Meanwhile, combine the soured cream and yogurt as a topping; spoon it over the enchiladas just before serving them.

SUGGESTED ACCOMPANIMENT: *curly endive salad.*

EDITOR'S NOTE: *The tomatillos called for in this recipe are also known as Mexican ground cherries and are closely related to the Cape gooseberry. If they are unavailable, substitute 350 g (12 oz) of fresh green unripe tomatoes, coarsely chopped.*

Turkey Curry with Puréed Yams

Serves 6
Working time: about 30 minutes
Total time: about 1 hour 45 minutes

Calories **335**
Protein **25g**
Cholesterol **75 mg**
Total fat **12g**
Saturated fat **6g**
Sodium **255mg**

600g	boneless dark turkey meat, skinned and cut into 2.5 cm (1 inch) cubes	1¼ lb
45 g	unsalted butter	1½
2	small yams or sweet potatoes, peeled and cut into 1 cm (½ inch) cubes	2
¾ litre	unsalted turkey or chicken stock	1¼ pints
2	medium onions, finely chopped	2
1	stick celery, finely chopped	1
2	garlic cloves, finely chopped	2
½ tsp	grated fresh ginger root, or ¼ tsp ground ginger	½ tsp
½ tsp	fresh thyme, or ⅛ tsp dried thyme	½ tsp
2 tbsp	curry powder	2 tbsp
5 tbsp	fresh lemon juice	5 tbsp
¼ tsp	salt	¼ tsp
	freshly ground black pepper	
60 g	sultanas	2 oz
150 g	peas	5 oz

In a saucepan, bring 1 litre (1¾ pints) of water to the boil. Add the turkey, blanch for 1 minute, and drain.

In a large, heavy frying pan over low heat, melt half of the butter. Add the yams and cook them slowly, stirring frequently, until they are browned and tender — about 25 minutes. Purée the yams with ¼ litre (8 fl oz) of stock in a food processor or blender, and set them aside.

Over medium-low heat, melt the remaining butter in the frying pan. Add the onions, celery, garlic, ginger and thyme. Cook, stirring frequently, until the onions begin to brown — about 15 minutes.

Add the turkey, curry powder, lemon juice, salt and pepper. Reduce the heat to low and gently stir in the rest of the stock. Cover and simmer for 45 minutes. Uncover the frying pan and add the sultanas and the yam purée. Cover the pan again and cook, stirring occasionally, until the turkey cubes are tender — about 30 minutes more. Add the peas and cook another 5 minutes. Serve the curry immediately.

SUGGESTED ACCOMPANIMENT: *steamed rice with cashews.*

Turkey Escalopes with Citrus

Serves 4
Working (and total) time: about 30 minutes

Calories **265**
Protein **27g**
Cholesterol **65mg**
Total fat **11g**
Saturated fat **3g**
Sodium **125mg**

8	5 mm (¼ inch) thick turkey escalopes (about 500g/1 lb) pounded to 3 mm (⅛ inch) thickness	8
1	large navel orange	1
1	lime	1
	flour for dredging	
1½ tbsp	virgin olive oil	1½ tbsp
4 tbsp	dry white wine	4 tbsp
4 tbsp	unsalted turkey or chicken stock	4 tbsp
1 tbsp	finely chopped shallots	1 tbsp
1 tsp	chopped fresh thyme, or ¼ tsp dried thyme	1 tsp
1 tsp	chopped fresh sage, or ¼ tsp dried sage	1 tsp
½ tsp	sugar	½ tsp
⅛ tsp	salt	⅛ tsp
	freshly ground black pepper	
15 g	unsalted butter	½ oz
2 tbsp	coarsely chopped parsley	2 tbsp

Use a knife to cut the peel from the orange and lime, taking care to remove all of the bitter white pith. Cut the fruit into 5 mm (¼ inch) cubes and set aside.

Make 3 mm (⅛ inch) slits along the escalopes' edges at 2.5 to 5 mm (1 to 2 inch) intervals to prevent the turkey from curling while cooking. Dredge the escalopes in the flour and shake off the excess. Heat a large heavy frying pan over medium-high heat and add 1 tablespoon of the oil. Put four escalopes in the pan and sauté for 45 seconds. Turn them over and sauté until the pink around the edges has turned white — about 30 seconds more. Transfer them to a heated serving plate and keep warm. Add the remaining oil to the pan, sauté the rest of the escalopes, and keep warm.

To prepare the sauce, add the wine, stock and shallots to the pan and bring to the boil over medium-high heat. Reduce the liquid by half, stirring frequently. Lower the heat to medium and stir in the fruit, thyme, sage, sugar, salt and pepper. Whisk in the butter and simmer, stirring occasionally, for 5 minutes. Add the parsley at the last minute. Pour the sauce over the escalopes and serve immediately.

SUGGESTED ACCOMPANIMENTS: *burghul; peas.*

Chopped Turkey with Lime and Coriander

Serves 26 to 32 as a party snack, 8 as a main course
Working time: about 30 minutes
Total time: about 30 minutes

Calories **160**
Protein **16g**
Cholesterol **30 mg**
Total fat **6g**
Saturated fat **1g**
Sodium **200 mg**

350 g	cooked turkey breast meat, finely chopped	12 oz
Yogurt sauce		
¼ litre	plain low-fat yogurt	8 fl oz
1 tsp	finely chopped fresh coriander	1 tsp
1 tsp	sugar	1 tsp
2 tbsp	fresh lime juice	2 tbsp
⅛ tsp	salt	⅛ tsp
⅛ tsp	cayenne pepper	⅛ tsp
Turkey morsels		
30 g	fresh breadcrumbs	1 oz
1	lime, rind only, grated	1
5 tbsp	finely sliced spring onion greens	5 tbsp
2 tsp	finely chopped fresh coriander	2 tsp
¼ tsp	chili powder	¼ tsp
¼ tsp	salt	¼ tsp
1	egg white	1
4 tbsp	plain flour	4 tbsp
2 tbsp	safflower oil	2 tbsp

To prepare the sauce, pour the yogurt into a small bowl and whisk in the coriander, sugar, lime juice, salt and cayenne. Let stand 15 minutes.

Place the turkey in a bowl with the breadcrumbs, rind, spring onions, coriander, chili powder and salt. Add the egg white and knead by hand or mix with a spoon.

With dampened hands, gently form the meat mixture into balls the size of large marbles and lightly dust with flour. Heat the oil in a heavy frying pan over medium heat and fry as many balls as possible without crowding until brown all over — 5 to 6 minutes. Drain the balls on paper towels and transfer them to a warm platter. Serve with the sauce.

Chilled Turkey with Creamy Tuna Sauce

THIS RECIPE WAS INSPIRED BY VIITELLO TONNATO,
THE CLASSIC ITALIAN VEAL DISH.

Serves 6
Working time: about 30 minutes
Total time: about 40 minutes

Calories **285**
Protein **31g**
Cholesterol **70mg**
Total fat **15g**
Saturated fat **2g**
Sodium **125mg**

750 g	boneless turkey breast meat, skinned and cut into bite-size chunks	1 ½ lb
½ tsp	virgin olive oil	½ tsp
½ tsp	safflower oil	½ tsp
⅛ tsp	salt	⅛ tsp
12.5 cl	unsalted turkey or chicken stock, warmed	4 fl oz
	fresh sage, finely sliced, or chopped parsley	
Tuna sauce		
100 g	can tuna, packed in brine, drained	3½ oz
3 tbsp	virgin olive oil	3 tbsp
2 tbsp	safflower oil	2 tbsp
5 tbsp	buttermilk	5 tbsp
1 tsp	fresh lime juice	1 tsp
1 tsp	capers, rinsed and patted dry	1 tsp

Heat the oils in a large heavy frying pan over medium heat. Sauté the turkey pieces for 3 minutes and turn them over. Sprinkle with the salt and cook for another 3 minutes. Add the stock, lower the heat, and simmer for 2 minutes more. Remove each piece as it whitens. Set aside to cool. Reduce the stock to about 4 tablespoons and reserve for the sauce.

To make the sauce, purée the tuna with the stock in a food processor or a blender. Scrape down the sides with a rubber spatula and process another 10 seconds. With the motor still running, pour in the oils slowly. Add the buttermilk, lime juice and capers, and process for 1 minute more or until smooth. (Alternatively, pound the tuna to a paste in a mortar.) Transfer the sauce to a bowl and refrigerate.

To assemble the dish, pour a little sauce on individual plates. Put a portion of the turkey on each plate and dribble the remaining sauce over the turkey. Garnish with sage or with chopped parsley.

SUGGESTED ACCOMPANIMENTS: *julienned carrots; French bread.*

Turkey Escalopes with Pine-Nuts and Currants

Serves 4

Working (and total) time: about 50 minutes

alories **450**
rotein **33g**
holesterol **60mg**
otal fat **26g**
aturated fat **4g**
odium **485mg**

8	5 mm (¼ inch) thick turkey breast escalopes (about 500 g/1 lb), pounded to 3 mm (⅛ inch) thickness	8
3	egg whites	3
½ tsp	salt	½ tsp
	freshly ground black pepper	
3 tbsp	virgin olive oil	3 tbsp
2 to 3 tbsp	finely chopped shallots	2 to 3 tbsp
8 cl	white wine vinegar	3 fl oz
10	black peppercorns	10
3	bay leaves	3
3 tbsp	currants	3 tbsp
8 cl	safflower oil	3 fl oz
60 g	dry breadcrumbs	2 fl oz
30 g	fresh parsley, finely chopped	1 oz
2	garlic cloves, finely chopped	2
½	orange, rind only, finely chopped or grated	½
3 tbsp	pine-nuts, lightly toasted	3 tbsp

In a shallow bowl, beat the egg whites with the salt and pepper. Add the escalopes one at a time, turning them to coat them with the mixture.

In a small heavy-bottomed saucepan, heat the olive oil. Add the shallots and sauté over medium heat until translucent — about 5 minutes. Add the vinegar, 17.5 cl (6 fl oz) water, peppercorns and bay leaves, and simmer for 20 minutes. Stir in the currants and simmer for another 10 minutes, or until the liquid is reduced by half, to about 12.5 cl (4 fl oz).

In the meantime, heat the safflower oil in a large heavy frying pan. Spread the breadcrumbs in a plate. Dip the escalopes in the crumbs, then brown them in the hot oil over medium to high heat for 1 to 2 minutes on each side. Put them on a heated platter and cover with foil to keep warm.

To assemble, combine the parsley, garlic and rind. Strain the reduced sauce, reserving the currants, and pour it evenly over the turkey escalopes. Sprinkle with the currants, the parsley mixture and the pine-nuts. Serve warm or, if preferred, at room temperature.

SUGGESTED ACCOMPANIMENTS: *risotto; broccoli salad with julienned sweet red pepper.*

Turkey-Stuffed Pittas

Serves 8
Working time: about 45 minutes
Total time: about 1 hour and 30 minutes

Calories **370**
Protein **27g**
Cholesterol **45mg**
Total fat **14g**
Saturated fat **2g**
Sodium **135mg**

750 g	turkey breast meat, skinned	1½ lb
2 tsp	safflower oil	2 tsp
1	lime, juice only	1
8	small wholemeal (pocket bread) pittas	8
90 g	lettuce, shredded	3 oz
Dry marinade		
1 tbsp	paprika	1 tbsp
2 tbsp	finely chopped onion	2 tbsp
2	garlic cloves, finely chopped	2
¼ tsp	cayenne pepper	¼ tsp
¼ tsp	white pepper	¼ tsp
½ tsp	crushed fennel seeds	½ tsp
2 tsp	fresh thyme, or ½ tsp dried thyme	2 tsp
½ tsp	dried oregano	½ tsp
Vegetable filling		
1	large avocado, peeled and cut into 5 mm (¼ inch) cubes	1
½	lemon, juice only	½
2	large tomatoes, halved, seeded, coarsely chopped	2
125 g	onion, finely chopped	4 oz
1	large sweet green pepper, seeded, deribbed, cut into 5 mm (¼ inch) pieces	1
Yogurt dressing		
3 tbsp	fresh lime juice	3 tbsp
1 tbsp	red wine vinegar	1 tbsp
5 drops	Tabasco sauce	5 drops
1 tbsp	honey	1 tbsp
2 tsp	Dijon mustard	2 tsp
2	garlic cloves, finely chopped	2
2 tbsp	chopped fresh coriander	2 tbsp
¼ tsp	salt	¼ tsp
2 tbsp	safflower oil	2 tbsp
12.5 cl	plain low-fat yogurt	4 fl oz

In a small bowl, combine the marinade ingredients.

Use a sharp knife to crisscross both sides of the turkey with 1 cm (⅓ inch) deep cuts, 2 cm (¼ inch) apart. Rub in the marinade, making sure the seasonings fill the cuts, and refrigerate for 1 hour.

While the turkey is marinating, prepare the vegetable filling. In a bowl, sprinkle the avocado with the lemon juice and toss to keep it from turning brown. Combine with the tomato, onion and green pepper. Refrigerate until ready to serve.

Preheat the oven to 200°C (400°F or Mark 6). To prepare the dressing, combine the lime juice, vinegar, Tabasco sauce, honey, mustard, garlic, coriander and salt in a large bowl, and whisk vigorously. Whisk in the oil slowly. Then whisk in the yogurt and refrigerate.

In a large, shallow, fireproof casserole, heat the 2 teaspoons of safflower oil over medium-high heat. Sauté the turkey on one side until brown — about 5 minutes. Turn, cook for 1 minute, then place the casserole in the upper level of the oven. Roast the turkey until the flesh is firm and springy to the touch — 8 to 12 minutes. Remove from the casserole, squeeze the lime juice over the meat, and allow to stand for 5 minutes. Slice against the grain into 5 mm (¼ inch) thick pieces. Cut each into strips.

To assemble the pittas, place them in the hot oven for 1 minute to soften. Slice each open at the top, stuff some shredded lettuce inside and fill the rest of the pocket with the turkey and the vegetable mixture. Serve the yogurt dressing separately.

Turkey Escalopes with Red and Green Peppers

Serves 4
Working time: about 15 minutes
Total time: about 30 minutes

Calories **235**
Protein **27g**
Cholesterol **60mg**
Total fat **11g**
Saturated fat **2g**
Sodium **205mg**

8	5 mm (¼ inch) thick turkey escalopes (about 500 g/1 lb), pounded to 3 mm (⅛ inch) thickness	8
60 g	plain flour	2 oz
2 tbsp	safflower oil	2 tbsp
1 tsp	virgin olive oil	1 tsp
4 tbsp	finely chopped onion	4 tbsp
2	garlic cloves, finely chopped	2
17.5 cl	unsalted turkey or chicken stock	6 fl oz
2 tbsp	chopped fresh basil, or 2 tsp dried basil	2 tbsp
2 tbsp	balsamic vinegar, or 1 tbsp red wine vinegar	2 tbsp
¼ tsp	salt	¼ tsp
	freshly ground black pepper	
1	large sweet green pepper, julienned	1
1	large sweet red pepper, julienned	1

To prevent the turkey from curling while cooking, score the edges of the escalopes with 3 mm (⅛ inch) slits at 2.5 to 5 cm (1 to 2 inch) intervals. Dredge the escalopes in the flour and shake off the excess.

▶

Heat a large, heavy frying pan over medium-high heat and add half of the safflower oil. Put four escalopes in the pan and sauté them for 45 seconds. Turn them over and sauté them until their edges turn from pink to white — about 30 seconds more. Transfer the cooked escalopes to a heated platter. Add the remaining tablespoon of safflower oil to the pan and sauté the other four escalopes. Remove the pan from the heat and transfer the turkey to the platter. Cover loosely with aluminium foil and keep warm.

To prepare the peppers, reduce the heat to medium-low and heat the olive oil in the pan. Add the onion and garlic and cook until the onion is translucent — about 10 minutes. Then add the stock, basil, vinegar, salt, pepper and julienned peppers. Increase the heat to medium and simmer until the peppers are tender — about 5 minutes. Spoon the pepper mixture over the escalopes and serve the dish immediately.

SUGGESTED ACCOMPANIMENT: *spaghetti tossed with garlic and olive oil.*

Stir-Fried Turkey with Mixed Vegetables

Serves 4
Working time: about 30 minutes
Total time: about 40 minutes

Calories **210**
Protein **24g**
Cholesterol **45mg**
Total fat **10g**
Saturated fat **2g**
Sodium **350mg**

350 g	turkey breast meat, cut into 6 by 1 cm by 5 mm (2½ by ½ by ¼ inch) strips	12 o
4 tsp	safflower oil or peanut oil	4 ts
1	small sweet red pepper, seeded, deribbed and cut into 5 mm (¼ inch) wide strips	
75 g	broccoli florets	2½ o
45 g	mushrooms, thinly sliced	1½ o
30 g	mange-tout, with strings removed	1 o
4	spring onions, trimmed and coarsely chopped	
90 g	Chinese cabbage, sliced	3 o
Marinade		
1 tsp	dark sesame oil	1 ts
2 tbsp	low-sodium soy sauce, or naturally fermented shoyu	2 tbs
2 tbsp	finely chopped fresh ginger root	2 tbs
2	garlic cloves, finely chopped	
Sesame sauce		
12.5 cl	unsalted turkey or chicken stock	4 fl o
4 tsp	low-sodium soy sauce, or naturally fermented shoyu	4 ts
1 tbsp	red wine vinegar	1 tbsp
1 tbsp	sesame seeds	1 tbsp
1 tsp	dark sesame oil	1 ts
	freshly ground black pepper	

To prepare the marinade, combine the sesame oil, soy sauce, ginger and garlic. Add the turkey strips, toss, and set them aside to marinate for half an hour.

To make the sesame sauce, mix the stock, soy sauce, vinegar, sesame seeds, sesame oil and pepper in a small bowl, and set it aside.

Place a wok or heavy frying pan over high heat and add 2 tablespoons of the oil. When the oil is hot but not smoking, add the turkey strips and stir-fry them, turning them with a metal spatula or slotted spoon, just until the meat turns white — about 2 minutes. Remove the wok or pan from the heat and use a slotted spoon to transfer the turkey to a plate.

Heat the remaining 2 teaspoons of oil in the wok or pan. Add the red pepper, broccoli, mushrooms and spring onions, and stir-fry them for 1 minute. Add the mange-tout and cabbage, and cook the vegetables 1 minute more, stirring and tossing rapidly. Pour in the sauce and cook the mixture an additional 2 minutes, stirring constantly. Stir in the turkey and heat it through. Serve hot.

SUGGESTED ACCOMPANIMENT: *steamed rice.*

EDITOR'S NOTE: *Stir-frying is designed to sear meats and cook vegetables quickly, without sacrificing their colour, texture or flavour. It must be executed speedily so the meats will not toughen and the vegetables will not wilt.*

Turkey Satays with Peanut Sauce

SATAY IS AN INDONESIAN WORD FOR SKEWERED TITBITS OF GRILLED MEAT.

Serves 8
Working time: about 30 minutes
Total time: about 6 hours and 15 minutes

Calories **235**
Protein **29g**
Cholesterol **60mg**
Total fat **10g**
Saturated fat **2g**
Sodium **285mg**

1 kg	turkey breast meat, skinned and cut into 2.5 cm (1 inch) cubes	2 lb
Marinade		
¼ litre	plain low-fat yogurt	8 fl oz
4 tbsp	safflower oil	4 tbsp
1 tbsp	grated fresh ginger root	1 tbsp
½ tsp each	ground cardamom and ground coriander	½ tsp each
¼ tsp	salt	¼ tsp
½ tsp	freshly ground black pepper	½ tsp
2 tsp	paprika	2 tsp
Peanut sauce		
90 g	peanut butter	3 oz
¼ litre	boiling water	8 fl oz
2	garlic cloves, finely chopped	2
2 tbsp	fresh lemon juice	2 tbsp
2 tbsp	low-sodium soy sauce, or naturally fermented shoyu	2 tbsp
¼ tsp	crushed red pepper flakes	¼ tsp
2 tbsp	molasses	2 tbsp

Whisk the marinade ingredients together. Add the cubed turkey and refrigerate for 6 hours or overnight, stirring occasionally to keep the pieces well coated.

If you plan to cook the turkey over charcoal, light the coals about 30 minutes before cooking time; for grilling, preheat the grill with its rack and pan in place about 10 minutes beforehand.

To make the peanut sauce, first heat the peanut butter in a heavy-bottomed saucepan over low heat. Whisk in the boiling water, then stir in the garlic, lemon juice, soy sauce, red pepper and molasses. Bring the mixture to the boil and whisk it until it thickens — about 2 minutes. Taste the sauce and add more red pepper or molasses if desired. Pour into a sauceboat.

Thread the turkey cubes on to skewers, preferably square or flat-bladed, so the cubes will not slip when turned and cook unevenly. Cook the cubes over charcoal, turning them several times, for about 8 minutes. Grilling may take as long as 15 minutes — about 4 minutes for each side. To test for doneness, make a small cut in a turkey cube to see whether its centre has turned from pink to white. Arrange the satays on a heated platter and serve the sauce separately.

SUGGESTED ACCOMPANIMENT: *fried rice.*

Meanwhile, blanch the parsley leaves in boiling
water for 1 minute, drain and refresh them under cold
water. Put the parsley in a food processor or blender,
add the reduced poaching liquid, and purée. Keep
the sauce warm.

In a heavy frying pan, cook the leek in half the butter
over low heat until soft — about 10 minutes. Transfer
to a plate. Cook the radishes in the remaining butter
for 1 minute.

To assemble, slice the turkey rolls thinly on the
diagonal and arrange in an attractive pattern on individual plates. Decorate with the leeks and radishes,
and pour a little sauce on each plate, taking care not to
cover the meat or vegetables.

SUGGESTED ACCOMPANIMENT: *braised bulb fennel.*

Rolled Turkey Escalopes Stuffed with Buckwheat

Serves 6
Working time: about 45 minutes
Total time: about 45 minutes

Calories **245**
Protein **24g**
Cholesterol **45mg**
Total fat **8g**
Saturated fat **2g**
Sodium **345mg**

8	5 mm (¼ inch) thick turkey breast escalopes (about 500 g/1 lb), pounded to 3 mm (⅛ inch) thickness	8
350 g	fresh spinach, stemmed and washed	12 oz
Buckwheat stuffing		
15 g	unsalted butter	½ oz
1	medium onion, finely chopped	1
1	small celery stick, diced	1
100 g	roasted buckwheat groats (kasha), preferably whole kernels	3½ oz
4 tbsp	dry white wine	4 tbsp
125 g	fresh mushrooms, thinly sliced	4 oz
2	garlic cloves, finely chopped	2
1 tsp	fresh thyme, or ¼ tsp dried thyme	1 tsp
1 tbsp	virgin olive oil	1 tbsp
¼ litre	unsalted turkey or chicken stock	8 fl oz
½ tsp	salt	½ tsp
	freshly ground black pepper	
4 tbsp	wheat germ	4 tbsp
1	egg white, lightly beaten	1
Madeira sauce		
12.5 cl	Madeira or medium-dry sherry	4 fl oz
1 tbsp	finely chopped shallot	1 tbsp
1 tsp	fresh thyme, or ¼ tsp dried thyme	1 tsp
¼ litre	unsalted turkey or chicken stock	8 fl oz
2 tbsp	balsamic vinegar, or 1 tbsp red wine vinegar	2 tbsp
⅛ tsp	salt	⅛ tsp

Blanch the spinach for 1 minute and refresh with cold
water. Squeeze out the water and set aside.

To make the stuffing, melt the butter in a heavy-
bottomed saucepan over medium-low heat, and cook
the onion and celery until the onion is translucent —
about 10 minutes. Stir in the buckwheat groats and

Turkey Rolls with Parsley Sauce

Serves 4
Working time: about 1 hour
Total time: about 1 hour

Calories **365**
Protein **44g**
Cholesterol **180mg**
Total fat **14g**
Saturated fat **6g**
Sodium **455mg**

8	5 mm (¼ inch) thick turkey breast escalopes (about 500 g/1 lb), pounded to 3 mm (⅛ inch) thickness	8
250 g	skinned, finely chopped turkey leg meat	8 oz
2	egg whites, plus 1 whole egg	2
4 tbsp	finely chopped parsley	4 tbsp
½ tsp	salt	½ tsp
	freshly ground black pepper	
½ litre	unsalted turkey or chicken stock	16 fl oz
12.5 cl	dry white wine	4 fl oz
125 g	fresh parsley leaves	4 oz
1	medium-sized leek, cut into 7.5 cm (3 inch) sections, finely sliced lengthwise	1
30 g	unsalted butter	1 oz
8	radishes, thinly sliced	8

In a food processor or blender, combine the chopped
turkey leg meat with the egg whites and the whole egg,
and process until smooth. Transfer the mixture to a
bowl; add the chopped parsley, salt and pepper, mixing
well. Put an eighth of this stuffing on the centre of each
escalope, wrap the sides of the escalope round it and secure with wooden toothpicks.

Place the turkey rolls in a large shallow sauté pan. Add
the stock and wine. Bring the liquid to the boil, reduce
the heat and simmer, covered, until tender — about 20
minutes. With a slotted spoon, transfer the rolls to a
heated plate and cover with foil to keep warm. Reduce
the poaching liquid to about 17.5 cl (6 fl oz).

cook for 1 minute. Add the wine, mushrooms, garlic, thyme, oil, stock, salt and pepper. Bring to a simmer, reduce the heat, and cover. Cook until the liquid is absorbed — 10 to 15 minutes. Off the heat, stir in the wheat germ. Add the beaten egg white and blend thoroughly. Set the mixture aside to cool.

Lay the escalopes on a flat surface and cover them with spinach leaves. Place 3 tablespoons of the stuffing on each escalope and roll up tightly. Sprinkle with pepper. Wrap each roll in aluminium foil, making sure that the packages are watertight. Pour enough water into a large, deep pan to fill it 5 cm (2 inches) deep. Bring the water to the boil and add the rolls. Reduce the heat and simmer, turning the rolls after 10 minutes — about 20 minutes in all.

To make the sauce, put the Madeira, the shallot and the thyme in a small saucepan. Bring to the boil, then lower the heat and reduce the liquid by half. Add the stock, vinegar and salt, and bring back to the boil. Reduce the heat again and simmer for 10 minutes.

To serve, remove the foil from the turkey and slice each roll diagonally into 1 cm (½ inch) pieces. Arrange the slices on a warmed serving platter and spoon the sauce over them.

SUGGESTED ACCOMPANIMENT: *steamed Savoy cabbage.*

Turkey Salad with Feta Cheese

Serves 4
Working time: about 20 minutes
Total time: about 20 minutes

Calories **495**
Protein **42g**
Cholesterol **105mg**
Total fat **33g**
Saturated fat **8g**
Sodium **710mg**

500 g	cooked turkey breast meat, skinned and cut into 1 cm (½ inch) cubes	1 lb
1	small cucumber, peeled, halved, seeded and thinly cut on the diagonal	1
8	red radishes, diced	8
8	large Greek black olives, stoned and halved	8
125 g	feta cheese, cut into cubes	4 oz
500 g	fresh spinach, stemmed, washed and dried	1 lb
Basil vinaigrette		
2	garlic cloves, finely chopped	2
2 tbsp	chopped fresh basil, or 2 tsp dried basil	2 tbsp
½ tsp	sugar	½ tsp
1 tbsp	grainy mustard	1 tbsp
	freshly ground black pepper	
2 tbsp	fresh lemon juice	2 tbsp
2 tbsp	red wine vinegar	2 tbsp
2 tbsp	safflower oil	2 tbsp
4 tbsp	virgin olive oil	4 tbsp

To prepare the vinaigrette, place all the ingredients in a screw-top jar with a tight-fitting lid and shake vigorously until thoroughly blended — about 30 seconds.

Combine the turkey, cucumber, radishes, olives and cheese in a large bowl, add the dressing, and toss. Arrange the spinach on plates and spoon the salad on top.

Turkey Salad with Yogurt and Buttermilk Dressing

Serves 6
Working time: about 30 minutes
Total time: about 30 minutes

Calories **330**
Protein **27g**
Cholesterol **53mg**
Total fat **14g**
Saturated fat **3g**
Sodium **215mg**

500 g	cooked turkey breast meat, skinned and cut into 1 cm (½ inch) cubes	1 lb
600 g	small new potatoes	1¼ lb
2 tbsp	virgin olive oil	2 tbsp
90 g	medium mushrooms, quartered	3 oz
⅛ tsp	salt	⅛ tsp
1	large sweet green pepper, seeded, deribbed, cut into 1 cm (½ inch) chunks	1
2 tbsp	dry white wine	2 tbsp
30 g	watercress leaves	1 oz
60 g	spring onions, chopped	2 oz
1	lettuce, washed and trimmed	1
2	medium tomatoes, sliced	2
1	small cucumber, sliced	1
1	medium onion, thinly sliced	1
Yogurt and buttermilk dressing		
1	spring onion, chopped	1
2 tbsp	red wine vinegar	2 tbsp
1 tbsp	fresh lemon juice	1 tbsp
½ tsp	celery seeds	½ tsp
4 drops	Tabasco sauce	4 drops
¼ tsp	salt	¼ tsp
	fresh ground black pepper	
3 tbsp	virgin olive oil	3 tbsp
4 tbsp	buttermilk	4 tbsp
4 tbsp	plain low-fat yogurt	4 tbsp
1	garlic clove, chopped	1

Drop the potatoes into boiling water, cover, and cook until tender — about 20 minutes. Drain. When they are cool enough to handle, cut the unskinned potatoes into 2 cm (¾ inch) cubes. Set aside in a warm place.

Heat the 2 tablespoons of olive oil in a small heavy-bottomed non-reactive saucepan over medium heat. Add the mushrooms and the salt and cook for about 1 minute. Add the green pepper and the wine and continue cooking for 5 minutes, stirring occasionally.

Meanwhile, in a large bowl, combine the turkey, warm potatoes, watercress and spring onions. Toss in the mushroom-and-pepper mixture. Set aside.

To prepare the dressing, place all the ingredients in a screw-top jar with a tight-fitting lid and shake vigorously until thoroughly blended — about 30 seconds.

Add the dressing to the turkey mixture and toss lightly. Arrange lettuce on individual plates and place a generous portion of the salad on each. Garnish with slices of tomato, cucumber and red onion.

Turkey and Black Bean Salad

Serves 10
Working time: about 30 minutes
Total time: about 1 day

Calories **395**
Protein **30g**
Cholesterol **45mg**
Total fat **16g**
Saturated fat **2g**
Sodium **260mg**

750 g	cooked turkey breast meat cut into thin strips	1½ lb
300 g	black kidney beans, soaked for 8 hours	10 oz
1	medium onion, coarsely chopped	1
2	garlic cloves, chopped	2
7.5 cm	cinnamon stick, broken in half	3 inch
1½ tsp	fresh thyme, or ½ tsp dried thyme	1½ tsp
1	small dried hot red chili pepper, seeds removed (see caution, page 25), or ¼ tsp cayenne pepper	1
1	bay leaf	1
250 g	mange-tout, with strings removed, sliced into thin strips	8 oz
1	small melon, halved, seeded, flesh cut into small chunks	1
6	spring onions, trimmed and finely sliced	6
3	medium tomatoes, skinned, seeded, coarsely chopped	3
1	small sweet green pepper, seeded, deribbed and chopped	1
1	round-heart or oak leaf lettuce	1
Coriander dressing		
17.5 cl	red wine vinegar	6 fl oz
1	lemon or lime, juice only	1
2 tbsp	Dijon mustard	2 tbsp
2 tbsp	honey	2 tbsp
15 drops	Tabasco sauce	15 drops
¼ tsp	salt	¼ tsp
	freshly ground black pepper	
2	garlic cloves, chopped	2
5 tbsp	chopped fresh coriander	5 tbsp
8 cl	safflower oil	3 fl oz
4 tbsp	virgin olive oil	4 tbsp

Drain the soaked beans and put them into a 4 litre (7 pint) fireproof casserole with the onion, garlic, cinnamon, thyme, chili pepper and bay leaf. Add water to cover by 5 cm (2 inches), bring to the boil, and boil for 10 minutes. Lower the heat and skim off the foam. Cover and simmer just until the beans are tender — 1 to 1½ hours. Drain the beans in a colander and rinse with cold water. Remove the chili pepper, cinnamon and bay leaf and allow the beans to drain further.

Blanch the mange-tout in boiling water for 15 seconds and refresh them in cold water. Drain and place on paper towels to dry.

Put all the dressing ingredients, except the oils, in a food processor or blender and process for 15 seconds. Add the oils slowly and process until smooth — about 30 seconds more.

In a large bowl, combine the melon, spring onions, tomatoes, green pepper and turkey. Add the mange-tout and beans. Pour half the dressing over the salad and toss lightly. Serve on lettuce leaves arranged on a platter and pass the remaining dressing.

Roast Breast of Turkey with Fruit Stuffing

Serves 8
Working time: about 30 minutes
Total time: about 1 hour

Calories **255**
Protein **23g**
Cholesterol **60mg**
Total fat **7g**
Saturated fat **3g**
Sodium **90mg**

850 g to 1 kg	boneless turkey breast, with skin	1¾ to 2 lb
⅛ tsp	salt	⅛ tsp
1 tbsp	safflower oil	1 tbsp
	chopped fresh sage or parsley for garnish	
Fruit stuffing		
30 g	unsalted butter	1 oz
6 tbsp	finely chopped onion	6 tbsp
1	large cooking apple, peeled, cored, diced	1
1 tsp	sugar	1 tsp
1 tsp	chopped fresh sage, or ¼ tsp dried sage	1 tsp
¼ tsp	ground cloves	¼ tsp
125 g	dried apricots, cut into small pieces	4 oz
60 g	seedless raisins	2 oz
3 tbsp	unsalted turkey or chicken stock	3 tbsp
4 tbsp	apple juice	4 tbsp
Cider sauce		
1 tbsp	finely chopped onion	1 tbsp
2 tbsp	dry white wine	2 tbsp
¼ litre	apple juice	8 fl oz
12.5 cl	unsalted turkey or chicken stock	4 fl oz
1 tsp	red wine vinegar	1 tsp

To make the stuffing, melt the butter in a heavy-bottomed saucepan over medium heat. Sauté the onion until it is translucent — about 10 minutes. Add the apple and sugar and continue cooking, stirring occasionally, until the apple is tender but not mushy — about 5 minutes. Stir in the sage, cloves, apricots, raisins, stock and apple juice. Reduce the heat and cover the pan tightly. Cook until all of the liquid is absorbed — about 5

minutes — stirring once. Transfer to a bowl and allow to cool. (The stuffing can be prepared a day ahead and refrigerated.)

Preheat the oven to 180°C (350°F or Mark 4). Put the turkey, skin side down, on a flat surface. Using a sharp knife, cut a flap in the breast by slicing from the long, thin side towards the thicker side, being careful not to cut all the way through. Open the flap and place the turkey between two pieces of plastic film. Pound lightly to flatten to an even thickness of about 1 cm (½ inch). Sprinkle the turkey with the salt and mound the stuffing in the centre. Wrap the flap round the stuffing and roll the breast snugly to form a cylinder with the skin on the outside. Tuck in the ends and tie securely with string.

Heat the oil in a roasting pan and brown the skin side of the roll for 3 to 4 minutes. Turn the turkey skin side up and put the pan in the oven. Roast for 20 to 25 minutes, or until the juices run clear when the meat is pierced with the tip of a sharp knife. Remove the turkey from the pan and keep warm.

To make the sauce, pour off any fat in the pan and discard. Add the onion and wine and cook over medium-high heat, stirring to deglaze the pan. Add the apple juice, stock and vinegar and continue cooking until the sauce is reduced by a quarter — about 10 minutes.

To serve, remove the string and cut the turkey into 2 cm (¾ inch) slices. Arrange on a heated serving platter and garnish with fresh sage or parsley. Pass the sauce separately.

SUGGESTED ACCOMPANIMENT: *peas and pearl onions.*

Roast Gingered Turkey Breast

Serves 6
Working time: about 10 minutes
Total time: about 1 day

Calories **160**
Protein **26g**
Cholesterol **60mg**
Total fat **5g**
Saturated fat **1g**
Sodium **165mg**

750 g	turkey breast, skinned and boned	1½ lb
2 tsp	safflower oil	2 tsp
	Ginger marinade	
3	garlic cloves, finely chopped	3
¾ tsp	ground cinnamon	¾ tsp
2 tbsp	peeled and grated fresh ginger root	2 tbsp
4 tbsp	unsalted turkey or chicken stock	4 tbsp
1 tsp	dark sesame oil	1 tsp
1 tbsp	low-sodium soy sauce, or naturally fermented shoyu	1 tbsp

To make the marinade, combine the garlic, cinnamon, ginger, stock, sesame oil and soy sauce in a shallow bowl just large enough to hold the turkey breast. Using a knife with a sharp point, poke several 1 cm (½ inch) deep slits in the thick part of the meat to allow the marinade to penetrate. Put the turkey in the bowl with the marinade and turn it to coat it. Cover and refrigerate for 8 to 24 hours, turning occasionally.

Preheat the oven to 180°C (350°F or Mark 4). Remove the turkey from the marinade, scraping any clinging garlic and ginger back into the bowl. Reserve the marinade and allow the turkey to come to room temperature. Heat the safflower oil in a shallow fireproof casserole over medium-high heat. Sauté the turkey until golden on one side — about 4 minutes — and turn. Use a pastry brush to baste with the accumulated juices and continue cooking for 1 minute. Put the casserole in the oven and roast the turkey until it feels firm but springy to the touch —15 to 20 minutes — basting once with the reserved marinade. Let the turkey rest for at least 5 minutes before slicing. Serve hot or cold.

SUGGESTED ACCOMPANIMENT: *radicchio salad.*

Honey-Glazed Roast Turkey

Serves 12
Working time: about 1 hour
Total time: about 5 hours

Calories **480**
Protein **50g**
Cholesterol **150mg**
Total fat **15g**
Saturated fat **6g**
Sodium **370mg**

5.5 kg	fresh or thawed turkey, the neck, gizzard and heart reserved for gravy	12 lb
¾ tsp	salt	¾ tsp
	freshly ground black pepper	
2 tbsp	honey	2 tbsp

Orange and sweet potato stuffing

1	lemon, rind only, cut into fine strips	1
4	navel oranges, the rind of 2 cut into fine strips	4
6	medium sweet potatoes, peeled and cut into 1 cm (½ inch) cubes	6
90 g	unsalted butter	3 oz
3	large onions, chopped	3
4 tbsp	fresh lemon juice	4 tbsp
12.5 cl	unsalted turkey or chicken stock	4 fl oz
⅛ tsp	salt	⅛ tsp
	freshly ground black pepper	
½ tsp	ground cloves	½ tsp
¾ tsp	dry mustard	¾ tsp
6	slices wholemeal bread, cut into cubes and lightly toasted	6
2 tbsp	brandy	2 tbsp

Port and orange gravy

	the turkey neck, gizzard and heart	
1 tbsp	safflower oil	1 tbsp
1	carrot, chopped	1
1	stick celery, coarsely chopped	1
2	medium onions, coarsely chopped	2
1	garlic clove, coarsely chopped	1
¼ litre	white wine	8 fl oz
1	bay leaf	1
1 tsp	fresh thyme, or ¼ tsp dried thyme	1 tsp
	roasting juices from the turkey, degreased	
1	orange, rind grated, juice strained	1
1 tbsp	red wine vinegar	1 tbsp
2 tbsp	cornflour	2 tbsp
8 cl	port	3 fl oz
½ tsp	salt	½ tsp
	freshly ground black pepper	

To prepare the stuffing, blanch the lemon and orange rind in ¼ litre (8 fl oz) of boiling water for 1 minute. Drain and set aside. Using a sharp knife, peel the oranges and divide them into sections. Cut each section in half and set them aside.

In a large saucepan, bring 2 litres (3½ pints) of water to the boil. Drop in the sweet potato cubes and blanch them for 3 minutes. Drain and set aside.

In a large fireproof casserole, melt 60 g (2 oz) of the butter over medium-low heat. Add the onion and cook it until translucent, stirring occasionally — about 10 minutes. Add the lemon and orange rind, oranges, sweet potatoes, lemon juice, stock, salt and pepper. Cook until the sweet potato cubes are tender — 7 to 10 minutes. Remove from the heat and add the cloves, mustard, the remaining butter, the bread cubes and the brandy. Mix thoroughly. Allow to cool before using.

To make a stock for the gravy, chop the turkey neck into pieces. Heat the oil in a heavy-bottomed saucepan over medium-high heat. Add the neck, gizzard, heart, carrot, celery, onions and garlic. Sauté, stirring, until the vegetables begin to brown — about 5 minutes. Add the white wine, bay leaf, thyme and ¾ litre (1¼ pints) of water. Reduce the heat to low and simmer for 1 hour, skimming off impurities as necessary. Strain the stock, pushing down on the contents to extract all the liquid; there should be about 60 cl (1 pint). Set it aside.

Preheat the oven to 180°C (350°F or Mark 4). Rinse the turkey inside and out under cold running water and dry it thoroughly with paper towels. Rub the salt and pepper inside the body and neck cavities and on the outside of the bird.

To stuff the turkey, loosely fill both cavities. Tie the drumsticks together with string and tuck the wing tips under the bird. Put the turkey on a rack in a shallow roasting pan. Add ¼ litre (8 fl oz) of water to the pan.

To keep the turkey moist and prevent it from overbrowning, make a tent of aluminium foil. Use an extrawide sheet of foil (or two sheets of standard foil crimped together) that measure 45 cm (18 inches) longer than the pan. Lay the foil shiny side down over the turkey, and tuck it loosely round the inside edges of the pan. Roast the turkey in the oven for 2½ hours.

Take the turkey from the oven, and carefully remove the foil tent. Brush the turkey all over with the honey. Turn the heat down to 170°C (325°F or Mark 3), then return the turkey to the oven, and roast it uncovered for 1 hour. The bird is done when a meat thermometer inserted in the thickest part of the thigh reads 83°C (180°F). There should be about ¼ litre (8 fl oz) of roasting juices in the pan. Let the turkey stand for at least 20 minutes before carving it. In the meantime, remove the stuffing from the cavities and set it aside in a bowl loosely covered with foil to keep it warm.

To make the gravy, combine the stock, reserved (degreased) roasting juices, orange juice and rind, and vinegar in a saucepan. Bring the mixture to the boil. Mix the cornflour and the port and whisk them into the saucepan; return the gravy to the boil. Reduce the heat to low and simmer for 5 minutes. Add the salt and pepper and serve piping hot with the carved bird and the stuffing.

EDITOR'S NOTE: *To roast a larger turkey, increase the cooking time by 20 to 25 minutes per 500 g (1 lb), and leave the foil tent on until 1 hour of cooking time remains. To cook the turkey unstuffed, rub orange peel and ¼ teaspoon of cloves inside the cavity for extra flavour, and subtract 5 minutes per 500 g (1 lb) from the total cooking time.*

If you wish to cook the stuffing separately, put it in a baking dish with an additional 4 tablespoons of stock. Cover the dish with aluminium foil and bake in a preheated 170°C (325°F or Mark 3) oven for 45 minutes. Uncover the dish and return it to the oven for another 45 minutes.

Buckwheat Stuffing

Serves 10
Enough for a 4.5 to 5.5 kg (10 to 12 lb) turkey
Working time: about 30 minutes
Total time: about 1 hour and 30 minutes

Calories **215**
Protein **7g**
Cholesterol **10mg**
Total fat **12g**
Saturated fat **3g**
Sodium **190mg**

315 g	toasted buckwheat groats (kasha)	10½ oz
45 g	unsalted butter	1½ oz
250 g	mushrooms, wiped clean, thinly sliced	8 oz
1	stick celery, finely chopped	1
350 g	onions, chopped	12 oz
3	garlic cloves, finely chopped	3
60 cl	unsalted turkey or chicken stock	1 pint
12.5 cl	port or dry sherry	4 fl oz
½ tsp	salt	½ tsp
	freshly ground black pepper	
2	egg whites	2
1½ tsp	ground cinnamon	1½ tsp
150 g	blanched almonds, toasted in a moderate oven, then coarsely chopped	5 oz
125 g	parsley leaves	4 oz

Melt 15 g (½ oz) of the butter in a large, heavy frying pan over medium-high heat. Sauté the mushrooms until they begin to brown — about 7 minutes. Stir in the celery, onions and garlic. Reduce the heat to medium-low, cover, and cook for 3 minutes. Uncover and continue cooking, stirring occasionally, until the onions are translucent — about 5 minutes more. Set the mixture aside.

In a saucepan, bring the stock, port or sherry, salt and pepper to a simmer. While the stock simmers, beat the egg whites in a mixing bowl. Add the buckwheat groats and stir until the grains are well coated.

In a large, fireproof casserole, melt the remaining butter over medium-high heat. Add the coated buckwheat groats and stir constantly with a fork until the grains are dry and do not stick together — about 2 minutes. Pour in the simmering stock, then stir in the onion-and-

mushroom mixture and the cinnamon. Reduce the heat to low, cover, and simmer until the grains are soft — about 15 minutes. Remove the mixture from the heat, add the almonds and parsley, and blend well with a fork.

Roast the bird until only 1 hour of cooking time remains. Remove it from the oven and pour the juice and the fat from the breast cavity. Stuff the cavity with the buckwheat mixture, and finish roasting the turkey.

EDITOR'S NOTE: *If you wish to cook the stuffing separately, put in a baking dish and cover the dish with aluminium foil. Bake the stuffing in a preheated 170°C (325°F or Mark 3) oven for 20 minutes. Uncover the baking dish, add 12.5 cl (4 fl oz) of stock and return to the oven for another 20 minutes. If you roast turkey without stuffing, put some celery leaves, onion trimmings, parsley stems and a few garlic cloves in the breast cavity to give it extra flavour.*

Spinach, Beet Green and Pine-Nut Stuffing

Serves 10
Enough for a 4.5 to 5.5 kg (10 to 12 lb) turkey
Working time: about 30 minutes
Total time: about 30 minutes

Calories **265**
Protein **11g**
Cholesterol **7mg**
Total fat **8g**
Saturated fat **2g**
Sodium **385mg**

175 g	beet greens or Swiss chard, stemmed and chopped	6 o
1 kg	spinach, stemmed and chopped	2 l
30 g	fresh parsley, chopped	1 o
½ litre	unsalted turkey or chicken stock	16 fl o
125	sultanas	4 o
30 g	unsalted butter	1 o
750 g	onions, chopped	1½ l
3	garlic cloves, finely chopped	
2 tsp	chopped fresh thyme, or ½ tsp dried thyme	2 ts
¼ tsp	salt	¼ ts
	freshly ground black pepper	
45 g	pine-nuts, toasted	1½ o
1 tbsp	fresh lemon juice	1 tbs
4 tbsp	brandy	4 tbs
175 g	dry breadcrumbs	6 o

In a large pot, bring 12.5 cl (4 fl oz) of water to the boil. Add the beet greens and then the spinach and parsley. Cover the pot and steam just until all three are wilted — about 4 minutes. Drain and refresh with cold water. Squeeze out the excess moisture and set aside.

In a saucepan, bring the stock to the boil and reduce it to about 5 tablespoons. Remove from the heat. Add the sultanas and set aside to plump.

Meanwhile, melt the butter in a heavy frying pan. Add the onions and cook for about 5 minutes over medium-low heat, stirring frequently. Add the garlic, thyme, salt and pepper, and cook, stirring occasionally, until the onions are softened but not brown — about 5 minutes more. Add the sultanas and stock.

In a large bowl, combine the greens, the onion mix

1 tbsp	fresh lemon juice	1 tbsp
1½ tbsp	red wine vinegar	1½ tbsp
450 g	uncooked sweetcorn kernels, (about 5 ears of fresh corn)	15 oz
225 g	dry breadcrumbs	7½ oz

In a medium saucepan, bring the stock to the boil. Reduce the stock to about 12.5 cl (4 fl oz) and set it aside.

Heat 2 teaspoons of the olive oil in a large, heavy frying pan over medium heat. Add the mushrooms and sauté them for about 1 minute. Stir in the salt and aubergine, then cover. Cook until the aubergine begins to give off moisture — about 4 minutes. Uncover and cook, stirring frequently, for an additional 10 minutes. Transfer the mixture to a large bowl.

Place the pan back on the stove. Heat the remaining teaspoon of olive oil and the butter over medium heat, then add the leek or onions. Cover and cook for about 1 minute. Uncover and add the shallots, peppers, garlic, basil, rosemary, lemon juice and vinegar, and continue cooking until the peppers are tender — about 2 minutes more. Combine with the aubergine-and-mushroom mixture in the large bowl. Add the sweetcorn, breadcrumbs and stock, and mix well. If the mixture is sticky, add more breadcrumbs. Allow the stuffing to cool before using.

ture, pine-nuts, lemon juice and brandy. Mix in the breadcrumbs. Allow the stuffing to cool before using.

EDITOR'S NOTE: *If you wish to cook the stuffing separately, put it in a baking dish with an additional 8 cl (3 fl oz) of stock. Cover the dish with aluminium foil and bake the stuffing in a preheated 170°C (325°F or Mark 3) oven for 45 minutes. Uncover the dish and return it to the oven for another 45 minutes. If you roast a turkey without stuffing, put parsley stems, onion trimmings, a few garlic cloves, some thyme leaves and black pepper into the breast cavity for extra flavour.*

EDITOR'S NOTE: *If you wish to cook the stuffing separately, put it in a baking dish with an additional 4 tablespoons of stock. Cover the dish with aluminium foil and bake the stuffing in a preheated 170°C (325°F or Mark 3) oven for 45 minutes. Uncover the dish and return it to the oven for another 45 minutes. If you roast a turkey without stuffing, put the leek tops or onion trimmings, basil stems, a few garlic cloves and a piece of the lemon peel into the breast cavity for extra flavour.*

Red Pepper, Sweetcorn and Aubergine Stuffing

Serves 10
Enough for a 4.5 to 5.5 kg (10 to 12 lb) turkey
Working time: about 30 minutes
Total time: about 30 minutes

Calories **215**
Protein **8g**
Cholesterol **2mg**
Total fat **4g**
Saturated fat **1g**
Sodium **260mg**

30 cl	unsalted turkey or chicken stock	½ pint
3 tsp	virgin olive oil	3 tsp
350 g	mushrooms, quartered	12 oz
¼ tsp	salt	¼ tsp
2	medium-sized aubergines, unpeeled, cut into 1 cm (½ inch) cubes	2
10 g	unsalted butter	⅓ oz
1	large leek, trimmed and chopped, or 2 medium onions, chopped	1
2 tbsp	chopped shallots	2 tbsp
2	sweet red peppers, seeded, deribbed, cut into 1 by 2.5 cm (½ by 1 inch) strips	2
3	garlic cloves, finely chopped	3
1 tbsp	chopped fresh basil, or 1 tsp dried basil	1
1 tsp	chopped fresh rosemary, or ¼ tsp dried rosemary	1 tsp

Turkey Galantine

THIS RECIPE FOR A GRAND AND ELEGANT PARTY DISH OFFERS A
BOLD DEPARTURE FROM THE CLASSIC GALANTINE.

Serves 10
Working time: about 2 hours
Total time: about 3 hours and 30 minutes

Calories **405**
Protein **55g**
Cholesterol **165mg**
Total fat **13g**
Saturated fat **5g**
Sodium **430mg**

5.5 kg	fresh or thawed turkey	12 lb
½ tsp	salt	½ tsp
	freshly ground black pepper	
1 tbsp	honey	1 tbsp
Vegetable stuffing		
10 to 12	large mushrooms, wiped clean	10 to 12
1	lemon, juice only	1
3	small leeks, about 2 cm (¾ inch) in diameter, trimmed to 20 cm (8 inches) in length and left whole, washed thoroughly to rid them of any sand	3
½ tsp	salt	½ tsp
2	small yellow or green courgettes, cut lengthwise into 2.5 cm (1 inch) wide strips about 5 mm (¼ inch) thick	2
2	small carrots, peeled, quartered lengthwise, with cores removed	2
30 g	unsalted butter	1 oz
1	onion, finely chopped	1
3	garlic cloves, finely chopped	3
500 g	kale, stemmed and washed	1 lb
750 g	spinach, stemmed and washed	1½ lb
90 g	Parmesan cheese, freshly grated	3 oz
½ tsp	grated nutmeg	½ tsp
	freshly ground black pepper	
2	egg whites	2
Currant and wine sauce		
2	large onions, cut into 2.5 cm (1 inch) pieces	2
2	carrots, cut into 1 cm (½ inch) pieces	2
1	stick celery, cut into 2.5 cm (1 inch) pieces	1
3	garlic cloves, halved	3
1 tbsp	safflower oil	1 tbsp
	turkey carcass, neck, wings, heart, gizzard	
1	bay leaf	1
2 tsp	fresh thyme, or ½ tsp dried thyme	2 tsp
17.5 cl	red wine	6 fl oz
125 g	mushrooms, chopped, plus the mushroom trimmings from the vegetable stuffing	4 oz
¼ tsp	salt	¼ tsp
	freshly ground black pepper	
4 tbsp	currants	4 tbsp

Cutting away the back round the collarbone, exposing the "oyster" and the thighbone.

Cutting beneath the ridge of the breastbone to remove the carcass.

Place a thoroughly chilled turkey with its breast down, drumsticks facing you, on a wooden cutting board or other non-skid surface. Bend open a wing; using a boning knife or a small, strong, sharp knife, cut round the base of the wing and through the joint to remove the wing. Remove the second wing. Set both aside. Next, make a long slit from the neck to the tail, cutting through the skin to expose the long upper ridge of the backbone. Cut off the tail if it is still attached. With the knife blade held firmly against one side of the backbone, begin freeing the meat from that side of the bird. Using your other hand to lift away the skin and flesh, cut and scrape beneath the oyster-shaped morsel of meat shown on the left, and round and down the outside of the collarbone. Cut about one third of the way down the rib bones, working along the length of the carcass until you encounter the thigh joint. To locate the thigh socket, grasp the end of the drumstick and pull the leg towards you. Cut away the meat and cartilage round the joint. Sever the joint by cutting round the ball where it joins the socket. Continue cutting downwards to detach the leg, being careful not to slice through the bottom layer of breast skin. Repeat these steps on the other side of the turkey.

Cut the skin and flesh from round the neck and collarbone so that the back meat comes away from the carcass on both sides. Pressing the blade of the knife against the rib cage and then the breastbone, cut and scrape away the breast. Take care not to pierce the skin (that would allow filling to escape later) and stop when you reach the ridge of the breastbone. Cut away the breast on the other side, again holding the knife against the bone and halting when you reach the breastbone ridge. Scrape away the flesh on either side to expose the ridge and tip of the breastbone. Lift the carcass with one hand. Then starting at the tip of the breastbone free the carcass by cutting just beneath the entire breastbone ridge and through the cartilage with the knife, as shown on the left. Be careful not to puncture the skin; there is no flesh between the skin and the bone at this point. Starting at the detached end of one of the thighbones, cut into the flesh on either side of the bone along its length. Scrape away the flesh from the sides and detached end of the bone. Holding the bone with one hand, scrape down its length to the joint to expose it, a shown on the left. Sever the joint and tendons, and remove the thighbone. Repeat the process to remove the other thighbone. Now turn to the breast. Using your fingers to loosen and separate the connective membrane, peel the triangular fillets from the breast and set them aside *(centre left)*. Remove the white tendon from the thick end of each fillet by slicing through the flesh on either side of the tendon. So that the meat will uniformly encase the stuffing, make a horizontal cut in the thick part of each side of the breast as shown in the photograph below, on the left. Unfold the resulting flaps into the triangular space at the top of the heart-shaped flesh. Carefully trim off excess fat and membrane. Replace the fillets on the breast. Cover the breast with a sheet of plastic film and lightly pound the meat to flatten it evenly. Remove the plastic film and refrigerate the turkey until you are ready to stuff it.

To begin preparing the stock for the sauce, preheat the oven to 200°C (400°F or Mark 6). Then put the onions, carrots, celery and garlic in a roasting pan, and toss them with the oil. Cut the carcass and neck into pieces, and place these on top of the vegetables along with the wings, heart and gizzard. Put the pan in the oven. Roast until the bones are browned — about 30 minutes. While the turkey bones are browning, begin preparing the vegetable stuffing. Cut off the mushroom stems 5 mm (¼ inch) below the caps. Place the mushrooms on a cutting board, stems up, and slice off two opposite sides from each one so that the sides are flush with the stem; this allows the mushrooms to fit snugly against one another in a row when the stuffing is added. Reserve the trimmings for the sauce. Heat 17.5 cl (6 fl oz) of water with the lemon juice in a non-reactive shallow pan over medium heat. Add the mushrooms, leeks and ¼ teaspoon of the salt. Cover and cook for 7 minutes. Turn the leeks over and stir the mushrooms. Lay the courgette strips on top, skin side up, and continue cooking until the leeks are tender — about 5 minutes. Drain the vegetables on paper towels and discard the liquid in the pan.

Add 2.5 cm (1 inch) of water to the pan and bring it to the boil. Add the carrot strips, reduce the heat, and simmer until tender — about 5 minutes. Set the carrots aside with the other vegetables and discard the water. Melt the butter in the pan over medium-low heat; cook the onion and garlic in the butter, stirring occasionally, until translucent — about 10 minutes.

Bring a large pan of water — about 10 to 12 litres (17 to 20 pints) — to the boil. Add the kale and cook, covered, for 5 minutes. Add the spinach, stir, and cook for 2 minutes more. Drain the greens in a colander and run cold water over them until cool. Squeeze the greens firmly with your hands into two or three balls. Slice the balls into thin sections. Put the sections in a large mixing

bowl and combine them with the grated Parmesan cheese. Add the nutmeg, pepper, the remaining ¼ teaspoon of salt, and the sautéed onion and garlic. Whisk the egg whites until foamy, and mix them into the spinach, kale and cheese mixture.

Transfer the oven-browned bones and vegetables to a large pot. Deglaze the roasting pan with ½ litre (16 fl oz) of water. Add this liquid to the pot, and pour in enough water to cover the bones. Add the bay leaf and thyme. Bring the stock to the boil, reduce the heat to low, and simmer for 1½ hours, skimming foam from the surface as necessary.

To stuff the boned turkey, lay the bird on a work surface with its drumsticks pointing towards you; sprinkle the meat with ¼ teaspoon of the salt and some additional pepper. Spread the spinach mixture evenly over the breast to within 2.5 cm (1 inch) of the edges. Lay on alternating strips of courgette, skin side down, and carrot. Position the leeks on top. Arrange the mushrooms stem side up in a tightly packed row down the centre, as shown on the left. Preheat the oven to 180°C (350°F or Mark 4). Thread a trussing needle with a long piece of string. Wrap the thighs round the stuffing; if possible, get a helper to hold up the sides of the turkey while you begin sewing it. (Any mushrooms that tumble out can be tucked back in later on.) Sew together the sides of the back to enclose the stuffing snugly. Stitch all the way to the neck, then sew up the wing holes. Use a short length of string to tie the drumsticks together.

Place the galantine on a rack in the roasting pan. Sprinkle the outside with the remaining ¼ teaspoon of salt and some more pepper. Use an extra-wide sheet of foil or two smaller sheets crimped together to fashion a cooking tent about 45 cm (18 inches) longer than the pan. Lay the foil shiny side down over the turkey, and tuck the foil loosely around the inside edges of the pan. Place the pan in the oven and cook for 45 minutes.

Remove the pan from the oven and reduce the temperature to 170°C (325°F or Mark 3). Take off the tent and brush the outside of the turkey with the honey. Return to the oven for 45 minutes to an hour more; the galantine is done if the juices run clear when a thigh is pierced to the centre with the tip of a sharp knife.

While the galantine finishes roasting, strain the stock into a saucepan. Add the wine, chopped mushrooms and mushroom trimmings, salt, and pepper. Simmer until reduced to about ½ litre (16 fl oz).

Remove the galantine from the oven and let it rest for 20 minutes while you finish the sauce: add the currants to the stock-and-wine mixture and simmer for 10 minutes. Purée the sauce in a food processor or blender and pour it into a sauceboat.

Use a carving knife to cut the galantine into 5 mm (¼ inch) slices, supporting each slice with a spatula as you remove it. Pass the sauce separately.

3 First steamed, then roasted, a duck stuffed with garlic, rosemary and pear is served with watercress and stuffed tomatoes (recipe, page 117).

Updating Some Old Favourites

No cookery book on poultry would be complete without duck, goose and the domesticated pigeon squab. And two other birds demand inclusion: pheasant and quail, once acquired only as hunters' bounty, are now produced on farms and brought fresh or frozen to market. They are well worth cooking, if not perhaps as family fare then certainly as food for entertaining.

Of the five birds represented in this section, duck and goose are most readily available and feature in the largest number of recipes. Fortunately, both can be cooked in ways that significantly reduce their fat content. Because most of their fat exists under the skin in a thick pad, it can be removed with the skin, or steamed or roasted away.

Roasting is the most popular method of cooking duck and goose. The trick is to prick the skin all over to permit the melting fat to trickle out during roasting. This should be repeated when the birds are about half cooked. At the same time, the fat that collects in the pan should be poured off or removed with a basting bulb, and discarded. The recipe for goose on page 121 first steams the bird to sweat out much of the fat, then roasts it. A goose treated in this way will emerge moist and tender from the oven under a sheath of crisply done skin, and the apple-and-red cabbage stuffing will have none of the greasiness so often associated with goose.

Because of their tendency to put on fat, geese are generally killed when they are three to four months old and weight 3 to 6 kg (6 to 12 lb). Their fat and bone structure make them appear meatier than they are. Thus it is a good idea to allow about 350 g (12 oz) of uncooked goose for a 90 g (3 oz) serving.

Ducks are slaughtered young — at about seven to eight weeks of age and between 1.75 and 3 kg (3½ and 6 lb) in weight. Like geese, they appear to have more flesh on them than in fact they do. Of the breeds that are raised for the table, the most popular in Britain is the Aylesbury duck, though new breeds such as the Barbary duck are being introduced.

Ducks are usually sold whole, but can be cut up at home and grilled or sautéed. Lately, boneless duck breasts have become available in shops. Two recipes for breast appear in this section and call for the meat to be cooked lightly and served pink; any resistance to the idea will be overcome with the first taste.

Duck has much to recommend it nutritionally. A good source of protein, it is lower in cholesterol than turkey. And the meat is only slightly more fatty than the leanest sirloin.

Duck Breasts with Red Wine and Juniper Berries

Serves 6
Working time: about 45 minutes
Total time: about 45 minutes

Calories **475**
Protein **24g**
Cholesterol **90mg**
Total fat **11g**
Saturated fat **4g**
Sodium **185mg**

6	duck breasts, skinned and boned, fat removed	6
1 tsp	safflower oil	1 tsp
¼ tsp	salt	¼ tsp
Red wine and juniper sauce		
1 litre	full-bodied red wine	1¾ pints
½ litre	unsalted chicken stock	16 fl oz
125 g	shallots, or onion, thinly sliced	4 oz
½ tsp	fennel seeds	½ tsp
1 tbsp	juniper berries, crushed	1 tbsp
8	black peppercorns	8
½ tsp	fresh thyme, or ¼ tsp dried thyme	½ tsp
1	bay leaf	1
2 tbsp	sugar	2 tbsp
4 tbsp	balsamic vinegar, or 3 tbsp red wine vinegar	4 tbsp
1 tsp	honey	1 tsp
2	garlic cloves, crushed	2
½ tsp	cornflour, mixed with 2 tsp water	½ tsp

To begin the sauce, combine the wine, stock, sliced shallots or onion, fennel seeds, crushed juniper berries, peppercorns, thyme and bay leaf in a non-reactive saucepan and cook at a slow boil until the liquid is reduced by half — about 25 minutes.

Meanwhile, melt the sugar in a small, heavy-bottomed saucepan over low heat, stirring constantly with a wooden spoon until the sugar turns golden-brown. Standing well back to avoid being splattered, add the vinegar all at once. Stir to dissolve the sugar, then add this mixture to the reduced wine and stock mixture. Stir in the honey and garlic, and simmer the sauce for 10 minutes. Strain it, then return it to the pan. Cook the sauce, skimming occasionally, until it is reduced to about 30 cl (½ pint). Stir in the cornflour mixture and cook until thick and shiny — about 1 minute.

Heat the oil in a large, heavy frying pan over medium-high heat and sauté the duck breasts for 5 minutes. Turn them over, sprinkle with the salt, and cook for 3 minutes more. Remove the breasts from the pan, set them aside and keep them warm. Deglaze the pan with about 4 tablespoons each of water and sauce. Stir the deglazed pan juices into the sauce.

To serve, cut each breast diagonally into about 10 slices and arrange on heated plates or a heated serving platter. Spoon hot sauce over the duck and serve.

SUGGESTED ACCOMPANIMENTS: *mashed potatoes; braised red cabbage or carrot and courgette strips.*

Duck Breasts with Sour Apple

Serves 4
Working time: about 20 minutes
Total time: about 30 minutes

Calories **310**
Protein **24g**
Cholesterol **95mg**
Total fat **18g**
Saturated fat **7g**
Sodium **150mg**

4	duck breasts, skinned and boned, fat removed	4
1 tbsp	virgin olive oil	1 tbsp
⅛ tsp	salt	⅛ tsp
15 g	unsalted butter	½ oz
1	cooking apple, peeled, cored, thinly sliced and tossed with 2 tbsp fresh lemon juice	1
1	shallot, finely chopped	1
½ tsp	fresh thyme, or ¼ tsp dried thyme	½ tsp
3 tbsp	balsamic vinegar, or 1½ tbsp red wine vinegar	3 tbsp
1 tbsp	honey	1 tbsp
1	garlic clove, finely chopped	1
¼ litre	unsalted chicken stock	8 fl oz

Heat the oil in a large, heavy frying pan over medium-high heat. Sauté the breasts on one side for 5 minutes. Turn them over, sprinkle with the salt and reduce the heat to medium. Continue cooking until the meat feels firm but springy to the touch — about 3 minutes. Remove the breasts from the pan and keep warm.

Add the butter to the pan and sauté the apple slices for 2 minutes. Add the shallot, thyme, vinegar, honey and garlic, and cook, stirring frequently, until the apples are lightly browned — 2 to 3 minutes more. Add the stock and bring to the boil. Lower the heat and simmer the sauce until it is reduced by half — about 10 minutes.

Meanwhile, slice the breasts diagonally across the grain into 5 mm (¼ inch) thick pieces. Fan the slices out on a serving platter or on individual plates. Spoon the hot sauce and apples over them, and serve immediately.

SUGGESTED ACCOMPANIMENT: *steamed broccoli florets.*

Duck with Mushrooms and Mange-Tout

Serves 4
Working time: about 1 hour
Total time: about 3 hours

Calories **460**
Protein **30g**
Cholesterol **70mg**
Total fat **25g**
Saturated fat **8g**
Sodium **290mg**

2.5 kg	duck, cut into four serving pieces	5 lb
175 g	onion, chopped	6 oz
1	carrot, finely chopped	1
2 tbsp	flour	2 tbsp
3	garlic cloves, finely chopped	3
¼ tsp	salt	¼ tsp
	freshly ground black pepper	
¾ litre	unsalted chicken stock	1¼ pints
¼ litre	dry white wine	8 fl oz
3 or 4	parsley sprigs	3 or 4
1	small bay leaf	1
½ tsp	fresh thyme, or ¼ tsp dried thyme	½ tsp
½ tsp	grated lemon rind	½ tsp
125 g	mushrooms, halved, or quartered if large	4 oz
250 g	mange-tout, strings removed, blanched a few seconds in boiling water, refreshed in cold water, drained	8 oz

Preheat the oven to 230°C (450°F or Mark 8).

Heat a heavy frying pan over medium heat and put in the duck pieces skin side down, without overlapping any of them. Sauté until the skin turns golden-brown — 2 to 3 minutes. Turn the pieces and brown them on the other side — 1 to 2 minutes more. Transfer the duck pieces to a large, fireproof casserole.

Place the casserole in the oven and bake it for 10 minutes; this renders the fat from the duck. Remove the casserole, spoon off the fat, and turn the pieces. Bake for another 10 minutes.

Remove the duck pieces from the casserole and pour off all but 1 tablespoon of fat. Add the onion and carrot to the casserole and stir well to scrape up any bits of meat that have baked on to the bottom. Cook the vegetables over medium heat for 3 minutes.

Return the duck pieces to the casserole and sprinkle them on one side with 1 tablespoon of the flour. Turn the pieces and sprinkle them on the second side with the remaining tablespoon of flour. Bake the casserole in the oven for an additional 5 minutes.

Reduce the oven temperature to 200°C (400°F or Mark 6). Stir the garlic into the meat and vegetables and sprinkle in the salt and pepper. Add the stock, wine, parsley, bay leaf, thyme and lemon rind, and bring the mixture to a simmer over medium-high heat. Place aluminium foil directly over the casserole contents, then cover with a lid and bake for 20 minutes.

Remove the duck pieces from the casserole. Pour the sauce into a small saucepan. Return the duck pieces to

the casserole and allow them to cool. Cover and refrigerate both the duck and the sauce until the sauce jells — 2 hours or overnight.

Spoon off the layer of congealed fat from the top of the sauce and discard it. Bring the sauce to the boil over medium-high heat, then cook it until it is reduced to about 60 cl (1 pint) — 10 to 15 minutes. Pour the sauce over the duck in the casserole and reheat it over medium heat. Once the sauce is bubbling, add the mushrooms and cook for 5 minutes. Finally, stir in the mange-tout, cover, and cook for 1 minute more. Serve the duck and vegetables very hot.

Roast Duck Stuffed with Pears and Garlic

Serves 4
Working time: about 30 minutes
Total time: about 2 hours and 15 minutes

Calories **405**
Protein **25g**
Cholesterol **75mg**
Total fat **27g**
Saturated fat **10g**
Sodium **210mg**

2.5 kg	duck, rinsed and patted dry	5 lb
15 g	unsalted butter	½ oz
15 to 20	garlic cloves, peeled, large ones halved	15 to 20
500 g	pears, slightly underripe, cut into 2 cm (¾ inch) cubes and tossed with 1 tbsp fresh lime juice	1 lb
1 tbsp	fresh rosemary, or 1 tsp dried rosemary	1 tbsp
1 tsp	sugar	1 tsp
¼ tsp	salt	¼ tsp
1	bunch watercress for garnish	1

Trim any excess skin and fat from round the neck of the duck. Remove any fat from the cavity. Cover the bottom of a large pan with 2.5 cm (1 inch) of water and set a metal rack or steamer in the pan. Bring the water to the boil on top of the stove. To help release fat while steaming, lightly prick the duck all over with a wooden toothpick or skewer, taking care not to pierce the flesh below the layer of fat. Place the duck breast side down in the pan. Cover tightly and steam the duck for 30 minutes.

Preheat the oven to 180°C (350°F or Mark 4).

While the duck is steaming, melt the butter in a heavy frying pan over medium heat. Cook the garlic cloves in the butter, stirring frequently, until they begin to soften and brown — about 12 minutes. Stir in the pears, rosemary and sugar, and cook until the pears are soft — about 8 minutes more. Set the stuffing aside.

When the duck has finished steaming, sprinkle it inside and out with the salt. Place the duck on a rack in a roasting pan, breast side down, and roast it for 15 minutes. Remove the duck and reduce the oven temperature to 170°C (325°F or Mark 3). Turn the duck breast side up on the rack. Prick the breast and legs of the duck. Fill the cavity with the pear-garlic mixture. Return the bird to the oven and roast it until the skin turns a deep golden-brown — about 1½ hours. Cut the duck into quarters and garnish with the watercress.

SUGGESTED ACCOMPANIMENTS: *pearl barley; grilled tomatoes.*
EDITOR'S NOTE: *The process of steaming followed by roasting helps to defat the duck considerably, resulting in a crisp skin and fewer calories.*

Roast Duck
with Cranberry Compote

Serves 6
Working time: about 45 minutes
Total time: about 2 hours and 30 minutes

Calories **595**
Protein **33g**
Cholesterol **85mg**
Total fat **30g**
Saturated fat **10g**
Sodium **390mg**

Two	ducks, rinsed and patted dry, necks	Two
2.25 kg	chopped in 4 pieces and reserved	4½ lb
½ tsp	salt	½ tsp
2	onions, quartered	2
4	bay leaves, crumbled	4
Balsamic vinegar sauce		
1 litre	unsalted chicken stock	1¾ pints
1	onion, quartered	1
1	carrot, sliced into 5 mm (¼ inch) rounds	1
4	garlic cloves, crushed	4
½ tsp	dried thyme	½ tsp
12.5 cl	dry white wine	4 fl oz
2	tomatoes, skinned, seeded and diced	2
2 tbsp	balsamic vinegar, or 1½ tbsp red wine vinegar	2 tbsp
⅛ tsp	salt	⅛ tsp
	freshly ground black pepper	
1 tbsp	grainy mustard	1 tbsp
Cranberry compote		
30 cl	fresh orange juice	½ pint
150 g	raisins	5 oz
350 g	cranberries	12 oz
1 tbsp	sugar	1 tbsp

Trim any excess skin and fat from round the necks of the ducks. Remove any fat from the cavities. Pour enough water into a large roasting pan to fill it 2.5 cm (1 inch) deep, and set a metal rack or steamer in the water. Bring the water to the boil on the stove top. To release fat from the ducks without rendering their juices, lightly prick both legs with a wooden toothpick or a skewer, taking care not to pierce the flesh below the layer of fat. Place a duck breast side down in the pan. Cover and steam for 15 minutes. Remove the duck from the pan; steam the other duck. Preheat the oven to 190°C (375°F or Mark 5).

Lightly prick the legs of both ducks again and pour off their juices from their cavities. Sprinkle the ducks inside and out with the ½ teaspoon of salt. Place half of the onions and bay leaves in the cavity of each duck. Put the ducks breast side down on a rack in a large roasting pan, and roast them for 30 minutes. Remove the ducks from the oven and reduce the temperature to 170°C (325°F or Mark 3). Turn the ducks breast side up and prick the entire skin. Return them to the oven and roast until the skin turns a deep golden-brown — 1¼ to 1½ hours.

While the ducks are roasting, begin preparing the sauce. Place the duck necks, stock, onion, carrot, garlic and thyme in a large saucepan. Bring the liquid to a simmer over medium heat and cook until it is reduced to half — about 45 minutes. Pour the enriched stock through a fine sieve and reserve it.

While the stock is simmering, make the cranberry compote. Put the orange juice and raisins in a saucepan and bring the liquid to the boil. Reduce the heat to low, cover, and cook for 5 minutes. Remove the pan from the heat and let it stand, still covered, for 5 minutes more. Purée the raisins and juice in a food processor or blender. Return the purée to the saucepan and add the cranberries and sugar. Bring the mixture to the boil, then reduce the heat to low, cover, and simmer until the cranberries have burst and almost all the liquid has been absorbed — about 15 minutes. Pour the compote into a serving bowl.

When the ducks are done, place them on a carving board while you finish making the sauce. Pour off the fat from the roasting pan and then deglaze the pan with the wine over medium-low heat. Add the enriched stock, the tomatoes and vinegar, and bring the liquid to a simmer. Stir in the salt, some pepper and the mustard. Raise the heat to medium-high and cook rapidly until the sauce is reduced to about 45 cl (¾ pint). Carve the ducks and arrange the pieces on a serving platter. Pour the sauce over the pieces and serve the cranberry compote on the side.

SUGGESTED ACCOMPANIMENTS: wild rice; steamed baby carrots
EDITOR'S NOTE: The process of steaming followed by roasting helps to defat the duck considerably, resulting in a crisp skin and fewer calories.

Goose Breasts with Blackberry Sauce

THIS RECIPE AND THE ONE THAT FOLLOWS USE ONE WHOLE GOOSE BETWEEN THEM. SINCE GOOSE BREAST IS NOT NORMALLY SOLD SEPARATELY, THE LEGS ARE RESERVED FOR A SECOND DISH THAT IS PREPARED THE NEXT DAY. RATHER THAN BEING CONSUMED IMMEDIATELY, THE DISH MAY THEN BE FROZEN FOR A LATER MEAL.

Serves 4
Working time: about 1 hour
Total time: about 1 day

Calories **335**
Protein **26g**
Cholesterol **80mg**
Total fat **14g**
Saturated fat **4g**
Sodium **215mg**

4 to 4.5 kg	goose, gizzard, heart and neck reserved	9 to 10 lb
½ litre	red wine	16 fl oz
4 tbsp	balsamic vinegar, or 3 tbsp red wine vinegar	4 tbsp
2	onions, cut in eighths	2
2	carrots, sliced in 5 mm (¼ inch) rounds	2
1½ tsp	fresh thyme, or ¾ tsp dried thyme	1½ tsp
10	black peppercorns, crushed	10
1	bay leaf	1
2 tsp	safflower oil	2 tsp
¼ tsp	salt	¼ tsp
	freshly ground black pepper	
Blackberry sauce		
500 g	fresh or frozen blackberries, several whole berries reserved for garnish, the rest puréed and strained through a fine sieve	1 lb
1 tbsp	red wine vinegar	1 tbsp
2 tsp	sugar	2 tsp
2 tbsp	gin	2 tbsp

Lay the goose on its back. Cut through the skin where a thigh joins the body. Bend the leg outwards to find the hip joint. Free the leg by cutting round the ball at the end of the thigh bone and through the socket. Repeat the process to remove the other leg. With a heavy knife or meat cleaver, chop the knobs off the drumsticks.

Slit the breast skin lengthwise along the breastbone. Keeping the knife blade pressed against the breastbone and then the rib cage, cut away each breast. Pull the skin and fat away from the breast meat as much as possible with your hands, then use a small knife to finish the process. Pull the skin off the legs.

In a shallow dish, combine the wine, balsamic vinegar, one quarter each of the onions and carrots, one third of the thyme, and the peppercorns. Refrigerate the goose pieces in this mixture overnight.

Preheat the oven to 230°C (450°F or Mark 8).

To make the stock, first trim as much fat and skin from the goose carcass as possible. With a meat cleaver or a heavy knife, cut the carcass into two or three pieces. Trim and roughly cut up the giblets and neck. Place the bones and giblets in a heavy-bottomed roasting pan and brown them in the oven for 15 minutes. Then add the remaining onions and carrots and cook for 15 minutes more.

Transfer the contents of the roasting pan to a stockpot. Pour off the fat from the roasting pan, deglaze it with some water, and pour the liquid into the stockpot. Add enough water to the pot to cover the bones, then ▶

bring the liquid to the boil and skim off the scum. Reduce the heat to medium-low. Add the remaining thyme and the bay leaf. Simmer the stock for 2 hours, then strain it into a saucepan and reduce it to about 60 cl (1 pint). Allow the stock to cool overnight in the refrigerator.

The next day, remove the breasts from the marinade, reserving the legs and marinade in the refrigerator. Heat the oil in a heavy frying pan over medium-high heat. Sauté the breasts for 5 minutes on their smooth sides. Turn them in the pan and sprinkle ⅛ teaspoon of the salt and some pepper over the cooked sides. Sauté the breasts for 3 minutes more, then remove them from the pan.

To prepare the sauce, skim the fat from the refrigerated stock. Add ¼ litre (8 fl oz) of the stock to the pan along with the puréed blackberries, 2 tablespoons of the marinade, the remaining salt, the vinegar and sugar. Bring the mixture to a simmer over medium-low heat. Add the breasts to the pan and simmer them for 7 minutes, turning once. Remove them from the sauce and set aside to keep warm. Raise the heat to medium and pour in the gin. Cook the sauce, whisking frequently, until it is shiny and reduced to 17.5 cl (6 fl oz) — about 15 minutes.

Cut the breasts across the grain into very thin slices. Arrange them on a serving platter, pour the sauce over and garnish with the reserved whole blackberries.

SUGGESTED ACCOMPANIMENTS: *French beans; sautéed mushrooms.*

Braised Goose Legs with Shiitake Mushrooms

Serves 2
Working time: about 30 minutes
Total time: about 2 days

Calories **425**
Protein **28g**
Cholesterol **95mg**
Total fat **20g**
Saturated fat **8g**
Sodium **400mg**

2	goose legs, skinned, refrigerated overnight in red wine marinade from previous recipe	2
1 tsp	safflower oil	1 tsp
¼ tsp	salt	¼ tsp
	freshly ground black pepper	
1	onion, chopped	1
1	carrot, sliced in 5 mm (¼ inch) rounds	1
35 cl	unsalted goose stock from previous recipe	12 fl oz
10	whole black peppercorns, crushed	10
3 or 4	fresh marjoram or parsley sprigs	3 or 4
4	garlic cloves, crushed	4
15 g	unsalted butter	½ oz
125 g	shiitake or button mushrooms, wiped with a damp paper towel and sliced	4 oz

Heat the oil in a heavy frying pan over medium heat. Remove the goose legs from the marinade and reserve the marinade. Cook the legs on the first side until brown — about 5 minutes. Turn the legs and sprinkle them with ⅛ teaspoon of the salt and some pepper. Cook them on the second side until brown — about 5 minutes more. Transfer the legs to a fireproof casserole.

Preheat the·oven to 170°C (325°F or Mark 3).

Cook the onion and carrot in the pan until soft — about 5 minutes — and add them to the casserole. Pour the marinade into the pan through a strainer lined with a paper towel. Pour the stock into the pan. Bring the liquid to a simmer and pour it over the goose legs. Add the remaining salt, the peppercorns, marjoram or parsley, and garlic. Partially cover the casserole to allow some steam to escape. Braise the legs in the oven until they are tender — about 1¾ hours. Remove the casserole and strain the sauce into a large, shallow bowl, gently pressing down on the vegetables to extract all their juices. Discard the vegetable solids. Set the legs aside in the casserole. Pour the sauce into a bowl set in a cold-water bath. When the sauce has cooled to room temperature, remove the bowl from the water bath and place it in the freezer so that the fat will congeal quickly.

Heat the butter in a heavy frying pan over medium-high heat. Sauté the mushrooms until they are lightly browned all over — about 15 minutes.

Spoon off the fat from the surface of the chilled sauce. Pour the sauce over the legs in the casserole, add the mushrooms and warm over low heat until the sauce comes to a simmer. Serve immediately.

SUGGESTED ACCOMPANIMENT: *fettucini tossed with yogurt and poppy seeds.*

Goose with Apple and Red Cabbage Stuffing

Serves 6
Working time: about 45 minutes
Total time: about 3 hours

Calories **445**			
Protein **30g**	4.5 kg	goose, with fat trimmed, gizzard, heart and neck reserved	10 lb
Cholesterol **750mg**	½	lemon	½
Total fat **17g**	1 tsp	salt	1 tsp
Saturated fat **5g**	3	red onions, thinly sliced	3
Sodium **320mg**	½ litre	dry white wine	16 fl oz
	1 kg	red cabbage, thinly sliced	2 lb
	2	cooking apples, peeled and cored, cut lengthwise into 8 slices	2
	2 tbsp	grated fresh ginger root	2 tbsp
	½ litre	red wine	16 fl oz
	4 tbsp	red wine vinegar	4 tbsp
	4 tbsp	sugar	4 tbsp
		freshly ground black pepper	
	12	small shallots, peeled	12
	1 tsp	cornflour, mixed with 1 tbsp water	1 tsp

Rinse the goose and pat it dry with paper towels. Prick the skin all over with a toothpick or a skewer, taking care not to penetrate the meat lest the juices seep out.

Rub the goose inside and out with the lemon half, squeezing out its juice as you go. Rub the inside with ¼ teaspoon of the salt. Place half of the onion slices in the cavity of the goose. Tie the legs together with string and tuck the wing tips underneath the back.

Pour ½ litre (16 fl oz) of water and the white wine into a large, deep roasting pan with a lid. Put a flat perforated steamer in the pan and place a large plate on it. Set the goose breast side down on the plate. Cover the pan, and steam the goose over high heat for 10 minutes. Reduce the heat to medium so that the liquid bubbles gently and steam still rises from its surface, and cook for 40 minutes more. Uncover the goose and prick its skin again. Steam for 1½ hours more.

Transfer the goose to a platter. Pour the cooking liquid into a bowl and set the bowl in a cold-water bath to reduce the temperature, then place the bowl in the freezer so that the fat will congeal quickly.

While the goose is steaming, cover the giblets and neck with 1 litre (1¾ pints) of water in a saucepan. Add the remaining onion slices and simmer, uncovered, for about 2 hours. Strain the stock into a saucepan and reduce it over medium-high heat to about ¼ litre (8 fl oz). Discard the neck, giblets and onions. Refrigerate the reduced goose stock.

While the stock is simmering, make the stuffing. In a large saucepan combine the cabbage, apples, ginger, ¼ litre (8 fl oz) of water, half of the red wine, the vinegar, sugar, ½ teaspoon of the salt and some pepper. Simmer the mixture for 30 minutes. Add the shallots and cook for 30 minutes more. Drain all the liquid from the stuffing and reserve it for the sauce.

Preheat the oven to 170°C (325°F or Mark 3).

Loosely fill the goose's cavity and neck with the drained stuffing. Close up the openings with metal skewers. Sprinkle the remaining salt over the outside of the bird. Place the goose breast side down on a rack set in a large roasting pan and roast it for 25 minutes. Turn ▶

the goose breast side up and roast it until well browned — about 35 minutes more.

Meanwhile, make the sauce. Take the cooled cooking liquid from the freezer. Remove the fat from the top and spoon the stock beneath it into a saucepan. Remove any fat from the refrigerated giblet stock and add the stock to the saucepan along with the drained stuffing liquid. Pour in the remaining red wine and cook the sauce over medium-high heat until reduced by two thirds — approximately 35 minutes. There should be about ½ litre (16 fl oz) of liquid in the pan. Add the cornflour-and-water mixture and whisk the sauce until it thickens.

Place the goose on a platter, spoon a little sauce round it and serve the rest in a gravy boat.

SUGGESTED ACCOMPANIMENT: *carrot and turnip purée spiced with nutmeg.*

EDITOR'S NOTE: *The process of steaming followed by roasting helps to defat the goose considerably, resulting in a crisp skin and fewer calories.*

Twice-Cooked Quail

ROASTING THE BIRDS AT HIGH HEAT GIVES THEM A CRISP, RICHLY COLOURED EXTERIOR. THE BRAISING YIELDS A SAUCE THAT INCORPORATES EVERY BIT OF THE ROASTING JUICES.

Serves 4
Working time: about 20 minutes
Total time: about 40 minutes

Calories **395**
Protein **43g**
Cholesterol **115mg**
Total fat **22g**
Saturated fat **6g**
Sodium **400mg**

8	quail (about 1 kg/2 lb)	8
	freshly ground black pepper	
½ tsp	salt	½ tsp
8	small sprigs fresh rosemary, or ½ tsp dried rosemary	8
2	garlic cloves, thinly sliced	2
1½ tsp	safflower oil	1½ tsp
¼ litre	strong unsalted chicken stock	8 fl oz
1 tbsp	Madeira	1 tbsp

Preheat the oven to 230°C (450°F or Mark 8).

Season the cavity of each quail with the pepper, salt, rosemary and garlic. To truss the birds, place them on their backs and run a piece of string, about 25 cm (10 inches) long, lengthwise beneath each one. Pull the ends of the string over the centre of the breasts and knot them. Push the drumsticks under the string.

Spread ½ tablespoon of the oil over the bottom of a fireproof roasting pan that is large enough to hold the quail snugly. Brush the remaining oil over the quail and place them in the pan, breast side up. Roast for 20 minutes without basting.

Put the roasting pan on the stove top over medium heat. Combine the stock with the Madeira and pour it into the pan. Simmer the stock for 2 to 3 minutes, turning the birds over and over in the liquid as you work. Cut away the string. Place two quail on each of four heated plates, and moisten the birds with 1 to 2 tablespoons of the sauce. Rotate each plate to distribute the sauce evenly round the quail. Serve the birds immediately.

SUGGESTED ACCOMPANIMENT: *sautéed radishes; green beans.*

Quail Stuffed with Wild Mushrooms and Rice

Serves 4
Working time: about 45 minutes
Total time: about 1 hour

Calories **690**
Protein **50g**
Cholesterol **115mg**
Total fat **26g**
Saturated fat **8g**
Sodium **585mg**

8	quail (about 1 kg/2 lb)	8
175 g	long-grain white rice	6 oz
60 cl	unsalted chicken stock	1 pint
¾ tsp	salt	¾ tsp
30 g	unsalted butter	1 oz
30 g	ceps or other dried mushrooms, soaked in cold water for 20 minutes, then finely chopped, the soaking liquid reserved	1 oz
1	stick celery, finely chopped	1
1	onion, finely chopped	1
1 tbsp	fresh thyme, or ¾ tsp dried thyme	1 tbsp
	freshly ground black pepper	
1¼ tsp	safflower oil	1¼ tsp
1	shallot, finely chopped	1
125 g	small or pickling onions, blanched for 30 seconds in boiling water, drained and peeled	4 oz
12.5 cl	Madeira	4 fl oz
1 tbsp	cornflour, mixed with 1 tbsp water	1 tbsp

Preheat the oven to 170°C (325°F or Mark 3). Combine the rice, ½ litre (16 fl oz) of the stock and ¼ teaspoon of the salt in a fireproof casserole over medium-high heat. Bring the liquid to a simmer, then cover the casserole tightly and put it in the oven. Cook until all the liquid has been absorbed and the rice is tender — about 25

minutes — and let it stand, covered, for 10 minutes.

While the rice is cooking, melt half of the butter in a heavy frying pan over low heat. Add the mushrooms, celery, onion and half of the thyme. Cook, stirring, until the celery is tender — about 5 minutes. Remove the pan from the heat.

When the rice is ready, stir the vegetable mixture into it and set it aside uncovered. Raise the oven temperature to 220°C (425°F or Mark 7).

To prepare the quail, rinse out their cavities with cold water and pat them dry. Sprinkle the birds with ¼ teaspoon of the salt and some pepper. Stuff the quail with the rice mixture, reserving the excess stuffing for an accompaniment. Spread ¼ teaspoon of the oil over the bottom of a fireproof casserole large enough to hold the birds in a single layer. Set the quail breast side up in the casserole and roast them until their breasts feel firm but springy to the touch — 15 to 17 minutes.

Meanwhile, start the sauce. Heat the remaining oil in a heavy-bottomed saucepan over low heat. Add the shallot and sauté it for 2 minutes. Stir in the small onions, Madeira, 12.5 cl (4 fl oz) of the reserved mushroom-soaking liquid, the remaining stock and the rest of the thyme. Cover tightly and simmer the mixture until the small onions are translucent — about 10 minutes.

When the quail are ready, transfer them to a warmed serving platter and pour the excess fat from the casserole. Put the reserved stuffing in a small baking dish, and cover it with foil. Turn off the oven and place the rice mixture in the oven to heat it through.

Place the casserole over low heat and deglaze it with some of the liquid from the saucepan. Return the mixture to the saucepan. Push the onions to one side, whisk in the cornflour and water, and simmer for 2 minutes. Finish the sauce by adding the remaining salt, some pepper and the remaining butter to the saucepan. If the sauce is too thick, thin it with 2 tablespoons of the mushroom-soaking liquid. Pass the sauce separately.

SUGGESTED ACCOMPANIMENT: *steamed spring greens.*

Squab Breasts with Shallot-Cream Sauce

Serves 4
Working time: about 1 hour
Total time: about 2 hours and 40 minutes

Calories **390**
Protein **16g**
Cholesterol **75mg**
Total fat **25g**
Saturated fat **10g**
Sodium **155mg**

Four	pigeon squabs, necks reserved, giblets	Four
400 g	discarded	14 oz
¼ tsp	salt	¼ tsp
¼ litre	dry white wine	8 fl oz
2	onions, coarsely chopped	2
1	carrot, sliced in 5 mm (¼ inch) rounds	1
20	garlic cloves, crushed	20
10	black peppercorns, crushed	10
1 tsp	fresh thyme, or ½ tsp dried thyme	1 tsp
15 g	unsalted butter	½ oz
2	shallots, finely chopped	2
2 tbsp	double cream	2 tbsp
2 tbsp	brandy	2 tbsp
	freshly ground black pepper	
1 tsp	safflower oil	1 tsp

To remove the squab breasts, cut the skin between the legs and breasts and bend the legs down to the cutting surface. Remove each breast with its breastbone intact by cutting through the rib cage and round the wing socket. Sprinkle ⅛ teaspoon of the salt over the skin side of the breasts and put them in the refrigerator.

Cut up the backs, legs, wings and necks. Heat a large, fireproof casserole over medium heat. Sauté the chopped bones, watching that they do not burn, until they are well browned and the bottom of the pan is lightly caramelized — 10 to 15 minutes.

Deglaze the casserole with the wine. Add the onions,

carrot, garlic, peppercorns, and enough water to ju[st] cover the bones. Bring the liquid to the boil ov[er] medium-high heat, skim off the impurities, and add th[e] thyme. Reduce the heat to medium-low and simmer th[e] stock for 30 minutes. Add ½ litre (16 fl oz) of water an[d] simmer for 1 hour more. Strain the stock into a sm[all] saucepan and discard the solids. Reduce the stock ov[er] medium-high heat to 35 cl (12 fl oz).

Preheat the oven to 200°C (400°F or Mark 6).

Melt the butter in a saucepan over medium heat an[d] cook the shallots in it until they are translucent — abo[ut] 3 minutes. Whisk in the cream, and cook for 1 minut[e,] whisking. Pour in 17.5 cl (6 fl oz) of the stock and simm[er] for 4 minutes over medium-high heat, whisking co[n]stantly. Add the remaining stock and the brandy. Simm[er] for 15 to 20 minutes more, stirring occasionally, un[til] the sauce has thickened slightly. There should be abo[ut] 17.5 cl (6 fl oz) of sauce. Stir in the remaining salt an[d] some pepper.

While the sauce is simmering, heat the oil in a larg[e] shallow fireproof casserole over high heat. Sauté th[e] squab breasts skin side down for 3 minutes on each si[de] of the breast. Put the casserole in the oven and roast th[e] breasts skin side up for 6 to 8 minutes. Remove th[e] breasts and let them stand for 3 minutes. With a sma[ll] sharp knife, cut each breast off the bone in one piec[e.] Then cut the breasts against the grain into thin slice[s.] Arrange the slices on individual plates and spoon som[e] sauce around them. Pass the rest of the sauce separatel[y.]

SUGGESTED ACCOMPANIMENTS: *peas; pumpkin.*

Pheasant Breasts in Parchment

Serves 4
Working time: about 30 minutes
Total time: about 30 minutes

Calories **270**
Protein **21g**
Cholesterol **50mg**
Total fat **7g**
Saturated fat **1g**
Sodium **170mg**

4	pheasant breasts, skinned and boned (about 500 g/1 lb), bones reserved for stock	
1 tbsp	safflower oil	1 tb[sp]
1	garlic clove, crushed	
¼ tsp	salt	¼ ts[p]
	freshly ground black pepper	
1 tbsp	finely chopped fresh ginger root	1 tb[sp]
1	shallot, finely chopped	
12.5 cl	pear liqueur	4 fl [oz]
2	pears, quartered, cored, and cut lengthwise into 5 mm (¼ inch) thick slices	
12.5 cl	unsalted chicken stock, or pheasant stock made from the reserved bones	4 fl [oz]
2 tsp	chopped parsley	2 t[sp]

Heat the oil in a heavy frying pan over medium-hig[h] heat. Rub the garlic clove over both sides of the breast[s,] then sauté the breasts for 1 minute. Turn them over an[d] sprinkle them with the salt and some pepper. Sauté the breasts on the second side for 1 minute, then remove them from the pan and set them aside.

Preheat the oven to 190°C (375°F or Mark 5).

Add the ginger and shallot to the frying pan and cook them over low heat, stirring frequently, until the shallot is translucent — about 2 minutes. Remove the pan from the heat and stir in the pear liqueur. Return the pan to the stove again and simmer, stirring often, until the liquid is reduced to about 3 tablespoons — 2 to 4 minutes more.

Add the pear slices and toss them gently to coat them with the pear liqueur. Pour in the stock and simmer until the liquid is reduced by half — about 3 minutes. Remove the pan from the heat.

Cut four sheets of parchment paper or aluminium foil, each about 30 cm (12 inches) square. Place a breast diagonally in the centre of each square; spoon a quarter of the pears and sauce over each breast. Sprinkle ½ teaspoon of the parsley over each breast. Lift one corner of a parchment or foil square and fold it over to the opposite corner, forming a triangular papillote. Crimp closed the two open sides of the triangle, sealing the meat within. To crimp the parchment paper, make a series of overlapping folds along the open sides. Repeat the process to enclose the other breasts. Bake the papillotes on a baking sheet for 8 to 10 minutes. Put the papillotes on individual plates and let each diner open his or her own to savour the aroma.

SUGGESTED ACCOMPANIMENTS: *lightly buttered noodles; mixed lettuce and radicchio salad.*

4 A golden soufflé from the microwave oven stands ready to serve. The topping conceals a surprise filling of chicken stew and peas (recipe, opposite).

Poultry in the Microwave Oven

A microwave oven presents a fast and easy way to cook poultry with a minimum of fuss. A whole, unstuffed 1.5 kg (3 lb) chicken, for example, requires only about 20 minutes' roasting time, plus another 7 minutes of standing time during which the meat continues to cook. Chicken joints need only 6 to 7 minutes' cooking per 500 g (1 lb) — about one quarter the usual amount — and a 2.5 kg (5 lb) turkey breast will be ready to take from the oven in just 40 minutes. Even a whole 5.5 kg (12 lb) turkey can be roasted to a fine succulence in a microwave oven in a little over an hour.

In addition to its speed, microwave cookery offers some healthy bonuses. It can render more fat from chicken, say, than conventional methods do. And because the meat cooks for a much shorter time, fewer of its nutrients are lost in the process.

Most microwave ovens are ineffective in browning foods since the air within the oven does not heat up in the same way as the food does and thus cannot affect the food's surface. Taking this drawback into account, Healthy Home Cooking has created eight microwave poultry dishes that please the eye as much as the palate by including colourful vegetables and appropriate sauces. Only one recipe calls for use of a browner, a glass-ceramic grill or dish with a tin-oxide coating that allows foods to take on naturally a little of the appearance of meat roasted or baked in a conventional oven.

The recipes have been tested in both 625-watt and 700-watt ovens. Though power settings often vary among different manufacturers' ovens, the recipes use "high" to indicate 100 per cent power, "medium high" for 70 per cent, "medium" for 50 per cent and "medium low" for 30 per cent. To guard against overcooking a dish, use the shortest time specified; you can then test the food for doneness and cook it longer if need be. And remember that the food will go on cooking for several minutes after you have removed it from the oven.

Chicken Stew with Soufflé Topping

Serves 4
Working time: about 30 minutes
Total time: about 50 minutes

Calories **280**
Protein **26g**
Cholesterol **55mg**
Total fat **700g**
Saturated fat **2g**
Sodium **590mg**

4	chicken thighs, skinned	4
500 g	butternut squash, marrow or sweet potatoes	1 lb
17.5 cl	evaporated milk	6 fl oz
⅛ tsp	grated nutmeg	⅛ tsp
¾ tsp	salt	¾ tsp
	freshly ground black pepper	
1 tsp	fresh thyme, or ½ tsp dried thyme	1 tsp
1	onion, finely chopped	1
1	stick celery, finely chopped	1
2 tbsp	tomato paste	2 tbsp
75 g	shelled peas	2½ oz
1 tsp	unsalted butter	1 tsp
6	egg whites	6

Prick the squash, marrow or sweet potatoes in three or four spots and place on a paper towel in the microwave oven. Cook on high for 10 to 12 minutes. Remove from the oven, cover with a paper towel, and allow to stand until tender when pierced with a fork — 5 to 10 minutes. Cut the vegetables in half lengthwise, discarding any seeds, and scoop the pulp into a food processor or blender. Add the milk, nutmeg, ½ teaspoon of salt and a little pepper; purée until smooth.

Rub the thighs with the thyme and some more pepper. In a 1.5 litre (2½ pint) soufflé dish, combine the onion, celery, tomato paste, the remaining salt and a bit more pepper. Put the dish in the microwave oven and cook on high for 2 minutes. Stir the mixture, then add the chicken thighs, with their thicker ends facing the edges of the dish. Cook on high for 4 minutes. Turn each piece of chicken to expose the other side, then mound the peas in the centre. Rub the inside of the soufflé dish with the butter.

Transfer the purée to a large mixing bowl. If you are using a food processor, thoroughly wash and dry its work bowl. Whip the egg whites in the processor or with an electric mixer until they form stiff peaks. Stir about one quarter of the egg whites into the purée to lighten it, then fold in the remaining egg whites.

Add the mixture to the soufflé dish, filling it to the top. Microwave on medium low for 18 to 20 minutes, turning the dish a quarter turn every 5 minutes; the top of the soufflé will crack slightly when it is done. Serve the souf-flé immediately, while it is still puffy.

SUGGESTED ACCOMPANIMENTS: *watercress salad; French bread.*

To prepare the marinade, combine all the ingredients except the chicken and the green spring onion slices in a deep bowl. Add the thighs and stir to coat them evenly. Marinate the thighs for 2 hours at room temperature or overnight in the refrigerator.

When you are ready to cook the chicken, preheat a microwave browning dish on high for the maximum time allowed in the instruction manual. Remove the chicken from the marinade, wiping off and discarding the garlic, ginger and spring onion. Set the thighs on the browning dish and microwave them on high for 3 minutes. Turn the pieces over, sprinkle them with the green spring onion slices, and cook them on high for 90 seconds more. Serve immediately.

SUGGESTED ACCOMPANIMENTS: *steamed brown rice; cucumber salad.*

EDITOR'S NOTE: *If you do not have a microwave browning dish, cook the chicken in an uncovered baking dish for 5 to 6 minutes.*

Teriyaki Chicken

Serves 4
Working time: about 15 minutes
Total time: about 2 hours

Calories **170**
Protein **20g**
Cholesterol **75mg**
Total fat **9g**
Saturated fat **2g**
Sodium **120mg**

4	large chicken thighs, skinned and boned	4
2 tbsp	low-sodium soy sauce, or naturally fermented shoyu	2 tbsp
1 tbsp	dry sherry	1 tbsp
½ tsp	honey	½ tsp
1	garlic clove, sliced	1
1 tbsp	finely chopped fresh ginger root	1 tbsp
⅛ tsp	crushed black peppercorns	⅛ tsp
1	spring onion, white part chopped and green part sliced diagonally into 2.5 cm (1 inch) strips	1

Chicken in a Tortilla Pie

SALSA IS A VITAMIN-RICH SAUCE OF MEXICAN ORIGIN.

Serves 4
Working time: about 20 minutes
Total time: about 30 minutes

Calories **550**
Protein **54g**
Cholesterol **170mg**
Total fat **29g**
Saturated fat **12g**
Sodium **395mg**

1.5 kg	chicken, wings removed, the rest skinned and quartered	3 lb
12.5 cl	unsalted chicken stock	4 fl oz
¼ tsp	ground coriander seeds	¼ tsp
⅛ tsp	cayenne pepper	⅛ tsp
¼ tsp	ground cumin	¼ tsp
1	sweet green pepper, seeded, deribbed and finely chopped	1
4	spring onions, finely chopped	4
¼ tsp	dried oregano	¼ tsp
1 tbsp	virgin olive oil	1 tbsp
	freshly ground black pepper	
175 g	low-sodium cheddar or Emmenthal cheese, grated	6 oz
Two 25 cm	flour tortillas (see Editor's note, opposite)	Two 10 inch
⅛ tsp	chili powder	⅛ tsp
Salsa		
2	large ripe tomatoes, skinned, seeded and finely chopped	2
1 or 2	hot green chili peppers, seeded and very finely chopped (see caution, page 25)	1 or 2
2	garlic cloves, finely chopped	2
1	lime, juice only	1
1 tbsp	chopped fresh coriander or parsley	1 tbsp
¼ tsp	salt	¼ tsp
	freshly ground black pepper	

Place the chicken pieces in a baking dish with the meatier part of each piece towards the edge of the dish. Pour in the stock, and sprinkle the chicken with the coriander, cayenne pepper and ⅛ teaspoon of the cumin. Cover the dish with greaseproof paper and microwave on high for 10 minutes; half way through the cooking time, turn the pieces over. Remove the breasts from the dish and microwave the leg quarters for 2 minutes more. Then let the chicken stand in the cooking liquid until it is cool enough to handle. Discard the liquid and shred the meat with your fingers.

Combine the green pepper, spring onions, oregano, oil, black pepper and the remaining cumin in a bowl. Cover the bowl tightly with plastic film. Cook for 2 minutes on high, then remove the bowl from the oven and mix in the shredded chicken.

In a separate mixing bowl, stir together the salsa ingredients. Add 12.5 cl (4 fl oz) of the salsa and half of the cheese to the chicken mixture. Place a tortilla on a large plate, cover it with the chicken mixture and put the other tortilla on top. Sprinkle the pie with the remaining cheese and the chili powder. Microwave on high until the cheese melts — about 3 minutes. Cut the pie into wedges and serve it with the remaining salsa.

EDITOR'S NOTE: *To make flour tortillas, if ready-made ones are not available, rub 30 g (1 oz) of white vegetable fat into 100 g (3½ oz) of plain flour mixed with ⅓ teaspoon of salt. Gradually add 3 tablespoons of warm water and knead into a dough — about 1 minute. Add more flour if the dough is sticky. Rest the dough for 15 to 20 minutes. Divide it into two, and roll each piece out on a floured worktop to make a 25 cm (10 inch) circle, 4 mm (⅛ inch) thick. Fry in a lightly greased crêpe or frying pan until bubbles form and the surface is lightly speckled — about half a minute. Using a wooden spoon or spatula, flatten the bubbles, then turn the tortilla over and cook for 30 seconds on the other side.*

Chicken Parmesan

Serves 4
Working time: about 15 minutes
Total time: about 40 minutes

Calories **370**
Protein **33g**
Cholesterol **95mg**
Total fat **17g**
Saturated fat **5g**
Sodium **695mg**

8	chicken drumsticks, skinned, rinsed and patted dry	8
1	small onion, chopped	1
1	apple, peeled, cored and finely grated	1
1 tbsp	safflower oil	1 tbsp
35 cl	puréed tomatoes	12 fl oz
2 tbsp	tomato paste	2 tbsp
2 tbsp	Madeira	2 tbsp
1	garlic clove, finely chopped	1
1 tbsp	chopped fresh basil, or 1 tsp dried basil	1 tbsp
¼ tsp	dried oregano	¼ tsp
	freshly ground black pepper	
45 g	cornflakes, crushed	1½ oz
60 g	Parmesan cheese, freshly grated	2 oz
12.5 cl	plain low-fat yogurt	4 fl oz

Combine the onion and apple with the oil in a bowl.

Cover with a paper towel and microwave on high for 1 minute. Stir in the puréed tomatoes, tomato paste, Madeira, garlic, basil, oregano and some pepper. Cover the bowl with a paper towel again and microwave on medium (50 per cent power) for 9 minutes, stirring the sauce three times during the cooking. Remove the bowl from the oven and let it stand.

While the sauce is cooking, prepare the drumsticks. Sprinkle them with some pepper. Mix the cornflake crumbs and the Parmesan cheese. Dip the drumsticks into the yogurt, then dredge them in the crumb-cheese mixture, coating them evenly. Arrange the drumsticks on a microwave roasting rack with the meatier parts towards the outside of the rack. Microwave on high for 15 minutes, turning the dish once half way through the cooking time. Remove the drumsticks and let them stand for 7 minutes; then arrange them on a serving platter. Reheat the sauce on high for 1 minute and pour some of it over the chicken. Pass the remaining sauce separately.

SUGGESTED ACCOMPANIMENT: *spaghetti or macaroni.*

Barbecued Chicken

PRECOOKING THE CHICKEN IN THE MICROWAVE ALLOWS FOR A
DRAMATIC REDUCTION IN GRILLING TIME.

Serves 4
Working time: about 20 minutes
Total time: about 40 minutes

Calories **345**
Protein **42g**
Cholesterol **125mg**
Total fat **11g**
Saturated fat **3g**
Sodium **390mg**

1.5 kg	chicken, wings and backbone removed, the rest skinned and cut into serving pieces	3 lb
1	small onion, chopped	1
1	garlic clove, finely chopped	1
¼ tsp	safflower oil	¼ tsp
¼ litre	puréed tomatoes	8 fl oz
1 tbsp	cider vinegar	1 tbsp
2 tbsp	chutney	2 tbsp
4 drops	Tabasco sauce	4 drops
2 tbsp	dark brown sugar	2 tbsp
¼ tsp	dry mustard	¼ tsp
	freshly ground black pepper	

Light the charcoal in a barbecue grill about 30 minutes before grilling time.

To prepare the barbecue sauce, combine the onion, garlic and oil in a bowl. Cover with plastic film and micro-wave on high for 2 minutes. Add the puréed tomatoes, vinegar, chutney, Tabasco sauce, brown sugar, mustard and pepper, and stir well. Cover the bowl with a paper towel and microwave on medium high (70 per cent power) for 3 minutes. Stir the sauce again and micro-wave on medium high for 3 minutes more. Remove the sauce from the oven and let it stand while you precook the chicken.

Place the chicken pieces on a microwave roasting rack with their meatier portions towards the outside of the rack. Microwave the chicken on high for 6 minutes. Set aside any pieces that have turned from pink to white, then rearrange the remaining pieces with their uncooked portions towards the outside of the rack. Continue to microwave on high for periods of 2 minutes, removing the pieces that turn white.

Brush the chicken with the barbecue sauce. Grill the pieces over the hot coals for approximately 10 minutes, turning them once during the cooking and basting them often with the remaining sauce.

SUGGESTED ACCOMPANIMENT: *corn on the cob.*

Turkey Ring

Serves 6
Working time: about 20 minutes
Total time: about 35 minutes

Calories **265**
Protein **23g**
Cholesterol **45mg**
Total fat **12g**
Saturated fat **3g**
Sodium **315mg**

500 g	turkey breast meat, cut into 5 cm (2 inch) cubes	1 lb
1	small onion, finely chopped	1
3 tbsp	virgin olive oil, plus 1 tsp	3 tbsp
75 g	dry breadcrumbs	2½ oz
17.5 cl	semi-skimmed milk	6 fl oz
12.5 cl	plain low-fat yogurt	4 fl oz
4 tbsp	Parmesan cheese, freshly grated	4 tbsp
2 tbsp	chopped fresh basil, or 1 tsp dried marjoram	2 tbsp
	freshly ground black pepper	
1	green courgette, julienned	1
1	yellow squash or courgette, julienned	1
1	sweet red pepper, julienned	1
2	garlic cloves, finely chopped	2
¼ tsp	salt	¼ tsp

Combine the onion and 3 tablespoons of the oil in a small bowl. Cover lightly with plastic film and microwave on high until the onions are translucent — about 3 minutes. Uncover the onions and let them cool.

Mince the turkey in a food processor and mix in the breadcrumbs, milk and yogurt. Add the onion, cheese, 1 tablespoon of the basil or ½ teaspoon of the marjoram, and some pepper. Operate the processor in short bursts to combine the ingredients.

With your hands, press the turkey mixture round the edges of a round dish 25 cm (10 inches) in diameter, forming a ring with a 10 cm (4 inch) diameter hollow at the centre. Cover tightly with plastic film, leaving a corner open for steam to escape, and microwave on high for 6 minutes, turning the dish a quarter turn every 2 minutes. Let the turkey ring stand while you cook the vegetables.

Combine the courgette, squash and red pepper in a bowl with the remaining oil, the remaining basil or marjoram, the garlic, salt and some pepper. Cover with plastic film and microwave on high for 4 minutes, stirring once half way through the cooking time. Arrange some of the vegetables in a thin band around the outside of the turkey ring and mound the remaining vegetables in the centre. Serve hot.

SUGGESTED ACCOMPANIMENTS: *corn muffins; oak leaf lettuce salad.*

EDITOR'S NOTE: *The turkey ring may be assembled in advance and then reheated for serving. To reheat the dish, cover it with plastic film or greaseproof paper and microwave it on medium high (70 per cent power) for 4 minutes, turning once.*

Poussins with Barley Stuffing

Serves 4
Working time: about 25 minutes
Total time: about 1 hour

Calories **385**
Protein **29g**
Cholesterol **95mg**
Total fat **20g**
Saturated fat **8g**
Sodium **435mg**

Four 500 g	poussins, rinsed and patted dry	Four 1 lb
½ tsp	salt	½ tsp
100 g	pearl barley	3½ oz
4 tbsp	Parmesan cheese, freshly grated	4 tbsp
30 g	unsalted butter	1 oz
1	small onion, chopped	1
75 g	sweet red pepper, finely chopped	2½ oz
2	garlic cloves, finely chopped	2
1 tsp	fresh thyme, or ¼ tsp dried thyme	1 tsp
90 g	fresh mushrooms, wiped clean and thinly sliced	3 oz
	paprika	

Add ¼ teaspoon of the salt to ¼ litre (8 fl oz) of warm water in a small bowl. Microwave on high for 2 minutes. Add the barley and stir. Cook for 9 minutes on high, stirring once after 5 minutes. Remove the bowl from the oven, cover it tightly with plastic film, and let it stand for 10 minutes. Take off the plastic film, add the cheese to the barley and stir.

Put 15 g (½ oz) of the butter in a bowl and microwave it on high for 30 seconds. Stir in the onion, red pepper, garlic and thyme. Cook for 1 minute on high. Add the mushrooms and the remaining salt, and mix well. Cook on high for 2 minutes, then combine this mixture with the barley.

Fill the body cavity of each bird with one quarter of the stuffing, taking care not to pack it tightly. Sew the cavities shut with a needle and heavy thread. Tuck the wing tips under the birds and tie each pair of legs ▶

together. Wrap each bird in plastic film and place breast side down in a baking dish. Cook the birds on high for a total of 12 minutes, turning them over every 4 minutes.

Remove the birds from the oven and unwrap them. Melt the remaining butter in a small bowl by microwaving it on high for 30 seconds. Brush each bird with the melted butter and sprinkle each one liberally with paprika. Replace the birds on the dish, breast side up. Microwave them on high for a total of 12 minutes more, turning them every 4 minutes. Let the birds stand for about 5 minutes before serving.

SUGGESTED ACCOMPANIMENT: *Brussels sprouts.*

Roast Turkey with Tarragon-Cream Sauce

Serves 12
Working time: about 30 minutes
Total time: about 1 hour and 30 minutes

Calories **305**
Protein **45g**
Cholesterol **90mg**
Total fat **12g**
Saturated fat **4g**
Sodium **255mg**

5.5 kg	turkey, rinsed and patted dry	12 lb
½ tsp	salt	½ tsp
1	onion, chopped	1
2 tbsp	low-sodium soy sauce, or naturally fermented shoyu	2 tbsp
1 tsp	paprika	1 tsp
1 tbsp	virgin olive oil	1 tbsp
12.5 cl	single cream	4 fl oz
2 tsp	chopped fresh tarragon, or chopped watercress	2 tsp
	freshly ground black pepper	
1 tbsp	cornflour, mixed with 2 tbsp water	1 tbsp

Rub the cavity of the turkey with ¼ teaspoon of the salt and put the chopped onion inside. Tie the legs together and tuck the wing tips under the bird. Cover the wings and the ends of the drumsticks with smalls bits of foil.

Combine the soy sauce, paprika and oil in a small bowl. Brush the underside of the turkey with about half of this mixture. Put the turkey in an oven cooking bag. Draw the bag closed, leaving a small opening for steam to escape. Secure the bag with a plastic strip or elastic band, not a metal twist tie. Place the turkey breast side down in a large rectangular dish and microwave it on high for 15 minutes. Rotate half a turn and cook the bird on high for 15 minutes more before removing it from the oven.

Pour the accumulated juices from the bag into a saucepan and set it aside; the juices will form the base for the sauce. Remove the foil from the wings and drumsticks. Turn the turkey breast side up and brush the wings and breast with the remaining soy sauce mixture.

Close the bag loosely once more and microwave the turkey on high for 15 minutes. Rotate the dish half a turn and cook on high for a final 15 minutes.

Remove the bird from the oven. Pour the additional roasting juices into the saucepan with the reserved juices. Let the turkey stand for 20 minutes, then test for doneness by piercing a thigh with the tip of a sharp knife; the juices should run clear. If they do not, microwave the bird on high for 5 to 10 minutes more.

During the standing time, prepare the sauce. Spoon as much fat as possible from the surface of the reserved roasting juices; there should be about ½ litre (16 fl oz). Bring the liquid to the boil on the stove top and cook rapidly until it is reduced to 35 cl (12 fl oz) — 5 to 10 minutes. Add the cream, the tarragon or watercress, the remaining salt and some pepper. Return the liquid to the boil. Whisk the cornflour mixture into the sauce and cook until the sauce boils and thickens slightly — about 1 minute. Pour the sauce into a sauceboat; carve the turkey and serve.

SUGGESTED ACCOMPANIMENTS: *new potatoes; steamed artichoke hearts.*

EDITOR'S NOTE: *If you use a frozen turkey you may find that it will render more juice than a fresh one; either discard the excess juice or reserve it for another use. Although this recipe calls for a 5.5 kg (12 lb) turkey, you can easily cook a bird as large as 7 kg (15 lb) in the microwave. Enclose the turkey in an oven cooking bag and microwave it on high for 5 minutes per 500 g (1 lb), turning the dish at three regular intervals during cooking and turning the bird over half way through. Avoid buying pre-basted turkeys for microwaving: their pockets of fat may explode during cooking. The pop-out thermometers imbedded in some turkeys will not be activated until the end of the standing time. Thawing a turkey in the microwave is not recommended.*

Techniques

Cutting a Chicken into Serving Pieces

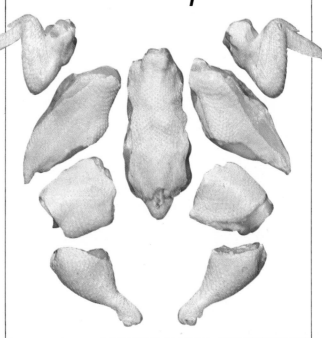

The waste-free and economical method of disjointing a whole chicken shown on these pages yields eight serving pieces (left). The backbone and any trimmings may be saved for the stockpot.

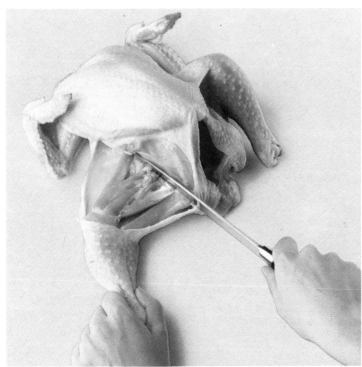

1 SEVERING THE LEGS. Lay a whole chicken breast side up on a cutting surface. Pull one leg away from the body; with a chef's knife, slice through the skin between breast and thigh. Bend the leg until the thighbone pops out of the socket. Cut through the tissue joining the thigh to the body (above) to free the leg. Repeat the process to remove the other leg.

2 DIVIDING THE LEGS. Place a leg on the cutting surface, skin side down, and locate the hard, round ball of the joint that connects the drumstick and thigh. With a single firm stroke, cut down through the joint to sever the drumstick from the thigh (above). Repeat the process with the other leg.

3 *DETACHING THE WINGS. Pull one wing away from the body. With a sawing motion, work the edge of the knife blade into the joint (below). Sever the joint by slicing down through the cartilage and skin, separating the wing from the carcass. Repeat the process to cut away the other wing.*

4 *SPLITTING THE CARCASS. Holding the carcass steady with one hand, begin cutting from tail to neck through the thin tissue that joins the breast to the back below it. When you reach the rib cage, use a sawing motion (below) to sever the rib bones. Continue cutting to separate the breast from the back.*

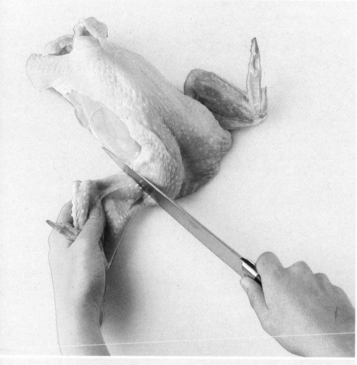

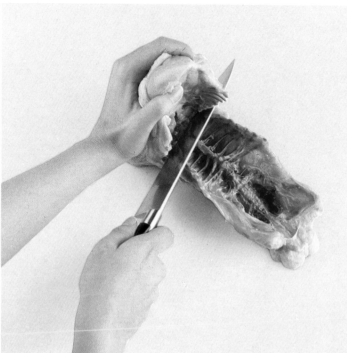

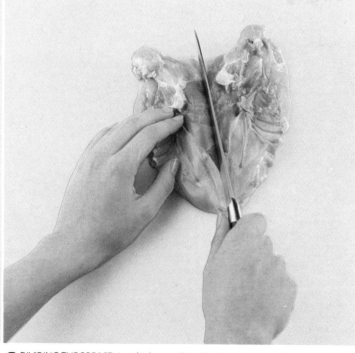

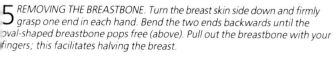

5 *REMOVING THE BREASTBONE. Turn the breast skin side down and firmly grasp one end in each hand. Bend the two ends backwards until the oval-shaped breastbone pops free (above). Pull out the breastbone with your fingers; this facilitates halving the breast.*

6 *DIVIDING THE BREAST. Lay the breast skin side down on the cutting surface. Using a firm, steady stroke to cut down the centre line of the breast, split it in two. If you need to add strength to the cutting motion, press the palm of your free hand upon the back of your other hand as you cut.*

Boning a Breast

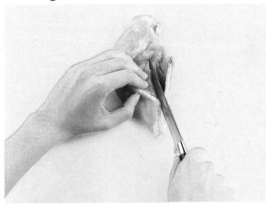

1 *STARTING THE CUT. At the thicker edge of a skinned breast, cut between the flesh and the bone with a sharp boning knife or utility knife, pressing the blade of the knife against the bone as a guide.*

2 *SEPARATING THE MEAT. With the tip of the knife blade, carefully cut the meat from the breastbone and ribs with repeated short slicing strokes, following the contours of the breastbone and rib cage. Detach the flesh in a single piece.*

Boning a Thigh

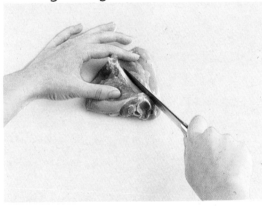

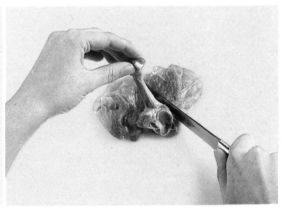

1 *CUTTING TO THE BONE. Steady a skinned thigh with its smooth side down. Use a sharp boning knife or utility knife to cut as deep as the bone and along its length, pulling the flesh away from the bone as you work.*

2 *FREEING THE MEAT. With the tip of the knife, scrape and cut away the flesh clinging to the thighbone. Once most of the bone has been exposed, grasp one end of it and cut free the remaining flesh (above).*

Trussing a bird

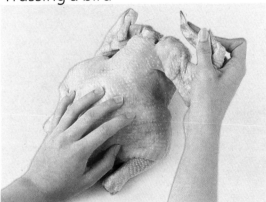

1 *TUCKING THE WINGS UNDER. Place a whole bird breast side down on a work surface. Bend a wing tip up and back towards the neck until it lodges behind the shoulder. Repeat the step to secure the other wing.*

2 *TYING THE DRUMSTICKS. Turn the bird over and cross the drumstick ends over the tail, pressing the legs firmly against the breast. Loop a 60 cm (2 ft) length of string several times round the ankles of the drumsticks to hold them together. Knot the string and trim the excess.*

Slicing Escalopes from a Turkey Breast

1 *MAKING THE FIRST CUT. Lay a whole skinned turkey breast on a work surface with the ridge of its breastbone facing up. Then, using a sharp boning knife or utility knife, carefully cut down along one side of the breastbone ridge.*

2 *SEPARATING A BREAST. Following the contour of the breastbone, carefully trim the meat in a single piece from the bone and ribs, using your free hand to pull away the flesh. Detach the long, thin fillet from the underside of the breast; reserve it for another use. Repeat the process to detach the other breast. Reserve the bones for stock.*

3 *SLICING ESCALOPES. Starting at the tapered end of a breast, slice diagonally across the grain of the meat with a sharp knife to detach the first escalope. Cut successive pieces about 5 mm (¼ inch) thick; slicing the meat on the diagonal produces thin escalopes with maximum surface area.*

4 *FLATTENING AN ESCALOPE. Lay an escalope on the work surface and gently pound it with the flat of a large chef's knife, the blade facing away from you, until the meat flattens to about half its original thickness. Repeat with the other escalopes. The slices may also be flattened by placing each one between two pieces of plastic film or greaseproof paper, then pounding with a wooden mallet or a flat-bottomed pan.*

Glossary

Aniseed: the liquorice-flavoured seed of a plant native to the Middle East. It is used in certain curries and poultry dishes.

Aquavit: a colourless, dry Scandinavian spirit often flavoured with caraway seeds.

Balsamic vinegar: a mild, extremely fragrant wine-based vinegar made in northern Italy. Traditionally, the vinegar is aged for at least seven years in a series of casks made of various woods.

Basil: a leafy herb with a strong, spicy aroma when fresh, often used in Italian cooking. Covered with olive oil and refrigerated in a tightly sealed container, fresh basil leaves may be kept for up to six months.

Baste: to help brown and flavour a food, and keep it from drying out, by pouring pan drippings or other liquid over it during cooking.

Bay leaves: the aromatic leaves of *Laurus nobilis* — a Mediterranean evergreen — used fresh or dried to flavour stocks and stews; also available in powder form. Dried bay leaves when broken have very sharp edges and can injure internally, so they should be removed before serving.

Blanch: to partially cook food by briefly immersing it in boiling water. Blanching makes thin-skinned fruits and vegetables easier to peel; it can also mellow strong flavours.

Braise: to cook meat, vegetables or a combination of the two with some liquids over low heat. Braising can be done in the oven or on top of the stove. It helps to moisten and tenderize the food.

Buckwheat groats (also called kasha): the nutty-tasting seeds of the buckwheat plant, hulled, steamed, dried, and sometimes ground; often also toasted to intensify flavour.

Bulb fennel: see Fennel.

Burghul (also called bulgur): a type of cracked wheat, where the kernels are steamed and then dried before being crushed.

Buttermilk: a tangy, low-fat, cultured milk product whose slight acidity makes it an ideal marinade base for poultry.

Calorie (or kilocalorie): a precise measure of the energy a food supplies when broken down for use in the body.

Caramelize: to heat sugar or a food naturally rich in sugar, such as garlic or onion, until it turns brown.

Cardamom: the bittersweet, aromatic dried seeds or whole pods of a herbaceous plant in the ginger family. Often used in curries.

Cayenne pepper: a fiery powder ground from the seeds and pods of red peppers. Used in small amounts to heighten other flavours.

Ceps (also called porcini): wild mushrooms with a pungent, earthy flavour that survives drying or long cooking. Dried ceps should be soaked in water before they are used.

Chervil: a lacy, slightly anise-flavoured herb often used as a companion to other herbs, such as tarragon and chives. Because long cooking may kill its flavour, chervil should be added at the last minute.

Chili peppers: hot or mild red, yellow or green members of the pepper family. Fresh or dried, most chili peppers contain volatile oils that can irritate the skin and eyes; they must be handled carefully *(see caution, page 25)*.

Chinese cabbage (also called Chinese leaves): an elongated cabbage resembling cos lettuce, with long broad ribs and crinkled, light green leaves.

Cholesterol: a wax-like substance made in the human body and found in foods of animal origin. Although a certain amount is necessary for body functioning, an excess can accumulate in the arteries, contributing to coronary ailments. See Monounsaturated fats; Polyunsaturated fats; Saturated fats.

Coriander (also called cilantro): the pungent, peppery leaves of the coriander plant or its earthy-tasting dried seeds. It is a common seasoning in Middle-Eastern, Oriental and Latin-American cookery.

Couscous: a fine-grained semolina pasta, served with the classic North African stew of the same name.

Cumin: the aromatic seeds of an umbelliferous plant similar to fennel, used whole or powdered as a spice, especially in Indian and Latin-American dishes. Toasting gives it a nutty flavour.

Dark sesame oil (also called Oriental sesame oil): a dark, polyunsaturated oil with a relatively low burning point, most often used as a seasoning; it should not be confused or replaced with lighter sesame cooking oils.

Deglaze: to dissolve the brown particles left in a pan after roasting or sautéing by stirring in wine, stock, water or cream.

Degrease: to remove the accumulated fat from stock or cooking liquid by skimming it off with a spoon or blotting it up with paper towels. To eliminate the last traces of fat, draw an ice cube through the warm liquid; the fat will cling to the cube.

Escalope: in poultry cookery, a boneless, skinless slice of breast meat, cut diagonally across the grain.

Fennel: a herb (also called wild fennel) whose feathery leaves and dried seeds have a mild anise flavour and are much used for flavouring. Its vegetable relative, the bulb — or Florence — fennel (also called finocchio) can be eaten raw in salads or cooked.

Fillet (also called tenderloin): in poultry cookery, one of two long muscles found on either side of a bird's breastbone. The fillets are approximately one quarter the size of the breast muscle itself.

Ginger: the spicy, buff-coloured root of the ginger plant. Fresh ginger can be grated, chopped, julienned, or cut into thin rounds and crushed with the flat of a large knife.

Julienne: the French term for vegetables or other food cut into strips.

Juniper berries: the berries of the juniper tree, used as the key flavouring in gin. They lend a resinous tang to marinades and sauces for game and goose.

Kasha: see Buckwheat groats.

Mace: the ground aril, or covering, that encases the nutmeg seed.

Mange-tout: flat green pea pods eaten whole, with only stems and strings removed.

Marjoram: sweet marjoram and its heartier relative pot marjoram are aromatic herbs related to oregano, but milder in flavour.

Millet: a nutritious whole grain whose nutty, mild taste makes it an ideal base for stuffings.

Monounsaturated fats: one of the three types of fats found in foods. Monounsaturated fats are believed not to raise the level of cholesterol in the blood.

Mozzarella: soft kneaded cheese from southern Italy, traditionally made from buffalo's milk, but now also made from cow's milk. Full-fat mozzarella has a fat content of 40 to 50 per cent, but lower-fat versions are available. The low-fat mozzarella used in the recipes in this book has a fat content of only about 16 per cent.

Non-reactive pan: a cooking vessel whose surface does not chemically react with food. This includes stainless steel, enamel, glass and some alloys. Untreated cast iron and aluminium may react with acids, producing discoloration or a peculiar taste.

Olive oil: any of various grades of oil extracted from olives. Extra virgin olive oil, which has a full, fruity flavour and the lowest acidity level, and virgin olive oil come from the first pressing of the olives. Pure olive oil, a processed blend of olive oils, has the lightest taste and the highest acidity.

Paprika: a slightly sweet, spicy powder produced by grinding dried red peppers. The best type of paprika is Hungarian.

Phyllo pastry: a paper-thin flour-and-water pastry popular in Greece and the Middle East. It can be made at home *(recipe, page 83)*, or bought, fresh or frozen, from delicatessens and shops specializing in Middle-Eastern food.

Pine-nuts: the seeds from the cones of the stone pine. The nuts' buttery flavour can be brought out by lightly toasting or sautéing them.

Poach: to cook gently in simmering liquid. The temperature of the poaching liquid should be approximately 94°C (200°F); and its surface should merely tremble.

Polyunsaturated fats: one of the three types of fats found in foods. They exist in abundance in such vegetable oils as safflower, sunflower, corn and soy bean. Polyunsaturated fats lower the level of cholesterol in the blood.

Prosciutto: an uncooked, dry-cured and slightly salty Italian ham, sliced paper-thin.

Purée: to reduce food to a smooth, even, pulplike consistency by mashing it, passing it through a sieve, or processing it in a blender or food processor.

Puréed tomatoes: purée made from skinned fresh or canned tomatoes. Available commercially, but should not be confused with the thicker, concentrated tomato paste sometimes labelled tomato purée.

Recommended Daily Amount (RDA): the average daily amount of an essential nutrient recommended for healthy people by the U.K. Department of Health and Social Security.

Reduce: to boil down a liquid in order to concentrate its flavour or thicken its consistency.

Ricotta: soft mild white Italian cheese, made from cow's or sheep's milk. Full-fat ricotta has a fat content of 20 to 30 per cent, but the low-fat ricotta used in recipes in this book has a fat content of only about 8 per cent.

Safflower oil: a vegetable oil that contains the highest amount of polyunsaturated fats.

Saffron: the dried, yellowish-red stigmas (or threads) of the saffron crocus, which yield a powerful yellow colour as well as a pungent flavour. Powdered saffron has less flavour than the threads.

Saturated fats: one of three types of fats found in foods. They exist in abundance in animal products and coconut and palm oils; they raise the level of cholesterol in the blood. Because high blood-cholesterol levels may cause heart disease, saturated-t consumption should be restricted to less than 15 per ent of the calories provided by the daily diet.

auté: to cook a food quickly in a small amount of hot t, usually in an uncovered frying pan.

ear: to brown meat by exposing it briefly to very high eat, sealing in natural juices.

esame oil: see Dark sesame oil.

esame paste: see Tahini.

hallot: a refined cousin of the onion, with a subtle avour and papery, red-brown skin.

hiitake mushroom: a variety of fresh or dried ushroom. The dried version should be stored in a cool, y place; it may be reconstituted by 20 to 30 minutes' aking in water before use.

chuan pepper (also called Chinese pepper, Japanese epper or anise pepper): a dried shrub berry with a tart, omatic flavour that is less piquant than black pepper.

mmer: to cook a liquid or sauce just below its boiling int so that the liquid's surface barely ripples.

odium: an essential nutrient required for maintaining e proper balance of body fluids. In most diets, a major urce of the element is table salt, made up of 40 per nt sodium. Excess sodium may contribute to high ood pressure, which increases the risk of heart sease. One teaspoon (5.5 g) of salt, with 2,132 illigrams of sodium, contains just over the maximum ily amount recommended by the World Health ganization.

y sauce: a savoury, salty brown liquid made from rmented soy beans and available in both light and rk versions. One tablespoon of ordinary soy sauce ntains 1,030 milligrams of sodium; lower-sodium riations, as used in the recipes in this book, may ntain half that amount.

patchcock: to split and flatten a bird, rendering it table for baking or grilling.

quab: a young pigeon, weighing from 300 to 500 g 0 oz to 1 lb) when sold. Domestic pigeons reared for

the table have paler flesh and a more mellow taste than wild pigeons.

Steam: to cover food and cook it in the steam created by a boiling liquid. It is an excellent means of releasing fat from a bird before roasting it. Steaming vegetables preserves the vitamins and flavours that are ordinarily lost in boiling.

Stir-fry: to cook cubes or strips of meat or vegetables, or a combination of both, over high heat in a small amount of oil, stirring constantly to ensure even cooking in a short time. The traditional cooking vessel is a Chinese wok; a heavy-bottomed frying pan may also be used for stir-frying.

Stock: a savoury liquid prepared by simmering meat, bones, trimmings, aromatic vegetables, herbs and spices in water. Stock forms a flavour-rich base for sauces and stews.

Sweet potato: either of two types of nutritious tuber, one with yellowish mealy flesh, the other with a moist, sweet, orange flesh. The latter is often sold as yam but should not be confused with the true yam, *(see below)*.

Tahini (also called sesame paste): a nutty-tasting paste made from ground sesame seeds that are usually roasted.

Tarragon: a strong herb with a sweet anise taste. In combination with other herbs it should be used sparingly, since its flavour may clash with rosemary, sage or thyme. Classically paired with chicken, it also marries well with turkey. Heat intensifies its flavour, so cooked dishes require smaller amounts.

Thyme: a versatile herb with a zesty, slightly fruity flavour and strong aroma. Of all herbs it is perhaps the perfect companion for poultry, intensifying the flavour of any bird.

Tomatillo: a small, green, tomato-like fruit, closely related to the Cape gooseberry, used as a vegetable. It is covered with a loose, papery husk and has a tart flavour.

Tomato paste: a concentrated tomato purée, available in cans and tubes, used in sauces and soups. See also Puréed tomatoes.

Total fat: an individual's daily intake of polyunsaturated, monounsaturated and saturated fats. Nutritionists recommend that fats provide no more than 35 per cent of the energy in the diet. The term as used in this book refers to all sources of fats in the recipes.

Truss: to secure the wings and legs of a bird against its body. This can be done by tying or sewing them with cotton or string. The wings may also be tucked back under the bird. The compact shape thus achieved helps to avoid overcooking any part of the bird and keeps the skin from splitting at the joints; it also simplifies the turning process.

Turmeric: a spice used as a colouring agent and occasionally as a substitute for saffron. It has a musty odour and a slightly bitter flavour.

Virgin olive oil: see Olive oil.

White pepper: a powder ground from the same dried berry as that used to make black pepper. Unlike black pepper, the berries are allowed to ripen and are ground without their shells. Used as a less visible alternative to black pepper in light-coloured foods.

Yam: a number of varieties of hairy tuber, rich in vitamin A and similar in taste when cooked to the potato. Sometimes known as the Indian potato, it should not be confused with the sweet potato, which is sometimes also sold as yam. The yam is less sweet and less widely available than the sweet potato.

Yogurt: a creamy, semi-solid cultured milk product made with varying degrees of fat. Yogurt makes an excellent low-fat substitute for soured cream in cooking. To keep it from separating, add 1 teaspoon of cornflour to 12.5 cl (4 fl oz) of yogurt before gently heating the mixture. Yogurt may also be combined with soured cream to produce a sauce or topping that is lower in fat and calories than soured cream alone.

ndex

Almonds: Braised chicken, and chick-peas, 48

ples:
Braised chicken with red and green, 38
Duck breasts with sour, 115
Goose with, and red cabbage stuffing, 121
Roast chicken with, turnips and garlic, 77
Turkey legs baked with yams and, 89
ricots: Sautéed chicken breasts with, bourbon and pecans, 24
paragus: Cold chicken and, with lemon-tarragon vinaigrette, 80
bergine:
Chicken, and tomato sauté, 20
Red pepper, sweetcorn and, stuffing, 109

Balsamic vinegar sauce, 118
nana: Chicken legs with dark rum, papaya, mango and, 43
rley stuffing: Poussins with, 133
rbecued chicken, 131
sil:
Chicken fan with, tomato sauce, 31
Grilled chicken with malt vinegar and, 71
Honey-, chicken, 54

Spatchcocked chicken with, yogurt sauce, 81
Vinaigrette, 102
Beans, black:
Poached chicken with, onion sauce, 28
Turkey and, salad, 103
Beans, haricot: Chicken braised with, and tomatoes, 39
Beet green: Spinach, and pine-nut stuffing, 108
Beetroot sauce: Turkey patties with, 86
Blackberry sauce: Goose breasts with, 119
Boning:
Chicken, 138
Turkey, 110-111
Bourbon: Sautéed chicken breasts with apricots, and pecans, 24
Broccoli: Stir-fried chicken with, red onions and cashew nuts, 23
Buckwheat:
Rolled turkey escalopes stuffed with, 100
Stuffing, 108
Buttermilk: Turkey salad with yogurt and, dressing, 102

Cabbage, Chinese: Plum-coated chicken with, 53
Cabbage, red:

Goose with apple and, stuffing, 121
Stir-fried chicken with, and chilies, 25
Cabbage, Savoy: Chicken on a bed of, 68
Calzones: Chicken-and-cheese-filled, 62
Capon: Roast, with sage cornbread stuffing, 76
Caraway seeds: Sautéed chicken with mustard, and chervil, 17
Carrots: Chicken breasts stuffed with garlic and, 18
Cashew nuts: Stir-fried chicken with broccoli, red onions and, 23
Celery: Braised chicken legs with, shallots and red onion, 32
Cheese:
Chicken-and-,-filled calzones, 62
Chicken Parmesan, 130
Spinach and, stuffing, 59
Turkey rolled with ham and, 88
Turkey salad with feta, 102
Chervil: Sautéed chicken with mustard, caraway seeds and, 17
Chicken, 11-83, 127-131, 133
Baked, 52-68
Boning, 138
Braised, 32-51
Chilled, couscous with lime, 82
Emerald roll, 79
Grilled, 69-73
Jointing, 136-137

Microwaved, 127-131
Pie, sage-flavoured, with phyllo crust, 82
Poached, 26-31
Poussins, 66, 74-75, 133
Roasted, 74-78
Sautéed, 12-25
Stock, 9
Trussing, 138
Chicken, baked:
on a Bed of Savoy cabbage, 68
Breasts stuffed with tahini, 55
Cajun, wings, 60
and-Cheese-filled calzones, 62
Crêpes filled with, and sweetcorn, 65
Honey-basil, 54
Legs stuffed with millet, 56
Oven-fried, 67
Peach-glazed poussins with ginger, 66
in Phyllo, 61
Pillows, 57
Plum-coated, with Chinese cabbage, 53
Rolled in vine leaves, 52
Spicy yogurt, thighs, 58
Spinach-stuffed, breasts, 59
Yogurt-, with pimientos and chives, 64
Chicken, braised:
Almonds and chick-peas, 48

Breasts with courgettes in red wine sauce, 44
Curried, with chutney and raisins, 42
Drumsticks cacciatore, 44
Fricassee with watercress, 50
with Haricot beans and tomatoes, 39
Jellied, with lemon and dill, 40
Legs with celery, shallots and red onions, 32
Legs with dark rum, papaya, mango and banana, 43
Legs stewed with prunes, 46
Lemon-mustard, with root vegetables, 47
Mole, 41
Orange-glazed, 34
with Orange and onion, 37
with Potatoes, leeks and kale, 51
with Plums and lemons, 36
with Red and green apples, 38
Saffron, stew, 34
Spanish-style, and saffron rice, 33
Chicken, grilled:
    Breasts with radishes, 72
    Lime and mint, 69
    with Malt vinegar and basil, 71
    Saffron, with yogurt, 70
    Thighs, with sherry and honey, 73
Chicken, microwaved:
    Barbecued, 131
    Parmesan, 130
    Poussins with barley stuffing, 133
    Stew with soufflé topping, 127
    Teriyaki, 128
    in a Tortilla pie, 128
Chicken, poached:
    with Black bean onion sauce, 28
    Cranberried, 29
    Emerald, roll, 79
    Fan with basil-tomato sauce, 31
    with Fennel, 26
    in Milk and curry, 30
    Red pepper and, spirals, 28
    Strips in gingered orange sauce, 27
Chicken, roast:
    with Apples, turnips and garlic, 77
    Capon with sage cornbread stuffing, 76
    Dry martini poussins, 74
    Poussins with pineapple and mint, 75
    Thyme-roasted, 78
Chicken, sautéed:
    Aubergine and tomato sauté, 20
    Breasts with apricots, bourbon and pecans, 24
    Breasts, with coriander, 15
    Breasts with livers and grapes, 13
    Breasts with raspberry sauce, 15
    Breasts stuffed with garlic and carrots, 18
    Breasts with tarragon and tomato, 22
    Cutlets with summer herbs and tomato sauce, 14
    with Mustard, caraway seeds and chervil, 17
    Paprika with yogurt, 21
    with Peanuts and ginger sauce, 16
    Riesling, 18
    Stir-fried, with broccoli, red onions and cashew nuts, 23
    Stir-fried chopped, on lettuce leaves, 12
    Stir-fried, with red cabbage and chilies, 25
Chicken, whole or jointed:

Barbecued, 131
on a Bed of Savoy cabbage, 68
Braised, almonds and chick-peas, 48
Braised, with potatoes, leeks and kale, 51
Braised, with red and green apples, 38
Braised, with haricot beans and tomatoes, 39
Cranberried, 29
Curried, with chutney and raisins, 42
Jellied, with lemon and dill, 40
Orange-glazed, 34
with Orange and onion, 37
Oven-fried cinnamon, 67
Plum-coated, with Chinese cabbage, 53
Poached, with black bean onion sauce, 28
Poached in milk and curry, 30
Roast, with apples, turnips and garlic, 77
Roast capon with sage cornbread stuffing, 76
Sautéed, paprika with yogurt, 21
Spanish-style, and saffron rice, 33
Spatchcocked, with basil-yogurt sauce, 81
Thyme-roasted, 78
in a Tortilla pie, 128
Yogurt-baked, with pimientos and chives, 64
Chicken breasts:
    Aubergine and tomato sauté, 20
    Braised, with plums and lemons, 36
    and-Cheese-filled calzones, 62
    Cold, and asparagus with lemon-tarragon vinaigrette, 80
    with Courgettes in red wine sauce, 44
    Crêpes filled with, and sweetcorn, 65
    Cutlets with summer herbs and tomato sauce, 14
    Fan with basil tomato sauce, 31
    Lemon-mustard, with root vegetables, 47
    with Peanuts and ginger sauce, 16
    Pillows, 57
    Poached in milk and curry, 30
    Poached, strips in gingered orange sauce, 27
    with Radishes, 72
    with Raspberry sauce, 15
    Rolled in vine leaves, 52
    Sautéed, with apricots, bourbon and pecans, 24
    Sautéed with coriander, 15
    Sautéed, with livers and grapes, 13
    Sautéed, with mustard, caraway seeds and chervil, 17
    Spinach-stuffed, 59
    Stir-fried, with broccoli, red onions and cashew nuts, 23
    Stir-fried minced, on lettuce leaves, 12
    Stir-fried, with red cabbage and chilies, 25
    Stuffed with garlic and carrots, 18
    Stuffed with tahini, 55
    with Tarragon and tomato, 22
    Wrapped in crisp phyllo, 61
Chicken drumsticks:
    Cacciatore, 44
    Parmesan, 130
Chicken legs:
    Baked, stuffed with millet, 56
    Braised, with celery, shallots and red onion, 32

with Dark rum, papaya, mango and banana, 43
Grilled, with malt vinegar and basil, 71
Honey-basil, 54
Poached, with fennel, 26
Saffron, stew, 34
Saffron, with yogurt, 70
Stewed with prunes, 46
Chicken livers: Sautéed chicken breasts with, and grapes, 13
Chicken thighs:
    Casserole with dried fruits and caramelized onions, 48
    Fricassee with watercress, 50
    Grilled with sherry and honey, 73
    Lime and mint, 69
    Mole, 41
    Spicy yogurt-baked, 58
    Stew with soufflé topping, 127
    Teriyaki, 128
Chicken wings: Cajun, 60
Chick-peas: Braised chicken, almonds and, 48
Chilies:
    Stir-fried chicken with red cabbage and, 25
    Turkey and green, enchiladas, 90
Chives: Yogurt-baked chicken with pimientos and, 64
Chutney: Curried chicken with, and raisins, 42
Cider sauce, 104
Cinnamon chicken: Oven-fried, 67
Cornbread sage stuffing, 76
Coriander:
    Chicken breasts sautéed with, 15
    Chopped turkey with lime and, 93
    Salad dressing, 103
Courgettes: Chicken breasts with, in red wine sauce, 44
Couscous: Chilled chicken, with lime, 82
Cranberried chicken, 29
[illegible]
118
Crêpes filled with chicken and sweetcorn, 65
Currants:
    Turkey escalopes with pine-nuts and, 95
    and Wine sauce, 110
Curry:
    on a Bed of Savoy cabbage, 68
    Chicken with chutney and raisins, 42
    Chicken poached in milk and, 30
    Sauce, 68
    Turkey, with puréed yams, 91

D̲ietary guidelines, 8
Dill: Jellied chicken with lemon and, 40
Dressing, yogurt, 97. See also Salad dressings
Duck: 113
    Breasts with red wine and juniper berries, 114
    Breasts with sour apple, 115
    with Mushrooms and mange-tout, 116
    Roast, with cranberry compote, 118
    Roast, stuffed with pears and garlic, 117
    Stock, 9

E̲nchiladas: Turkey and green chili, 90
Escalopes. See Turkey escalopes

F̲ennel: Poached chicken with, 26
Feta cheese: Turkey salad with, 102
Fricassee: Chicken, with watercress, 50
Fruit:
    Dried, chicken casserole with, and caramelized onions, 48
    Roast breast of turkey with, stuffing, 104
    Stuffing, 104

G̲alantine: Turkey, 110
Garlic:
    Chicken breasts stuffed with carrots and, 18
    Roast chicken with apples, turnips and, 77
    Roast duck stuffed with pears and, 117
    Tomato-, sauce, 57
Ginger:
    Chicken with peanuts and sauce, 16
    Marinade, 105
    Peach-glazed poussins with, 66
Gingered orange sauce: Poached chicken strips in, 27
Goose: 113
    with Apple and red cabbage stuffing, 121
    Braised, legs with shiitake mushrooms, 120
    Breasts with blackberry sauce, 119
    Stock, 9
Grapes:
    Chicken Riesling, 18
    Sautéed chicken breasts with livers and, 13
Gravy: Port and orange, 106

H̲am: Turkey rolled with, and mozzarella, 88
Herbs:
    Chicken cutlets with summer, and tomato sauce, 14
Honey:
    Basil chicken, 54
    Chicken thighs grilled with sherry and, 73
    Glazed roast turkey, 106

J̲uniper berries: Duck breasts with red wine and, 114

K̲ale: Braised chicken with potatoes, leeks and, 51

L̲eeks: Braised chicken with potatoes, and kale, 51
Lemon:
    Braised chicken with plums and, 36
    Cold chicken and asparagus with, tarragon vinaigrette, 80
    Jellied chicken with, and dill, 40
    Mustard chicken with root vegetables, 47
    Tarragon vinaigrette, 80
Lettuce leaves, stir-fried chopped: Chicken on, 12
Lime:
    Chilled chicken couscous with, 82

Chopped turkey with, and coriander, 93
Marinade, 69
and Mint chicken, 69
Turkey escalopes with citrus, 92

Madeira sauce, 100
Mange-tout: Duck with mushrooms and, 116
Mango: Chicken legs with dark rum, papaya, and banana, 43
Marinades:
Dry, for turkey-stuffed pittas, 97
Lime, for chicken, 69
Ginger, for turkey, 105
for Stir-fried turkey, 98
for Turkey satays, 99
Martini: Dry, poussins, 74
Microwave recipes, 127-135
Milk: Chicken poached in, and curry, 30
Millet: Baked chicken legs stuffed with, 56
Mint:
Lime and, chicken, 69
Poussins with pineapple and, 75
Mirin sauce, 28
Mole: Chicken, 41
Mozzarella: Turkey rolled with ham and, 88
Mushrooms:
Braised goose legs with shiitake, 120
Duck with mange-tout and, 116
Quail stuffed with wild, and rice, 122
Mustard:
Lemon-, chicken with root vegetables, 47
Sautéed chicken with, caraway seeds and chervil, 17

Nutritional guidelines, 8
Nuts. See individual nuts

Oils, cooking, 8
Onions:
Braised chicken legs with celery, shallots and red, 32
Chicken casserole with dried fruits and caramelized, 48
Chicken with orange and, 37
Poached chicken with black bean, sauce, 28
Stir-fried chicken with broccoli, red, and cashew nuts, 23
Orange:
Chicken with, and onion, 37
Poached chicken strips in gingered, sauce, 27
Port and, gravy, 106
and Sweet potato stuffing, 106
Turkey escalopes with citrus, 92

Papaya: Chicken legs with dark rum, mango and banana, 43
Paprika: Chicken, with yogurt, 21
Parmesan: Chicken, 130
Parsley sauce: Turkey rolls with, 100
Patties: Turkey, with beetroot sauce, 86
Peach-glazed poussins with ginger, 66
Peanut sauce, 99
Pine-nuts: Chicken with, and ginger sauce, 16

Pears:
Roast duck stuffed with, and garlic, 117
Pheasant breasts in parchment, 124
Pecans: Sautéed chicken breasts with apricots, bourbon and, 24
Peppers. See Chilies; Sweet peppers
Pheasant breasts in parchment, 124
Phyllo:
Chicken wrapped in crisp, 61
Sage-flavoured chicken pie with, crust, 82
Pies:
Sage-flavoured chicken, with phyllo crust, 82
Tortilla, chicken in a, 128
Pimientos: Yogurt-baked chicken with, and chives, 64
Pineapple: Poussins with, and mint, 75
Pine-nuts:
Spinach, beet green and, stuffing, 108
Turkey escalopes with, and currants, 95
Pittas: Turkey-stuffed, 97
Pizza:
Dough, for calzones, 62
Sauce, 87
Turkey crust, 87
Plums:
Braised chicken with, and lemons, 36
Coated chicken with Chinese cabbage, 53
Port and orange gravy, 106
Potatoes: braised chicken with, leeks and kale, 51
Poultry:
Buying guidelines, 7, 11
Cooking time, judging, 7, 9
Frozen, 7
Handling, 7
Wines for, 9
Poussins:
with Barley stuffing, 133
Dry martini, 74
Peach-glazed, with ginger, 66
with Pineapple and mint, 75

Quail:
Stuffed with wild mushrooms and rice, 122
Twice-cooked, 122

Radishes: Chicken breasts with, 72
Raisins: Curried chicken with chutney and, 42
Raspberry sauce: Chicken breasts with, 15
Rice:
Quail stuffed with wild mushrooms and, 122
Spanish-style chicken and saffron, 33
Riesling: Chicken, 18
Rum: Chicken legs with dark, papaya, mango and banana, 43

Saffron:
Chicken stew, 34
Chicken with yogurt, 70
Spanish-style chicken and, rice, 33
Sage:
Flavoured chicken pie with phyllo crust, 82

Roast capon with, cornbread stuffing, 76
Tomato sauce with, 88
Salad dressings:
Coriander, 103
Yogurt, 97
Yogurt and buttermilk, 102
Salads:
Chilled chicken couscous with lime, 82
Cold chicken and asparagus with lemon-tarragon vinaigrette, 80
Turkey and black bean, 103
Turkey, with feta cheese, 102
Turkey, with yogurt and buttermilk dressing, 102
Salsa, 129
Satays: Turkey, with peanut sauce, 99
Sauces:
Balsamic vinegar, 118
Basil-tomato, 31
Basil-yogurt, 81
Beetroot, 86
Black bean onion, 28
Blackberry, 119
Cider, 104
Currant and wine, 110
Curry, 68
Ginger, 16
Gingered orange, 27
Madeira, 100
Mirin, 28
Parsley, 100
Peanut, 99
Pizza, 87
Raspberry, 15
Red wine, 44
Red wine and juniper, 114
Salsa, 129
Sesame, 98
Shallot-cream, 124
Tarragon-cream, 134
Tomato, 14
Tomato-garlic, 57
Tomato and red pepper, 62
Tomato, with sage, 88
Tuna, 94
Yogurt, 93
Yogurt-tomato, 59
Sesame sauce, 98
Shallots:
Braised chicken legs with celery, and red onion, 32
Squab breasts with, cream sauce, 124
Sherry: Chicken thighs grilled with, and honey, 73
Slicing turkey escalopes, 139
Soufflé topping: Chicken stew with, 127
Spatchcocking a chicken, 81
Spices. See individual names
Spinach:
Beet green and pine-nut stuffing, 108
and Cheese stuffing, 59
Stuffed chicken breasts, 59
Squab breasts with shallot-cream sauce, 124
Stews:
Chicken, with soufflé topping, 127
Saffron chicken, 34
Stir-fried dishes:
Chicken with broccoli, red onions and cashew nuts, 23
Chopped chicken on lettuce leaves, 12
Chicken with red cabbage and chilies, 25
Turkey with mixed vegetables, 98

Stock:
Basic chicken, 9
Guidelines for, 6
Stuffing:
Apple and red cabbage, 121
Barley, 133
Buckwheat, 100, 108
Fruit, 104
Orange and sweet potato, 106
Red pepper, sweetcorn and aubergine, 109
Sage cornbread, 76
Spinach, beet green and pine-nut, 108
Spinach and cheese, 59
Sweetcorn, for crêpes, 65
Vegetable, 97, 110
Sweet peppers:
Red, and chicken spirals, 28
Red, sweetcorn and aubergine stuffing, 109
Turkey escalopes with red and green, 97
Sweet potato: Orange and, stuffing, 106
Sweetcorn:
Crêpes filled with chicken and, 65
Red pepper, and aubergine stuffing, 109

Tahini: Baked chicken breasts stuffed with, 55
Tarragon:
Chicken breasts with, and tomato, 22
Cold chicken and asparagus with, lemon vinaigrette, 80
Roast turkey with, cream sauce, 134
Teriyaki chicken, 128
Thyme-roasted chicken, 78
Tomato:
Chicken, aubergine and, sauté, 20
Chicken braised with haricot beans and, 39
Chicken breasts with tarragon and, 22
Chicken fan with basil-, sauce, 31
Cutlets with summer herbs and, sauce, 14
Garlic sauce, 57
and Red pepper sauce, 62
Sauce, with sage, 88
Yogurt-, sauce, 59
Tortilla pie: Chicken in a, 128
Trussing chicken, 138
Tuna sauce: Chilled turkey with creamy, 94
Turkey: 85-111, 132, 139
Boning, 110-111
Stock, 9
Stuffing for, 100, 104, 108-109, 110
Turkey, baked:
Crust pizza, 87
and Green chili enchiladas, 90
Legs with yams and apples, 89
Patties with beetroot sauce, 86
Rolled with ham and mozzarella, 88
Turkey, braised: Curry with puréed yams, 91
Turkey, grilled: Satays with peanut sauce, 99
Turkey, microwaved:
Ring, 132
Roast, with tarragon-cream sauce, 134
Turkey, poached:
Rolled, escalopes stuffed with buckwheat, 101

Rolls with parsley sauce, 100
Turkey, roast:
  Breast of, with fruit stuffing, 104
  Galantine, 110-111
  Gingered, breast, 108
  Honey-glazed, 106
  Stuffings for, 104, 106, 108-109, 110
  with Tarragon-cream sauce, 134
Turkey, salad:
  and black bean, 103
  with feta cheese, 102
  with yogurt and buttermilk dressing, 102
Turkey, sautéed:
  Chilled, with creamy tuna sauce, 94
  Chopped, with lime and coriander, 93
  Escalopes with citrus, 92
  Escalopes with pine-nuts and currants, 95
  Escalopes with red and green peppers, 97
  Stuffed pittas, 97
Turkey, Stir-fried: with mixed vegetables, 98

Turkey breast. *See also* Turkey escalopes
    and Black bean salad, 103
  Chilled, with creamy tuna sauce, 94
  Chopped, with lime and coriander, 93
  Ring, 132
  Roast, with fruit stuffing, 104
  Roast, gingered, 105
  Salad with feta cheese, 102
  Salad with yogurt and buttermilk dressing, 102
  Satays with peanut sauce, 99
  Stir-fried, with mixed vegetables, 98
  Stuffed pittas, 97
Turkey escalopes:
  with Citrus, 92
  Flattening, 139
  with Pine-nuts and currants, 95
  with Red and green peppers, 97
  Rolled with ham and mozzarella, 88
  Rolled, stuffed with buckwheat, 100
  Rolls with parsley sauce, 100
  Slicing, 139
Turkey legs: Baked with yams and apples, 89

Turnips: Roast chicken with apples, and garlic, 77

Vegetables. *See also individual names*
  Filling for turkey-stuffed pittas, 97
  Lemon-mustard chicken with root, 47
  Stir-fried turkey with mixed, 98
  Stuffing, 97, 110
Vinaigrette:
  Basil, 102
  Lemon-tarragon, 80
Vine leaves: Chicken rolled in, 52
Vinegar:
  Balsamic, sauce, 118
  Grilled chicken with malt, and basil, 71

Watercress: Chicken fricassee with, 50
Wine:
  Chicken breasts with courgettes in red, sauce, 44

Choosing, 9
Currant and, sauce, 110
Duck breasts with red, and juniper berries, 114
Red, and juniper sauce, 114

Yams:
  Turkey curry with puréed, 91
  Turkey legs baked with, and apples, 89
Yogurt:
  Baked chicken with pimientos and chives, 64
  Chicken paprika with, 21
  Dressing, 97
  Saffron chicken with, 70
  Sauce, 93
  Spatchcocked chicken with basil-, sauce, 81
  Spicy, baked chicken thighs, 58
  Tomato sauce, 59
  Turkey salad with, and buttermilk dressing, 102

Picture Credits

All photographs in this book were taken by staff photographer Renée Comet unless otherwise indicated:

Cover: James Murphy. 2 top and centre: Carolyn Wall Rothery. 5 bottom: David DiMicco. 6: illustration by Joan Tartaglia for Perdue Farms Inc. 15 bottom: Taran Z Photography. 33: Steven Biver. 40: Michael Latil. 49: Karen Knauer. 57: John Burwell. 59: John Burwell. 75: Karen Knauer. 77: Steven Biver. 80: Michael Ward. 81 bottom: Taran Z Photography. 86: Michael Ward. 87: David DiMicco. 88: David DiMicco. 91: Michael Ward. 92: David DiMicco. 93: Karen Knauer. 94: David DiMicco. 95: Aldo Tutino. 96: David DiMicco. 98: Michael Latil. 100: Michael Geiger. 101-104: David DiMicco. 107-109: Michael Ward. 115: Michael Ward. 136-139: Taran Z Photography.

Acknowledgements

The editors are particularly indebted to Ademas, Washington, D.C.; Nora Carey, Paris; Pat Alburey, Cambridge, England; China Closet, Bethesda, Md., U.S.A.; Chong Su Han, Grass Roots Restaurant, Alexandria, Va., U.S.A.; Kitchen Bazaar, Washington, D.C.; Brenda Tolliver, Washington, D.C.; CiCi Williamson, Arlington, Va., U.S.A.

The editors also wish to thank the following persons and institutions: The American Hand Plus, Washington, D.C.; American Heart Association, Dallas, Tex., U.S.A.; Jay Avram, Silver Spring, Md., U.S.A.; John Binstead, Ministry of Agriculture, Fisheries and Food, Wolverhampton, England; Leslie Bloom, Silver Spring, Md., U.S.A.; Dr. John Brown, Health Education Council, London; Ellen Brown, Washington, D.C.; Jackie Chalkley, Washington, D.C.; Nic Colling, Home Produce Company, Alexandria, Va., U.S.A.; Shirley Corriher, Atlanta, Ga., U.S.A.; Don Coubly, Art Center College of Design, Pasadena, Calif., U.S.A.; La Cuisine, Alexandria, Va., U.S.A.; Carolyn Dille, Rockville, Md., U.S.A.; Rex Downey, Oxon Hill, Md., U.S.A.; Jenny Fleetwood, Leiston, Suffolk, England; Marcia Fox, Alexandria, Va., U.S.A.; The Fresh Fruit and Vegetable Bureau, London; Richard Jeffery, New York, N.Y.; Lenore & Daughters, Alexandria, Va., U.S.A.; Martin's of Georgetown, Washington, D.C.; Suad McCoy, Vancouver, Canada; National Broiler Council, Washington, D.C.; National Cancer Institute, Bethesda, Md., U.S.A.; National Research Council, Washington, D.C.; National Turkey Federation, Reston, Va., U.S.A.; Lisa L. Ownby, Alexandria, Va., U.S.A.; Paxton and Whitfield Ltd., London; Jane Peterson, Alexandria, Va., U.S.A.; Joyce Piotrowski, Vienna, Va., U.S.A.; Vivian Portner, Silver Spring, Md., U.S.A.; Ann Ready, Alexandria, Va., U.S.A.; Christine Schuyler, Washington, D.C.; Sharp Electronics Corporation, Mahwah, N.J., U.S.A.; Sandra Smith, Mount Lebanon, Pa., U.S.A.; Jimmy Sneed, Alexandria, Va., U.S.A.; Lyn Stallworth, Brooklyn, N.Y., U.S.A.; Kathleen Stang, Washington, D.C.; Straight from the Crate, Inc., Alexandria, Va., U.S.A.; U.S. Department of Agriculture, Washington, D.C.; Williams-Sonoma, Washington, D.C.; Jolene Worthington, Chicago, Ill., U.S.A.

Typesetting by G. Beard and Son Ltd., Brighton, Sussex, England
Printed and bound by Brepols S.A., Turnhout, Belgium